THE SPIEGEL AFFAIR

BY DAVID SCHOENBAUM

HITLER'S SOCIAL REVOLUTION

DAVID SCHOENBAUM

THE SPIEGEL AFFAIR

1968

DOUBLEDAY & COMPANY, INC.,
GARDEN CITY, NEW YORK

Library of Congress Catalog Card Number 67–19119
Copyright © 1968 by David Schoenbaum
All Rights Reserved
Printed in the United States of America
First Edition

To Tamara

CONTENTS

PREFACE

In the debt they owe to other people, all authors of contemporary history, like Orwell's animals, are equal. But some authors are more equal than others. I cannot help claiming for myself a very superior brand of equality. Without the aid of others, this book could not have been written at all.

My thanks go above all to Professor Karl Dietrich Bracher who encouraged me to write it *now*. I am also obliged to Dr. Heinrich Pfeiffer of the Alexander-von-Humboldt-Stiftung, Bad Godesberg, who underwrote moral encouragement with the most practical kind, and to the History Department of Kent State University.

Like all writers of contemporary history, I am particularly indebted to those who placed their time and patience at my disposal to answer questions: Conrad Ahlers, Kenneth Ames, Joe Holt Anderson, Rudolf Augstein, Edward W. Barrett, Paul Bausch, Hans Detlev Becker, Ernst Benda, Antonius Berard, William M. Blair, Ulrich Blank, Siegfried Buback, Walter Busse, John Chaloner, Wolfram Dorn, Horst Ehmke, Johannes K. Engel, Hans Globke, Sydney Gruson, Karl-Günther von Hase, Graham Hovey, Claus Jacobi, Gerhard Jahn, Catherine McArdle Kelleher, Arthur Krock, Wellington Long, Ludwig Martin, Herman Nickel, Norbert Oberle, Will Rasner, Hermann Renner, Hellmuth Roth, Wilfried Saliger, Hans Schmelz, Helmut Schmidt, Armin Scllheim, Theo Sommer, Franz-Josef Strauss, Alois Strohmayr, Anthony Verrier, George Vine, and Alfred Wüste.

Finally, a word of thanks to those who read all or part of my manuscript, and so did what they could to save me from myself: Arnulf Baring, Horst Ehmke, Shirley McKim Gardner, Catherine McArdle Kelleher, Christian Soe, and F. N. Spotts.

D.S.
Kent, Ohio
July 1967

I.

THE SITUATION

Every country gets the affair that it deserves. The Federal Republic of Germany got its on and after the evening of Friday, October 26, 1962. Around 9:20 P.M. federal attorneys and police entered the Hamburg and Bonn offices of *Der Spiegel*, the country's most influential news magazine, with search and arrest warrants. The publisher and leading staff members were charged with nothing less than treason. The search warrant also included the possibility of bribery—a key, as soon became obvious, to the *Spiegel's* books.

The real dimensions of the affair became evident only during the weeks that followed. If the affair began with what could only be viewed as a reminiscence of the Third Reich, its subsequent course suddenly seemed like nothing so much as a compulsive recapitulation of the Weimar Republic. Students marched, professors signed petitions, an apparently indestructible government fell. In the wake of the Cuban crisis, the new Germany, the world's second greatest trader and third industrial power, the outstanding military might between the English channel and the Soviet border, apparently dissolved in chaos.

As strength, stability, law, freedom, and democracy were successively called into question, the affair successfully challenged the waning Cuban crisis for space on the world's front pages. London's *Daily Mail*, a symbolic deputy of world opinion, pulled its correspondent down from the Himalayas, where he was watching Chinese troops advance on India, and returned him to Bonn.

If the world had its reservations about Germany, Germans, it appeared, also had considerable reservations about one another. In 1950 German legislators had gone to considerable trouble to define treason. But in a divided country with a disastrous history, their constituents sometimes found it hard to follow the definitions. The appearance of a single policeman made them nervous. The sight of whole battalions of them in a newspaper office scared them witless. Since the war, individual editions of German papers—the *Spiegel* among them—had been seized, individual reporters investigated, and individual editors sued and brought to court. But there had never been anything like this.

The immediate cause of the action appeared in an edition of some 500,000 on October 8. It was the week's cover story, with the title "Conditionally Prepared for Defense" (*"Bedingt abwehrbereit"*), the most detailed and comprehensive critique of West German defense policy that had yet appeared in print. It began with the results of the recent September NATO exercise, "Fallex 62," then analyzed them in terms of the theoretical alternatives of "massive retaliation" and "flexible response" in probing its well-informed way to the very heart of West German defense policy. After demolishing the premises of the policy, it damned the man primarily responsible for it, Defense Minister Franz Josef Strauss.

On October 9, an employee of the Solicitor General's office in Karlsruhe approached Federal Attorney Alvin Kuhn during a recess of the Federal High Court (*Bundesgerichtshof*) with a copy of the *Spiegel*. The clerk wondered whether the contents of the article might not represent a breach of Paragraph 100 of the Penal Code, West Germany's official-secrets act. After he had read the article, Kuhn wondered too. He consulted the Ministry of Defense, which in due course confirmed his suspicions. An official investigation was initiated and warrants were issued. On October 26 Federal Attorney Siegfried Buback led federal and local Hamburg police to the *Spiegel*'s offices in the Pressehaus while his colleague, Federal Attorney Norbert Oberle, prepared to search the *Spiegel*'s Bonn bureau, a block from the Bundeshaus, the seat of the West German parliament.

The real origins of the affair, however, went back to 1961 when a weakened but victorious Konrad Adenauer formed his fourth government in coalition with a minority party that had just campaigned to unseat him; or to 1956 when the switch to tactical nuclear weapons identified with U. S. Admiral Arthur Radford precipitated a quiet revolution in Western strategic doctrine; or to 1953 when West German legislators accepted the principle of rearmament at the same time that a workers' uprising in East Germany killed the possibility of peaceful national reunification in the foreseeable future.[1] Perhaps the beginning was in 1949 when the Federal Republic was created in the face of Social Democratic (SPD) and liberal Free Democratic (FDP) reservations.

At each of these points in recent German history, the question was the same: How was German security to be combined with German reunification; or, alternatively, whether the integration of West Germany with its West European neighbors and its alliance with the Western occupying powers permitted reunification at all.

From the beginning the West German parties divided on these dilemmas of foreign policy as they did not divide on the domestic issues of federalism vs. centralism, secularism vs. a public role for the churches, or free enterprise vs. public ownership. Domestic issues divided the parties from within. Foreign policy divided them one from another. All parties ostensibly accepted the same basic premise: that the Federal Republic was provisional, pending a peace treaty and the national reunification that was to follow. But it was clear that for Chancellor Konrad Adenauer and his Christian Democratic Union (CDU), who equated security with Western integration, the Federal Republic was less provisional than it was for their coalition partner, the FDP, and their major opponent, the SPD, who put reunification first. Kurt Schu-

[1] The best account of the East German rising is Arnulf Baring's *Der 17. Juni 1953* (Cologne and Berlin, 1965).

macher, leader of the opposition, jeered Adenauer from the floor of the first Bundestag. "Chancellor of the Allies," he roared as Adenauer announced his decision to take the country into the proposed European Coal and Steel Community. "Are you still a German?"

During the next decade, the division deepened as Adenauer's CDU supported the abortive European Defense Community and the rearmament that went with it, the NATO alliance, the European Common Market. The SPD opposed them, and the FDP was torn. In 1956, a defection of FDP "Young Turks" to a coalition with the SPD in the provincial capital of Düsseldorf ended in disaster. If FDP politicians feared Adenauer, FDP voters feared the SPD still more. The party split, and barely survived the 1957 election. Meanwhile West Germany advanced into an increasingly irresistible status quo. The initial investments had been made. Adenauer, the CDU, and the majority of West Germans were collecting the dividends. Dedicating themselves to the proposition that the business of the nation was business, West Germans produced the "economic miracle" that astonished themselves and the world. The credit went to the incumbent government, in particular to its Economics Minister, Ludwig Erhard, who had pronounced the "laissez faire, laissez aller," with which the miracle began. Pointing to prosperity and security, the presence of Western troops in West Germany and Germans in Western councils, Adenauer fought the 1957 election with the single, invincible slogan, "No experiments." He won the first absolute majority in Germany's parliamentary history.

In early 1959 the SPD tried a last experiment of its own, a *Deutschland Plan* for the federation of West and East Germany at virtually any price. This was quashed by Soviet Premier N. S. Khrushchev himself who told a delegation of leading Social Democrats that no foreign power, naturally including the Soviet Union, was interested in reunifying Germany on any terms. The SPD began an agonizing reappraisal of its entire postwar course. A new program was ratified at Bad Godesberg in October 1959. The following June, the SPD's Herbert Wehner announced to astonished government deputies that his party now accepted NATO. The party's transformation was completed in June 1961 when it nominated the Mayor of Berlin, Willy Brandt, an outspoken proponent of rearmament and NATO, as its first formal candidate for Chancellor. Brandt's nomination formally identified the SPD with the *faits accomplis* of the preceding years. By choosing the Mayor of Berlin, the party also symbolically identified itself with the unattained goal of reunification. And by passing the banner to a member of the younger political generation, it both aligned itself with the new administration in Washington and underlined, for even the most simple-minded German voter, the contrast to an incumbent born in 1876.

Even so, the 1961 election might have been the 1957 election all over again but for two factors. One was Adenauer himself. In April 1959 he had announced his intention of leaving the Chancellorship to run for the largely ceremonial office of Federal President. In June he reversed his decision and remained deaf to protests. The party acquiesced, but from then on, the old Adenauer magic began to fail, even among his most devoted supporters. The second factor was the world situation. Here two developments coincided. Stalin's death had triggered the disintegration of the bipolar power structure that had dominated international affairs since 1945. At the same time, the Soviet Union, having achieved a thermonuclear stalemate with the West, had become a more differentiated and hence more complicated threat. Both developments raised growing doubts about the validity of the old answers to increasingly complicated new problems. These doubts included the question of defense.

The original German contribution to NATO was to have been a substantial conventional army, in effect the old Wehrmacht in new uniforms. But when American strategy shifted to the use of tactical nuclear weapons in 1956, the Federal Republic shifted too. Over the protests of the SPD, the FDP, the labor unions, the physicists, and the majority of German intellectuals, the Federal Republic accepted tactical nuclear weapons as the basis of its defense. The shift had important consequences for Franz Josef Strauss.

Strauss, the son of a Munich butcher, a onetime bicycle-racing champion, and the possessor of one of the most brilliant academic records in recent Bavarian history, was in many ways the new Germany's new man. He was articulate in High German, a particularly earthy Bavarian dialect, Latin, or English, as the situation required; he was confident, energetic, and refreshingly—or intimidatingly—free of complexes in a country full of them. A deputy at thirty-four, he was a cabinet member at thirty-eight, Minister of Atomic Affairs at forty, and, a year later in 1956, Minister of Defense.

In Strauss's hands, the new policy turned into real soldiers trained by American colleagues to use real atomic weapons. The Bundeswehr became Western Europe's most powerful army, at least on paper. The voice of the new Germany speaking Radford's words in a Bavarian accent was heard in Washington, in Paris, and, by way of Paris, even in North Africa. Strauss's interest in the progress of the Fourth Republic's infant atomic researches led as far as tripartite talks with France and Italy on co-production of atomic weapons. They came to an end only on General de Gaulle's return to power in May 1957.

On March 25, 1958, the CDU majority in the government, supported by its Bavarian sister party, Strauss's Christian Social Union (CSU), voted to equip the Bundeswehr with tactical nuclear weapons supplied by the United States, or, to be more accurate, with the means of their delivery—a point that was widely misunderstood. The SPD and FDP, which were leaning more and more toward the disengagement proposals advanced by George Kennan, Hugh Gaitskell, and Poland's Foreign Minister, Adam Rapacki, were opposed. Strauss was skeptical from the start about the possibility of winning over the SPD, but attempted to woo the FDP. "You're not like those pacifists from the SPD," he told FDP deputy Wolfgang Döring, like himself a member of the younger generation in politics and a reserve officer in the Bundeswehr. "You have a feeling for national power." The key to

Strauss's argument was no escalation without representation. If the Federal Republic was to bear the brunt of a Soviet attack, it was entitled to equality not only of weapons but of political status, at least with its West European allies.

The argument was both consistent and defensible, but its net result was a new set of problems for West Germany. As the target date approached for fulfillment of NATO's 1958 MC-70 planning paper, the Federal Republic was far from its set goals. It was, moreover, according to its finance ministers, extended to the limit of its capacity. Washington complained about the shortage of available divisions, Bonn about the delayed arrival of nuclear vehicles. With the advent of Kennedy, Taylor, and McNamara, the alternatives became more varied, already ranging from a modified Gaullism to the military and economic division of labor envisioned in Kennedy's Grand Design. By the beginning of the 1961 German election campaign it had become evident that an era was over. Adenauer's premises—and hence the premises of the Federal Republic—had been alliance with the United States, cooperation with France, and a hard front with respect to an undifferentiated East. Now it was time to think again.

The 1961 campaign introduced for the first time in Germany American-style consumer researchers with a full arsenal of poster, broadcast, and television "images." During the summer, the word "image" itself found its way into the language of Goethe. The CDU/CSU, its eyes fixed anxiously on the preservation of its absolute majority, found itself faced for the first time with the problem of carrying the Chancellor, instead of vice versa. The FDP, out for the Chancellor's aged head, had a single goal: return to the government after four years on the outside. The SPD, stylistically and substantively, translated Kennedy into German.

Behind the lines, staff workers began to organize the campaign to follow the campaign. In July the *Spiegel* reported that Strauss had got together with Erich Mende, the leader of the FDP, which was committed, barring an absolute CDU/CSU majority, to a coalition with the CDU/CSU. The object of the meeting was, in effect, a pre-coalition coalition. Strauss agreed to throw his considerable weight in favor of Adenauer's deputy, Economics Minister Erhard, as the Chancellor's successor. His reward was unclear —perhaps the Foreign Ministry.

Then, on Sunday morning, August 13, East German People's Police blocked the sector boundaries in the center of Berlin, annexing the Russian share of what had until then been a four-power city. Shortly afterward masons appeared and built a wall. The cornerstone of Adenauer's policy—the Atlantic alliance—and its entire rhetorical justification—reunification through strength, strength through alliance—was put to the test.

In this unprecedented and totally unexpected situation, the CDU lost its nerve and Adenauer his initiative. On Monday night he appeared on television to reassure his countrymen. But his speech, like the CDU's subsequent exploitation of the red herring of Willy Brandt's illegitimate birth, only made voters more skeptical of his grasp of the situation. While Brandt dominated the West Berlin scene, and Vice President Lyndon Johnson made a special appearance there as President Kennedy's envoy, Adenauer failed to leave the wings in Bonn—thanks, it was said, to U.S. pressure to keep him there. According to the usually reliable Allensbach public-opinion poll, the CDU had enjoyed a 49–39 per cent margin over the SPD at the end of July. The CDU now fell to 35 per cent, while the SPD rose to 46 per cent. In what appeared to be a classical test, not only had deterrence failed, retaliation had not even been considered—at least publicly.

Strauss himself led the chorus of those exhorting their countrymen to "calm and moderation." All that occurred to the CDU, so far as could be seen, was a new series of posters issued by its campaign manager, Schleswig-Holstein's Minister President Kai-Uwe von Hassel, showing Khrushchev banging a shoe on a flaming red background with the message: "CDU—Righter than Ever." Erhard confided to journalists that he found the posters abhorrent. They nonetheless remained on the billboards.

In subsequent weeks, the American Vice President's visit and the symbolic reinforcement of the Berlin garrison restored the morale of the German electorate but failed to save the CDU.

On September 17, when 31,500,000 West Germans went to the polls, 45.4 per cent of them voted for the CDU/CSU; 36.2 per cent for the SPD; and 12.8 per cent for the FDP. This meant 243 CDU/CSU deputies in the new Bundestag (252 with the addition of the indirectly elected Berlin deputies), 190 (203) from the SPD, and 66 from the FDP. The SPD had won a moral victory, but the FDP had won the election. The CDU/ CSU, dedicated to the single goal of retaining an absolute majority, had lost. On the Monday morning after the election, commentators proclaimed that the Adenauer era was over.

A popular German proverb distinguishes between "an end with horror" and "horror without an end." The day after the election, most observers anticipated the former. But it was the latter that came to pass. During the following weeks, as U.S. and Soviet tanks faced each other on Berlin's Friedrichstrasse, West Germany's future governing parties were scarcely more cordial to one another.

Only the SPD, represented in Berlin by Brandt and in Bonn by Wehner, attempted to relate the formation of the new government to international events; an attempt that was, to be sure, in its own interest. It demanded a joint review of foreign policy and suggested the possibility of an all-party government. Adenauer, perhaps to bring the FDP in line, received an SPD delegation on September 25. But he ignored the SPD proposal.

Meanwhile the latent tension between the CDU, CSU, and FDP had reached its first crisis. On September 19 the CDU's steering committee decided to nominate Adenauer Chancellor. Simultaneously the FDP unanimously agreed to refuse membership in an Adenauer cabinet. A day later Strauss expressed regret that the CSU had not been consulted. It would, he announced, support Adenauer's policy, but it endorsed Erhard for Chancellor. On September 21, Adenauer's floor leader, old Heinrich Krone —"the man with the oil can," as a CDU deputy called him—presented a CDU compromise proposal to Federal President Heinrich Lübke: The CDU/CSU would support Adenauer to succeed himself if he would agree to resign as soon as the international situation permitted. A day later the CSU made the same proposal. The Bavarians, their spokesman Hermann Höcherl reported, were prepared to see Adenauer remain in office another year if he would then yield to Erhard. After a week of conferences, the CDU/ CSU agreed to negotiate with the FDP on a new Adenauer government. But the FDP remained intransigent, until Adenauer received the SPD delegation, and Erhard announced his decision not to run for Chancellor. Its position destroyed, the FDP agreed on September 28 to negotiate with the qualification that its chairman, Mende, would refuse a ministerial position under Adenauer. A two-man FDP committee met with Adenauer and Strauss to establish government policy. To everyone's surprise, they reached agreement a few days later. Addressing the first session of the new Bundestag on October 17, Adenauer confirmed his intention to retire before the end of the four-year legislative period, but added that he resented the FDP's insistence on pinning him to a specific date.

On October 20 a formal agreement was concluded with the FDP and ratified by the party executive on October 21 by a vote of 60 to 37; in protest, two FDP regional leaders resigned from office. Three days later, the agreement fell apart when the CDU/ CSU demanded a revision of the inter-party pact. On October 27 an SPD spokesman repeated the proposal for an all-party government.

The issue was still Adenauer, but the FDP was weakening. This time, when CDU/CSU deputies again tried to reach agreement with the FDP but explicitly excluded Adenauer from the terms of negotiations, the FDP switched its fire and named Foreign Minister Heinrich von Brentano as the insuperable obstacle. Brentano loyally resigned, the second minister in the history of the Federal Republic to leave office voluntarily. He was succeeded by the incumbent Minister of the Interior, Gerhard Schroeder. Strauss, regarded at the time as Schroeder's most prominent rival for succession to the Chancellorship, voted with the majority for his appointment.

On November 2 the SPD once more demanded an all-party

government, and the FDP, by a vote of 52 to 7, rejected a CDU/CSU demand for a new preamble to the coalition agreement. Successful negotiations on this question were nullified a few days later by a new problem. To provide jobs and representation for a maximum of their own deputies in the new government, the FDP had proposed a new ministry for aid to underdeveloped countries. Erhard, who understandably regarded the new ministry as a threat to his own Ministry of Economics, chose this moment to test his authority with respect to both the FDP and Adenauer. He demanded that Adenauer refuse the FDP. To no one's surprise, he lost.

On November 7 the Bundestag finally ratified Adenauer's appointment as Chancellor. The FDP's new Minister of Justice, Wolfgang Stammberger, avoided the vote by retiring to the Bundeshaus restaurant for a cup of coffee. Adenauer promised Krone and Mende that he would resign in time to let his successor establish himself in office before the 1965 election. The basis of the new government was a marriage contract of formidable complexity and dubious constitutionality. Among its provisions was one for a committee of coalition deputies, which was to meet at the beginning of each week to set policy. The party floor leaders, meaning Mende who refused to join the government, were given the right to attend all cabinet meetings. The FDP was rewarded with the Ministries of Finance, Atomic Affairs, and Development Aid in addition to Justice. After seven stormy weeks, the crisis was apparently over, but the following weeks were to show that the compromise had only made it worse.

The effects were reflected in foreign and defense policy. The Berlin crisis had confirmed what European critics like Strauss had for several years anticipated: the limits of American power. A memorandum by Dean Acheson commissioned by the new administration in Washington had concluded that the logical response to a nuclear stalemate was reinforcement of NATO's conventional forces. This conclusion, leaked to the Washington *Post*, reverberated across the Atlantic. Strauss, who was in basic agreement with Acheson's premises, came to contrary conclusions: if

American deterrence were no longer effective, the logical response was to develop a European deterrent capable of operating independently if the situation required it. His counterattack began in December when he appeared in Paris with proposals for a NATO nuclear force, something the Kennedy administration preferred to dodge temporarily. Strauss began giving pointed interviews to Adelbert Weinstein, military correspondent of the *Frankfurter Allgemeine Zeitung,* and attacking U.S. policy in every public speech.

Considerations of strategy were compounded by considerations of money. Bonn's 1962 budget increased defense spending by over 30 per cent of its 1961 level. But the new defense budget also represented only 5.7 per cent of the Federal Republic's gross national product, a rate of military spending that put it in sixth place in the fourteen-nation North Atlantic Alliance. In percentage of the population actually under arms, the Federal Republic was in fact fourteenth. As American pressure for conventional troops and the American desire for a diplomatic solution to the problem of access to Berlin increased, relations between the Kennedy administration and Strauss, and Washington and Bonn, worsened.

Bonn insisted that if Washington were to save Berlin by negotiations likely to benefit the East Germans, who were included in the deal Washington apparently envisioned for guaranteeing the access routes to Berlin, the United States would have to risk losing Germany. Bonn's Ambassador Wilhelm Grewe repeated his government's arguments in Washington, citing the entire collection of postwar treaty commitments on the Federal Republic's succession to the German Reich, its claim to support in its ultimate goal of reunification, its position on the question of an eastern border with Poland pending a peace treaty, and the status of Berlin.

The background of the conflict appeared mysteriously in the Catholic, pro-Adenauer *Rheinische Merkur* in September 1962. The source was four dispatches to Bonn's Foreign Ministry from Washington and Paris in October 1961. German ambassadors reported that Kennedy had informed Soviet Foreign Minister Andrei Gromyko that a discussion of Germany's eastern border would follow settlement of the Berlin question; that U. S. Ambassador to NATO, Thomas K. Finletter, has asked his German colleague for a reaction to Washington's proposal for a demilitarized zone in West Germany; that Britain's representative on the ambassadorial steering committee in Washington, Lord Hood, had declared that East German authority over the transit routes to West Berlin must be recognized. Washington was irate over the leak, and Adenauer, who was aware of the increasingly inhospitable treatment Grewe was receiving in the U.S. capital, found it convenient to make him responsible for it. Grewe was brought home and almost immediately made West German ambassador to NATO.

Despite intensive investigations in the Foreign Ministry in Bonn, no one either could or would say how the story had reached the *Rheinische Merkur*. But its author, an American named Julius Epstein, had previously been employed by General Julius Klein, whose Chicago public relations firm numbered Konrad Adenauer among its clients. Foreign Minister Schroeder indicated before the Bundestag's foreign relations committee that the Chancellor was among the suspects. It was symptomatic of the state of German-American relations.

Meanwhile, Strauss became involved in another crisis connected with the United States. The *Spiegel* was the first to report it. In 1959, U.S. authorities had made inquiries about housing for American troops in southern Germany. A small-town publisher named Johannes Evangelist Kapfinger had allegedly connected Strauss with local contractors who were incorporated in a group known from its initials as "Fibag." Strauss, who was a friend of Kapfinger's, had apparently been supposed to recommend "Fibag" to the Pentagon. Although nothing ever came of the deal, Strauss did in fact permit recommendations to be written from his office. In the spring of 1962, on the instigation of the SPD and FDP, a Bundestag committee convened to investigate the matter. A bizarre collection of witnesses appeared to testify, but none of them was sworn in, and very little but confusion emerged from their testimony. Shortly before the state election in North Rhine-Westphalia in July, the CDU proposed an end to the investigation. The SPD, which had no affection for Strauss and found it hard to forget that Kapfinger's contribution to the 1961 campaign was a sleazy slick-paper magazine whose only evident object had been to defame Willy Brandt, naturally opposed adjournment. But so did the FDP, and together this meant a majority.

As it happened, the resulting imbroglio coincided with a fiasco of some relevance to the general administration of justice in the Federal Republic. Since 1961, when Solicitor General Max Güde had resigned to run for the Bundestag, the Solicitor General's office had been vacant. In July of the next year, it was discovered, with the not precisely disinterested help of the East Germans, that the Justice Ministry's candidate for the office had not been squeamish about the death penalty during his wartime career as prosecutor at the Reich High Court in Leipzig. His candidacy came to an abrupt end. For Strauss it was a minor triumph. Incensed by the FDP vote for continued investigation of the Fibag affair, he demanded investigation of Justice Minister Stammberger. Stammberger, with a sense of responsibility not overly common in West German politics, submitted his resignation and personally moved that proceedings be introduced against himself.

In the end both investigations came to nothing. Stammberger's resignation was rejected. In the early hours of the morning on October 25, Strauss attracted a small audience at Federal President Lübke's annual reception for Bundestag members at Schloss Brühl. Helmut Schmidt, a former SPD deputy and a strong critic of Strauss's defense policy, ought to be arrested as a traitor. he reportedly declared; SPD deputy Georg Kahn-Ackermann should be sentenced to at least six months; Gerhard Jahn, the SPD deputy who had asked most of the questions during the "Fibag" investigation, deserved to have his head broken. His final malediction was said to have been reserved for the *Spiegel*. Shortly afterward Strauss disappeared into the garden, where witnesses reported that he was very sick. In a letter to the magazine *Der Stern* a few weeks later, answering an attack on him by *Stern* columnist

Sibylle, Strauss claimed that he had been misunderstood. He was, he said, only being ironic. His physiological difficulties, he added, went back to a wartime attack of jaundice and the pressure of recent weeks, especially the Cuban crisis.

On October 25, the Bundestag majority, including the FDP, officially cleared Strauss of charges in the Fibag affair. The next day police entered Hamburg's Pressehaus, and the *Spiegel* affair began.

II.

THE *Spiegel*

Why the *Spiegel*? And why the fuss? The answers were both deceptively easy and provocatively hard. Freedom of the press, freedom of criticism in general, was obviously part of the issue. It was no secret that the *Spiegel* was both anti-Adenauer and anti-Strauss. But this was not a unique position. Neither was the *Spiegel*'s preoccupation with defense. Other German publications worried at least as knowledgeably as the *Spiegel*. Other publications had also come to similar conclusions—presumably via similar sources—about NATO's September maneuver, "Fallex 62."

What made the *Spiegel* unique was not so much its policy as its public. It is widely assumed that Germans repress their past. In fact, as the affair made obvious, they are obsessed with it. The remarkable events of November and December 1962 were only in part a matter of the Federal Republican present. They were also a part of German history. The entire affair took place in a haze of historical association—Weimar and Hitler, Goebbels, Gestapo, even Captain Dreyfus. Minus the historical dimension, the reaction is virtually inexplicable.

"To judge by many of the reactions," wrote Fred Luchsinger, the Bonn correspondent of the *Neue Zürcher Zeitung*, on November 1, "one has the impression that wide sections of West German public opinion still take a problematic stand on national defense, and that not even in so serious a situation as the Cuban crisis are the necessities of national defense appreciated as they should be. The problem appears to be a saturation with things military going back to the last phase of the Third Reich. When these things are mentioned, automatic negative reactions continue to play a role—not to mention the conscious aversion of many intellectuals, who now display towards a democratic state the resistance that they neglected to display towards the dictatorship."

Foreigners, particularly from small, prosperous, and neutral countries, could argue this way. Neither their collective history nor the history of the *Spiegel* permitted Germans a similar luxury.

In itself, the history of the *Spiegel* was a history of postwar Germany, both a mirror (in German "Spiegel") image and a heightened reflection of the world around it. For staff and readers alike, the *Spiegel* is a living example of one of its cover stories.

Like many of the best stories of postwar Germany, its origins go back to 1945 when a twenty-three-year-old lieutenant named Rudolf Augstein resourcefully talked himself out of U.S. hands in Bavaria. Rounded up with thousands of troops and civilians in an open field, he took his place beside a girl bystander and lined up with the civilians. She was his fiancée, he announced, and could testify that he had already been demobilized for weeks. As it happened, he had never seen the girl before and never saw her again. The GIs in charge declined to make an issue of it.

An hour later, Augstein exchanged a handful of cigarettes for a bicycle and rode home to his native Hanover and a job with one of the two local newspapers starting under the aegis of the British occupation. His teachers recall him as the best in his class and a talented schoolboy poet. He had originally planned to study literature and take up a literary career. Under the circumstances, writing came first—primarily *feuilleton*, the critical-essayistic writing for which American papers have never had much use but European papers have always had a great deal.

With the British forces was a Czech-born staff sergeant, Harry Bohrer, who decided one day that what postwar Germany needed was a weekly news magazine like *Time*. The idea found favor with his fellow staff sergeant, Henry Ormond, also in his time a refugee from Hitler's Europe. It also struck a responsive note from their superior officer, John Chaloner, deputy press officer for Lower Saxony and, at twenty-three, the youngest major in the British army. (Bohrer is now a London journalist; Chaloner, a highly successful newspaper and magazine importer with exclusive British distribution rights to the *Spiegel*, an occasional novelist and sometime farmer. Ormond remained with the *Spiegel* as business manager until 1950. He now practices law in Frankfurt, where he was co-prosecutor at the Auschwitz trial between 1963 and 1965.)

Chaloner got a favorable reaction from German friends at the local press, among them Augstein, whose efforts with a play intended for the Hanover theater had caught his attention. Ten days of intensive training followed. Chaloner gave his protégés a daily story to write, corrected the results, then handed out new assignments. At the end a pilot issue was set before a committee of occupation officers and approved. On November 7, 1946, the first issue appeared as *Diese Woche* ("This Week").

Unlike the name, which was to be short-lived, the red-orange cover with its inset news photo was to become a trademark. The price, one mark, survived until 1964. Fifteen thousand copies of the first twenty-four-page issue were printed and caused a modest sensation. The editors could write what they pleased, Chaloner had said. Emphatically quoting Victor Gollancz, whose book on Germany's postwar chaos, *In Darkest Germany*, had just appeared in London, the infant magazine entered the world with an attack on the British occupation: while Britons were preparing Christmas turkeys, millions of Germans were starving.

In subsequent weeks, as complaints from all four occupying powers rained down on British headquarters, it seemed desirable to introduce a higher degree of supervision. The magazine was henceforth teletyped to Berlin *in toto* every week before its appearance. As a result, it began appearing on a different day each week—at one point in a double issue because the reviewing process had exceeded the weekly limit. Reluctant to give way visibly to pressure either from home or from allies, British authorities in Germany finally decided to put the magazine in German hands. But not even Chaloner knew that British hands retained their grip on the deliberately minimal supply of paper. Augstein was given a deadline measured in hours to find for himself the necessary operating capital of RM (Reichsmark) 30,000, two more licensees to take control of the operation, and a new name. In the course of a frantic telephone conversation with his father he briefly considered and rejected "The Echo." On January 4, 1947, the magazine resumed publication as the *Spiegel.*

The history of the postwar German press is a history of successes, but none was quite like the *Spiegel's.* At once serious and frivolous, folksy and polemic, nationalistic and libertarian, businesslike and affecting a Quiz Kid omniscience, it was a phenomenon new to German journalism. Like *Time,* its operating model, the *Spiegel* was conceived as if "written by one man for one man" at the end of a multistage collective editorial process. Like *Time,* it reproduced reality in story form, describing the week's events, irrespective of subject and immediate relevance, in a shower of concrete detail new to Germany: age, shoe-size, prevailing wind and weather. Nothing, according to its own editorial canon, being so interesting to people as other people, its aim was to personify the news. The most abstract events and problems found their focus in individuals, in cover stories about politicians, industrialists, physicists, theologians, opera singers, film stars. Again like *Time,* the *Spiegel* also improved the language for its own purposes, producing a stylized, heavily inverted prose, rich in compound nouns hitherto undiscovered even in a language particularly congenial to them.

Short of funds in a world in which unreformed Reichsmarks were of little interest even to those who happened to have them, "The German news magazine," as it called itself from the start, early turned weakness into a virtue. It concentrated its attention on events within the range of staff bicycles and requisitioned Volkswagens and took the world beyond at second hand. A growing collection of foreign publications was conscientiously clipped, classified, and filed in an archive of elaborately systematized information. Practically from the start, the archive was not an accessory but the very heart of the enterprise. It continued to be even after a staff of foreign and regional correspondents had filled the gap that had originally brought it into being. In time, the archive came to fill a dozen good-sized rooms, maintaining subscriptions, by 1967 to 573 newspapers and periodicals, 173 of them foreign. There were also files of *Simplicissimus*, pre-Hitler Germany's greatest satirical weekly; Maximilian Harden's *Die Zukunft*, pre-1914 Berlin's most influential weekly; Carl von Ossietzky's *Die Weltbühne*, the Weimar Republic's most prominent opposition journal; the Viennese Karl Kraus's *Die Fackel*, perhaps the most remarkable piece of one-man journalism in history; and the complete works of Ossietzky's collaborator, Kurt Tucholsky—all revealing indications of Augstein's taste.

In October 1962 the archive employed a staff of fifty and the editorial department forty-eight with equal status accorded to both. From the beginning the *Spiegel* was not squeamish about expressing an editorial opinion, whether in a random adjective or a characteristically epic-length cover story, but it demanded an exquisite fastidiousness about facts. Every fact in every manuscript was "verified"—where possible by Ph.D.s.

None of this, not even the most conspicuous deviations from what Germans call the "Anglo-Saxon" prototype—extensive verbatim interviews (*"Spiegel-Gespräche"*) with public figures, and Augstein's editorials, published pseudonymously for many years under the names Jens Daniel and Moritz Pfeil—are exactly startling to American readers. German journalism, however, had never seen anything like it. (After the affair, the *Spiegel* departed further from *Time*-style by introducing long signed articles by special staff correspondents.)

But what made the *Spiegel* unique was only secondarily a matter of form. Primarily it was a matter of substance, an expression of editorial personality; West Germany is not the United States and Rudolf Augstein not Henry Luce. *Time* executives conceded that the *Spiegel* was the best of *Time*'s imitators, although under the immediate impact of the affair *Time* was less generous. "*Der Spiegel,*" *Time* reported on November 9, 1962, "was created in 1947 as a publication loosely patterned after *Time,* but it soon changed into a Teutonic version of *Confidential Magazine.* Editorially, it stood against almost everything and for almost nothing—except, perhaps, recognition of East Germany, which it has frequently proposed. Never particularly friendly to the United States, *Der Spiegel* blasted President Kennedy's action on Cuba as hypocritical, weak, and an incitement to thermonuclear war."[1]

The special quality of the *Spiegel* went back to the circumstances of its birth. Nineteen forty-five was the Year Zero of recent German history, but also a kind of Eden. The currency reform of 1948 was to usher Germans out of Eden and into prosperity. The years preceding it were years of deprivation and desperation. But in other ways, still recalled by thousands and even millions, they were a great time to be alive, particularly for twenty-three-year-old intellectuals. Aggressive, unintimidated, and irreverent, the *Spiegel* at its birth was the product of bright and hopeful twenty-year-olds. It was to become the product of disillusioned and then desperate thirty-year-olds, and later of respectable and perhaps slightly cynical forty-year-olds. But none of this could be foreseen in 1947. The *Spiegel*'s founding fathers, free of the guilt that hampered and infected the millions of their countrymen who had attained their seniority before 1933, had little to lose and a great deal to win. With respect to the victors as well as their own countrymen, they were free men. In marginal cases, a little diplomacy was enough to save the day. A British cartoon, reprinted on June 21, 1947, showed Stalin trimming his mustache Hitler-fashion. Not surprisingly, Soviet protests followed. Augstein was called to account by a British control officer. "Does this mean," Augstein asked with winning disingenuousness, "that I can't even quote *News of the World?*" As it turned out, it didn't.

Cf. footnote on p. 85.

The taste of the editors was matched by their readers, who honored the *Spiegel* with the highest black-market price of any magazine on the German stands. Used copies drew up to RM 15, fifteen times their official price. Between the first issue and the currency reform, circulation increased from 15,000 to 66,000, an estimated tenth of the actual readership. Shortly after the reform, a reader survey reported that 89 per cent of the *Spiegel*'s audience was satisfied with it. Only 5 per cent reported basic dissatisfaction, largely on grounds of excessive irony, colorlessness, a tendency to gossip, superficiality, a lack of seriousness, and heavy-handedness. Augstein observed later that a number of would-be readers simply complained that it was unavailable.

Among the critics of 1948 were the Dutch royal family, whose displeasure was heard in London after an issue called attention to the then-Crown Princess Juliana's legs and the German-born Prince Bernhard's—in fact innocent—honorary membership in an SS unit before his marriage. The result was a two-week suspension of publication. Chaloner's intervention at the Foreign Office reduced it to a week.

The critics of 1950 were closer to home. Under the headline "*Klug sein und Mund halten*" ("Be Smart and Keep Quiet") the *Spiegel* reported on September 27 that a number of deputies of the new Bundestag had been bribed to vote for lower coffee duties, higher oil prices, and Bonn, instead of Frankfurt, as capital of the new Federal Republic. For the first time the Bundestag reacted directly to a *Spiegel* story. A week later, an investigating committee had convened. It was to convene again thirty-seven times in the following thirty-four weeks. At the end five deputies resigned. Now if ever the *Spiegel* was made.

A second major coup followed in 1952. A man named Hans Konrad Schmeisser, the *Spiegel* reported, had reason to believe that Chancellor Konrad Adenauer and his foreign policy adviser, Herbert Blankenhorn, subsequently ambassador in Paris, had maintained unusually close relations to French intelligence in the years before 1949. Blankenhorn, Schmeisser claimed, had provided the French with considerable quantities of interesting information. The French, for their part, had guaranteed both gentlemen and their families a speedy exit to France in the event of a Soviet attack. It was also reported that Adenauer's CDU had approached the French for campaign funds. There was reason to believe that Schmeisser was a reliable source. It was he who, under the name of Levacher, had been Blankenhorn's French contact.

Adenauer declared the entire story a fabrication and sued those responsible for it, Augstein and reporters Jaene and Maus. What remained of the issue was seized on July 10, 1952, the day after its appearance. The resulting litigation went on for five years and led neither to clarification nor to conviction. Court costs were divided between the contending parties. A *Spiegel* suit before the Federal Constitutional Court (*Bundesverfassungsgericht*) in Karlsruhe ultimately won the release of the confiscated copies a year and a half after their publication.

In the meantime, good journalism had been consolidated as good business. In 1950 Augstein became sole licensee and set out in search of a publisher. To his good fortune, Axel Springer, already building a family firm into Europe's greatest publishing empire, showed no interest. The *Spiegel* was not made to be a journalistic province nor Augstein to be a viceroy. To Augstein's equally good fortune, John Jahr did show interest. Jahr, an experienced businessman and publisher of a successful women's magazine, immediately recognized the *Spiegel*'s weak point: too little advertising. In 1947 editorial content had comprised 85.7 per cent of an average *Spiegel* issue, advertising 14.3 per cent. By 950 advertising had risen to 15.9 per cent, by 1952 to 19.2 per cent. Under Jahr's direction, the *Spiegel* made industry aware that its increasing number of readers were also consumers.

In 1953 Augstein was invited to address the Düsseldorf Industry Club. A year later, advertising had increased to 29.5 per cent of an average issue. In 1959, for the first time, it surpassed 50 per cent. Circulation increased correspondingly—91,000 in 1950, 174,000 in 1954, 350,000 in 1959, 482,000 in 1962, the year of the affair. (In 1967 circulation was over 900,000.)

While polls reported that *Spiegel* readers could be found in all social groups, the average *Spiegel* reader tended to be better educated and to earn more than the average West German. North German readers outnumbered South Germans; it followed that Protestant readers slightly outnumbered Catholics. Most readers lived in cities. Among the regular readers were 40 per cent of West Germany's university students, and among the advertisers, some of the biggest names in German business. In the course of time, both the government and the Bundeswehr appeared among them.

But the editorial line remained firmly in the hands of the editors, who let neither gratitude nor obligation stand in their way. On January 1, 1957, West Germany's antitrust law went into effect. Between December 1959 and November 1960, the *Spiegel* attacked twenty-six firms by name for transgressing it; seventeen of them were *Spiegel* advertisers. In 1960 it undertook a campaign against "affluence-alcoholism," one of the unlovelier manifestations of the "economic miracle." Liquor ads at the time constituted 19 per cent of its advertising volume.

It showed as little sensitivity to the collective susceptibilities of its readers, regularly serving them large doses of recent history, systematically vivisecting the untidy mores of a parvenu society, and diligently kicking its sacred cows—for example, the hunting mania that seemed to have seized large parts of the business and political world, or the cult of Albert Schweitzer. In part as a deliberate corrective to the daily press, it spared neither the churches nor the refugee organizations, both of them among the most powerful pressure groups in postwar German life.

But it was in politics that the *Spiegel* exercised its independence most conspicuously. Germany's postwar atmosphere was fundamentally apolitical, even antipolitical. The *Spiegel* was conceived to report events, not to direct them. This corresponded with Augstein's own inclinations, which were those of an unusually intelligent but not atypical middle-class German intellectual.

In the German intellectual tradition, Augstein's revolutionary heart beat on the stage rather than in the newspaper; the German revolution, Tucholsky once observed, took place in the theater. Augstein's first large-scale political statement was, characteristically, a play that transposed the postwar German scene back to the middle ages. Produced for the first and only time in Hanover in 1947, it got a friendly review in *Die Zeit* and a very bad one in the *Spiegel*. Augstein was only twenty-five at the time, but the failure of his play seems to have caused a personal crisis. As a long-time acquaintance has written, it was around this time that the *Spiegel* ceased to be his toy and turned into Augstein's full-time occupation.

Augstein's personal situation again coincided with the situation around him. Objective events were thrusting politics on Germany as they were on the *Spiegel*. The provincial beginnings of parliamentary democracy in West Germany, and their subsequent consolidation on a quasi-national basis in the Federal Republic, were a natural object of journalistic interest. The vanity, the marginal corruption, the sometimes dubious past and uneasy present of a new political generation preoccupied the *Spiegel* staff as aspiring democrats. The decisive factor, however, was the course of events itself—the bolshevization of the Soviet Zone, the single-mindedly Western orientation of the new administration in Bonn, and, above all, the Cold War. These things engaged them as Germans—young, mostly Protestant, largely Northerners.

If it was foreign policy that primarily interested Adenauer, from 1951, at the latest, it was foreign policy that primarily interested Augstein. But beginning with the Saar controversy—Adenauer, in the interest of French goodwill, was prepared to renounce the Saar, the *Spiegel* was not—agreement between them was minimal. What there was of it was negative, like common opposition to the Communist regime in East Germany. But even here the priorities were different. For Augstein, the division of Germany was a catastrophe equal to the war itself, in effect the sell-out of seventeen million fellow countrymen. Convinced that reunification was the only legitimate goal of German foreign policy, and that it could be achieved—provided that the Federal Republic committed itself to a different policy than Adenauer's

—the *Spiegel* turned increasingly into a journal of opinion. Though opinions were signed Jens Daniel or Moritz Pfeil, there was no doubt whose opinions they were. Here *Spiegel*-style gave way to Augstein-style, syntactical gymnastics to a prose distinguished by clarity, brilliance of expression, and at least a trace of fanaticism. *Ad politicem* and, as the Schmeisser affair showed, *ad hominem*, the fight continued through 1955 when the occupation ended officially and a basically sovereign West Germany joined NATO.

By now the *Spiegel* was an institution whose very critics testified to its independence and its influence. "The *Spiegel* gets its directions from East Berlin," declared a CDU deputy, Paul Bausch. "Line for line, the whorish West German journal reveals itself as the agent of overseas aggressors and their loyal allies, the boundary revisers in Bonn," declared *Red Star*, the journal of the Red Army. "The *Spiegel* represents tangible British interests and most likely not only industrial ones," declared a student paper in Marburg. "The German, distinctly left-wing and anti-Adenauer *Spiegel* . . ." declared an Amsterdam weekly. "Politically the *Spiegel* is right-wing," declared the *Nieuwe Rotterdamse Courant*. "The *Spiegel* has been no friend of ours for some time," an FDP candidate was to declare. "What has the *Spiegel* left undone in its effort to wage a campaign against Erich Ollenhauer, the SPD chairman?" asked an SPD paper in Mainz.

Advertisers, readership, a mounting collection of casualties, even its sources testified to its journalistic success. The *Spiegel* was at once admired, feared, and used. "That couldn't happen here," a high-school student is reported to have said after a performance of Ibsen's *An Enemy of the People*. "We have the *Spiegel*." The bribery count attached to the Fallex charges in 1962 by the Solicitor General's office merely convinced the *Spiegel*'s attorney of how little the federal attorneys understood their fellow countrymen. Like the uniquely Central European institution of the political cabaret, the *Spiegel* was an organ of indirect protest for a vast, loyal, insatiable, yet basically passive audience. Only its subsequent interest in Strauss was to cost it significant amounts of time and money.

With this exception, material came by itself—far more than the editors could use. Ex-General Reinhard Gehlen, director of the U.S.-sponsored *"Organisation* Gehlen," later the Bundes-nachrichtendienst (BND), the Federal Republic's foreign intelligence service, gave Hans Detlev Becker, Augstein's second-in-command, the first substantial story on the organization's origins, methods, and purposes. Government ministers came too, and even the federal Solicitor General. But so did the man on the street, the man addressed inside the cover every week as "Dear *Spiegel* Reader."

The combination of conscientious reporting, accessible sources, and a receptive audience had a regular impact: after the *Spiegel* reported a secret meeting of the neo-Nazi Socialist Reich Party in August 1952, the party was broken up. The *Spiegel* forced the resignation of a functionary of a right-wing pressure group after complaints to the Ministry of the Interior about the man's Nazi past had been brushed off and disregarded. On the basis of a *Spiegel* story, the Lower Saxon Ministry of Education introduced proceedings against an anti-Semitic high-school teacher named Zind. The man was convicted and escaped imprisonment only by a timely escape to Egypt. The Finance Minister of Rheinland-Palatinate resigned after evidence of corruption in office appeared in the *Spiegel*. In 1958 the *Spiegel* broke the story of how Mercedes had provided a car free of cost to an official close to the Chancellor. It was the first to report that the "Red Hand," a French terrorist organization, was operating against Algerian nationalists in the Federal Republic. After cover-story treatment in the *Spiegel* in 1960, William S. Schlamm, a militantly anti-Communist ex-Communist and U.S. citizen who had been conducting a West German speaking tour of Peter-the-Hermit dimensions, ceased to be a major influence on domestic German opinion.

For tens of thousands of Germans, Monday, the *Spiegel's* publication day, was a high point of the week. It was said—not entirely in jest—that public business stopped. "In conference," in the mouths of government secretaries, came to have very specific associations on Monday morning. The Federal Ministry of the Interior, the *Deutsche Zeitung* reported, classified its *Spiegel* copies. Although it was sold on the street at the next corner, the *Spiegel* was available within the ministry only to those with the highest security clearance.

By 1957, the summit of the Adenauer era, both the *Spiegel* and the Federal Republic had come a long way. The voices of both could be heard in the world. In Hamburg's Pressehaus, where the *Spiegel* had lodged since leaving Hanover in 1952, the economic miracle could be seen and felt in all its intensity. By 1962 the underheated bohemianism of surplus furniture and requisitioned cars had been replaced by glass, thick carpets, and teak—the wood postwar Germans like best to knock on. Editors wore tweeds, drove Jaguars, played golf. Editorial conferences resembled board meetings. In a curious way, the atmosphere combined Madison Avenue and Kafka. Glass walls separated the receptionists from the world around them; they also surrounded one of Augstein's secretaries. Anonymous doors to nameless offices, departments, and laboratories opened off interminable corridors right and left of the entrance. Behind each of them, observed an awed visitor, "sat an Emperor of China," with his own massive teak desk, telephone, and intercom box whose correlates, at least theoretically, included Augstein.

That they actually did so less and less was partly a result of the increasing intricacy and sophistication of Becker's editorial machine, partly because of Augstein himself. The *Spiegel*'s course, like the Federal Republic's, was set by the mid-50s, and both tended to be carried by their own inertia. For many staff members, the *Spiegel* was a way of life. Characteristically the defendants of 1962—Augstein, Becker, the editors-in-chief Claus Jacobi and Johannes K. Engel, the Bonn bureau chief Hans Dieter Jaene, and the authors of the incriminated article, Conrad Ahlers and Hans Schmelz—had spent all or most of their working lives as *Spiegel* editors.

"If the *Spiegel* is lucky, it will grow into a national task," Augstein had remarked in 1953. "If it is not, it will petrify in its own routine and hollow, self-satisfied narrow-mindedness, in an undernourished, pharisaical cleverness, and cease to matter." And although both readership and advertising revenue continued to rise, there was evidence that the *Spiegel* was running out of luck.

It had begun by opposing specific measures of the occupying powers. It had attacked those at home who had so spectacularly led Germany to disaster and those in the Soviet Zone who, in their own way, were doing their best to continue the disaster. It had struck out against the musty utopias of the domestic left and the corny "European" mysticism of the domestic right. It had fought clericalism, corruption, and rearmament—the last not because it was pacifist in principle but because it opposed Adenauer's foreign policy. By the mid-50s it showed signs of opposing everything, of becoming an organ of opposition for opposition's sake and at any price. A symptomatic libel decision in 1954 awarded damages to the plaintiff, Richard Schmid, presiding judge of Stuttgart's Oberlandesgericht (district court) and, in fact, a man temperamentally sympathetic to the *Spiegel*. In its decision, the Federal Constitutional Court declared that the offending article "presented a distorted picture of the plaintiff's political position, not only in the repetition of a number of incorrect contentions, but above all in the conscious omission of facts relevant to an accurate depiction of his views."

In these years, a perceptive observer wrote during the affair, the *Spiegel* advanced from the first phase of its development into the second. Hitherto determined to influence the course of events, it now resigned itself to tendentious observation. The youthful idealism of the first postwar years had been replaced by a kind of precocious cynicism whose indiscriminate hit-'em-again tendency appealed to its readers' critical sensibilities, but also to their collective weaknesses for vicarious window-peeking, for *Schadenfreude*, for self-pity and self-hate. A journal of opinion in no very specific sense, it was paradoxically a journal of little *but* opinion.

Like a whole generation of postwar German intellectuals, it was esteemed, indulged, patronized, feared, and ignored at the same time, the darling of a people prepared to encourage opposition in any way except by voting it into office.

In a society with a reasonable tolerance of friction, which the Federal Republic is not, the most frequent criticisms, e.g., "The Spiegel is nihilistic," could have been taken with a grain of salt. Adenauer's ritual declarations that "the situation has never been so grave" tended, with repetition, to lose some of their gravity. The situation nonetheless was grave. Augstein was as convinced of this as Adenauer. The early 50s, the years of the Federal Republic's great debates, were a period of high and genuine political passions. The tendency of those responsible to equate the state with the incumbent government and even with virtue was often understandable and sincere. Under the circumstances, however, it left something to be desired as a formula for measuring the Spiegel.

The criticism of potential friends like Hans Magnus Enzensberger, a very good poet and, in moments of grace, a very good critic, was more plausible. In 1957 Enzensberger was invited by the South-West German Radio to discuss "The Language of the Spiegel." Six years younger than Augstein and at least as disaffected with the course of events, Enzensberger had sharp words for a society that needed and supported a Spiegel. But he concentrated his fire on the Spiegel itself. What the Spiegel offered, Enzensberger contended, was not so much criticism as an elaborate substitute for it. Not only was it not the news magazine it claimed to be, it was the vehicle of a style that obscured rather than clarified what it had to say. What it offered its readers was not orientation but disorientation. "The magazine has the power to force a corrupt official from office, to attack a minister publicly, to expose official lies to public ridicule," Enzensberger declared. "But it also has the power to corrupt the views of millions of readers." Dead-pan, the Spiegel reprinted large portions of Enzensberger's attack in its issue of March 6.

Augstein had meanwhile drawn his own conclusions. In 1956

he joined the FDP. His entrance into the party happened to coincide with the "Young Turk" rebellion in Düsseldorf, and Wolfgang Döring, the engineer of the Düsseldorf action, happened to be a close friend of his, and later of the *Spiegel*'s.

For a while, a close acquaintance reports, Augstein considered giving up the *Spiegel* and going into politics full time. Becker and Jahr talked him out of it. He nevertheless appeared on the FDP's 1957 list of candidates for the Bundestag in North Rhine-Westphalia. Since his candidacy required formal residence in North Rhine-Westphalia, he registered at a Düsseldorf address, a detail that, like the political engagement that preceded it, was to play a role in the events of October 1962.

He also considered founding a new political journal. Before giving up the plan, he had hired half the staff of Springer's *Die Welt*, all of them disquieted by their publisher's increasingly right-wing course. Again Jahr dissuaded him. He was skeptical that the planned paper could make an economic go of it, and proposed instead to sell his own share of the *Spiegel* to the publishers of *Die Zeit*, Bucerius and Richard Gruner. In return, Augstein would get 50 per cent of *Die Zeit* and with it the political paper that he was after. Bucerius' doubts frustrated the project in its original form. But Gruner, the owner of a mammoth printing shop in Schleswig-Holstein, bought half of Jahr's share in the *Spiegel*. The other half went to Augstein, who now controlled 75 per cent of the *Spiegel*, more than at any time since its creation.

Of greater importance to both Augstein's and the *Spiegel*'s fortunes, however, was an impetus from the outside. At the end of 1956 Franz Josef Strauss became the Federal Republic's second minister of defense. From mid-1957 the *Spiegel* had a story worthy, in its own terms, of the apparatus at hand to report it. By 1961 the story had become a mission.

The first contacts between Strauss and the *Spiegel* were marked by a combination of curiosity and tentative goodwill on both sides. The first Strauss cover story was critical but not unfriendly. While it poked at the minister's habitual unpunctuality—Strauss had arrived at his first NATO meeting in December 1956 a quarter of an hour late—it also commended his English. Strauss's relatively unproblematic relationship to the past corresponded with that of the editors'. An anecdote recording Strauss's refreshingly self-confident entry on the international scene was quoted with approval. At a Euratom meeting he had slipped a note to his senior colleague, Brentano, recommending that he cease apologizing for Germany's presence: the Germans, after all, had been invited. Strauss's biography, including the campaign that had finally displaced his predecessor Theodor Blank, was reported in detail but without any particular edge. The program with which Strauss took office—de-facto reduction of West Germany's troop contribution, increased emphasis on tactical nuclear weapons—was criticized. But Strauss was given the opportunity to defend it in the first verbatim "*Spiegel-Gespräch.*" An accompanying photo showed Strauss smiling affably at the interviewer, Conrad Ahlers.

A subsequent Augstein-Daniel editorial on May 1, 1957, was a civil and faithful reproduction of the issues at stake. It attacked the minister's policy but not the minister. Tactical nuclear weapons, Augstein declared, were not crucial to NATO's effectiveness and were likely to lead only to similar pressure on the Russians from their East German satellite. This, he argued, would remove the possibility of reunification by yet another step. In West German hands they were a potential step toward World War III, he charged. But the final shot was aimed at Adenauer, not at Strauss: "The Chancellor believes dogmatically that the Soviet system can be undermined and brought down with the help of NATO. All the shortcomings of German foreign policy derive from this fundamental error."

The turning point seems to have come in the late summer of 1957. An inner circle of long-time *Spiegel* editors made a habit of inviting public figures to informal stag evenings. It occurred to Augstein that it might be interesting to spend an evening face-to-face with Strauss. Hans Schmelz, the author of the first Strauss cover story, delivered the invitation and succeeded in extricating Strauss from an election rally in Hamburg's cavernous Ernst-

Merck-Halle and hustling him out to Augstein's house. Strauss seems to have looked forward to the evening with as much anticipation as his hosts.

The evening was not a success. A very Bavarian Bavarian found himself surrounded by professionally bitter, ineradicably well-bred, and, deep down, very conservative North Germans—a Texan, in effect, confronted by the Yankee conscience. Large quantities of beer didn't help. Augstein, determined to conduct a serious conversation, soon gave up in despair.

He drove Strauss to the last train for Munich; they missed it, and Strauss compounded the embarrassment by proposing to the eminently law-abiding Augstein that they save time by driving down a one-way street in the wrong direction and through a red light.

The diminutive Schmelz remembered that at some point in the proceedings Strauss had, with innocent geniality, grabbed his right hand, which happened to be injured. Schmelz, in a reflex of pain, had pushed him back with his left hand. The minister, with a considerable quantity of beer in him, had seemed to rock on his heels. "*Nichts für ungut* (nothing personal)," Schmelz had said in ironic apology. "*Alles für Deutschland.*" "*Jawohl, nichts für uns* (nothing for us)," Strauss replied with emphatic misunderstanding. "*Alles für Deutschland.*" The evening was a disaster that Augstein recalled years afterward. Nothing was ever quite the same again. A qualified political opponent heretofore, Strauss had convinced Augstein in the course of a single evening that he was an unqualified public danger.

The first attack, appropriately, concerned Strauss the motorist. One of Bonn's most interesting squabbles in 1958 was precipitated by Strauss's effort to go through a major intersection against traffic. Lights blazing, horn blaring and the ministerial flag flapping conspicuously from a front fender, Strauss's car was held up by the policeman on duty. The *Spiegel* reported the contretemps with relish. It also reported Strauss's determined—and unsuccessful—efforts to get the cop demoted, and his chauffeur's not inconsiderable police record.

Subsequent attacks concerned Strauss the orator, Strauss the Christian Social politician, Strauss the strategic thinker, Strauss the peacetime commander-in-chief, Strauss the man about town. Single shots each, they were finally collected in a massive salvo in a cover story, the third on Strauss, which appeared on April 5, 1961. The West German press had seldom been freer—in every sense. The story was scarcely conceivable in the United States. Existing libel laws alone made it virtually unthinkable in Britain. An injunction prevented the distribution of the greater part of an English-language edition.

It was an elementary truth that divided countries should be kept away from nuclear weapons, the *Spiegel* declared, since it was obvious that a future war was likely to be a preventive-preventive war. China, Israel, the Federal Republic, were not qualified to possess nuclear weapons. "Despite this world-wide stream of rationality, a man has grown great in the Federal Republic who has unceasingly encouraged distrust between the great powers and demanded weapons for the Federal Republic that could bring about the 'suicide' of a Soviet aggressor and with it the suicide of the human race."

Strauss's election as chairman of the CSU was meant to be the last step to the chancellorship, the *Spiegel* continued. A record of contempt for the courts, for legal majorities, and finally for democracy itself was thus likely to become national policy. As chancellor, the *Spiegel* maintained, Strauss could be expected to fix the election law to produce permanent majorities, reintroduce the death penalty for political offenses, introduce a super libel law that would suppress the last vestiges of free expression, and, in all of these measures, to enjoy the support of both church and industry.

Although he was an autocrat to his subordinates, he claimed a unique freedom for himself, the *Spiegel* said. He exploited his friends, his colleagues, the army itself; he could be expected to shoot down the incumbent Foreign Minister von Brentano as he had previously shot down his predecessor as Defense Minister, Theodor Blank. He was, the *Spiegel* charged, a man prone to appeal to Nazi instincts, basically corrupt. Unlike Adenauer, who was, with all reservations, a man of principle, Strauss wanted power for its own sake.

"As little as Strauss wants an atomic war, so little does he presumably want to stamp out parliamentary democracy. But the means and methods he applies with an almost naïve self-confidence are more than the successor to Hitler's Reich can tolerate. Parliaments die these days without noticing it. Radio and television are neutralized by the inter-party agreements that govern them." The national press, the article continued, was no less impotent.

"The SPD has sold its soul," the *Spiegel* declared. "The FDP is a voluntary victim of political flattery." Although everything depended on the CDU, "whether the CDU or the SPD wins the next election is increasingly unimportant. The only important thing is whether Franz Josef Strauss advances another step toward the office that he will scarcely leave again, bar war and revolution."

With the cover story of April 1961, the *Spiegel* had visibly left behind a second stage in its history and entered a third. No longer a frustrated observer of events, it now conceived of itself as the Federal Republic's last line of resistance, its only national opposition.

In practice, opposition meant opposition to Strauss. This continued with the story of the Fibag scandal, which resulted in a parliamentary investigation. It was followed by the story of Lieutenant Colonel Barth. On September 16, 1961, a Bundeswehr plane had lost its course over West Germany and found itself over East Germany before the error was discovered. It landed in West Berlin and was returned to the Federal Republic by rail. Barth, commander of the unit to which the plane was assigned, was made to take the blame and transferred from his command —in effect demoted. He protested before a military tribunal. Evidence was presented that Strauss had ordered witnesses not to testify. A subsequent parliamentary investigation by the SPD's Gerhard Jahn established that Strauss, in reporting the incident, had falsified the tribunal's verdict.

The *Spiegel* attack continued with the story of "Uncle Aloys." On September 19, 1962, the magazine had announced the Fallex story for its next issue. Then Strauss decided to remain in Bonn after having been invited to return to Munich to lead the Bavarian government, and the *Spiegel* substituted a report of a new scandal involving military orders for Strauss's cronies. In this case, the beneficiaries appeared to be a long-time CSU member who had, in palmier days, produced anti-Semitic tracts for Julius Streicher, and a friend of Frau Strauss's family, a lawyer known to her since childhood as "Uncle Aloys." The *Spiegel* suggested that Strauss had got both real-estate and cash kickbacks in return for his favors.

The Fallex article was delayed until October 8 (the issue dated October 10). Eighteen days later the affair began.

III.

THE STORY

While the consequences of the Fallex article were complex, its origins were disarmingly simple. The *Spiegel* was looking for a story. A colonel in the Defense Ministry, Alfred Martin, who had one to tell, was looking for an author. By something of a coincidence they got together.

Martin's problem, like the *Spiegel's*, was Strauss. A member of the army planning staff with several years at NATO headquarters in Paris behind him, he found himself increasingly disturbed by the atmosphere around him.

Strauss, to his credit, had asserted civilian control over the military like no defense minister in German history. But the practical results were at some variance from conventional democratic theory. Strauss was a democratic politician with the democratic prerogatives of responsibility and patronage, and at the same time an absolute monarch as minister—at least from the point of view of his skeptical subordinates. "By and large," a former staff officer recalls, "the officers around Strauss hadn't yet caught on to the fact that ministers are politicians who come and go. Having been brought up in an absolutist tradition themselves, they regarded Strauss as an *ersatz* king. And they behaved like courtiers."

While controversy nominally ended at the doors of the Ermekeil Kaserne, the seat of the ministry, and usually long before that, while conscientious provincial commanders were known from time to time to guard their files with pistols, Strauss himself broadcast their contents as he saw fit. The *Frankfurter Rundschau* recalled during the affair how Strauss had announced the contents of NATO's MC 70 planning paper to reporters in December 1959; how he had leaked a secret U.S. report on Soviet strength, and, in early 1960, a rundown on the forthcoming winter NATO exercise to the *Frankfurter Allgemeine;* how he had published in the *Welt* a survey of current military air projects under way in the NATO countries in November 1960.

Staff officers divided neatly on the subject of Strauss's high-handedness, inaccessibility to views contrary to his own, and habitual unpunctuality. But the majority was for him. When Strauss wanted support for his tactical nuclear weapons policy, he had no trouble finding generals. A strong memo on the subject presented to parliament and the public in 1960 was inspired by Strauss, but it was generals who signed it. Germans like the *Zeit's* Countess Marion Dönhoff who uneasily recalled the Weimar Republic were shocked to see that generals were apparently again making policy.

In later interrogations by the Solicitor General's staff, Martin emphasized that, as a man, he had fundamental reservations about Strauss's style, his conduct of office, and his treatment of military subordinates. As an army officer he also had fundamental reservations about Strauss's policy.

The conflict between army and air force, endemic in all military establishments since World War II and intensified by the invention of the jet engine and the nuclear bomb, had been latent in the integrated Bundeswehr since its creation. Germany's air arm, which had been institutionally autonomous since Hermann Goering's days in the mid-30s, retained its autonomy when the Bundeswehr was created. Thanks to the ministry's curious organizational plan, which reflected the general indecision about what the Bundeswehr was in fact to do, the respective arms, land, sea, and air, were formally equal to one another. But the general staff, the *Führungsstab der Bundeswehr*, was equal—not superior—to all three. Delimitation and coordination of the two major branches remained a debating point. The army leaned toward the view that the air force was there to provide support for ground troops. The air force, under the leadership of its commanding general, Josef Kammhuber, inclined to the opinion that its appropriate mission was air defense.

Strauss's advent as Defense Minister and the tactical nuclear weapons debate coincided with the air force's growing realization that air defense of the Federal Republic, an area the size of Oregon with a population equal to that of the entire United States west of the Mississippi, was an absurdity. Kammhuber, a Bavarian like Strauss, drew his own conclusions. They juxtaposed conveniently with Strauss's. If air defense was impossible, then air deterrence and, potentially, air offense was the only alternative. If tactical weapons were the logical conclusion of such a policy, then the air force would carry them. With Bavarian solidarity, Strauss and Kammhuber examined the current output of the major Western aircraft producers and settled on Lockheed's F-104, the "Starfighter," as the vehicle of Germany's deterrent.

The Starfighter, which its designer had intended as a daylight interceptor, was reconstructed to meet Strauss's and Kammhuber's specifications, gaining a third again of its original weight in the process. The resultant F-104G differed fundamentally from the F-104, the two having, as the Swiss journal *Interavia* observed, "only certain basic parts and a profile in common." Speculating that NATO would reconsider Europe's nuclear role late in 1959 and early 1960, Strauss ordered yet another improvement on the original model, a "dual-timer" device to aim air-to-surface rockets.

A small number of prominent military men—among them the army's Kielmansegg, Baudissin, and Heusinger, and the air force's Steinhoff—rebelled against being faced with budgetary, strategic, and political *faits accomplis*. The consequences of their rebellion, which included honorific exile to Paris or Washington, only increased the frustration of dissidents who remained in Bonn, adding discontent with the minister's treatment of their exiled colleagues to general discontent with his conduct of office and with official policy. As the pro-Strauss majority increased, his remaining opponents found themselves more and more isolated.

This was the situation at the end of 1961 when Strauss commissioned an analytic study of German defense policy on his own premises. An air force general, Helmut Bertram, was made responsible for the study. "How would the Federal Republic look if worst came to worst?" was the question fed into the Defense Ministry's modest research apparatus. "Catastrophic" was the answer. The first part of the so-called war study (*Kriegsbildstudie*), an analysis of the consequences of a Soviet nuclear attack, reached the conclusion that 75 per cent of West Germany's potential in industry, transportation, and manpower would be destroyed at the outset of fighting. The information was passed on to the public in an article by Strauss's press officer, Colonel (now Brigadier General) Gerd Schmueckle, which appeared in Bundestag Speaker Gerstenmaier's resolutely Protestant and generally pro-government *Christ und Welt* in January 1962, under the title "The Transformation of the Apocalypse" (*Die Wandlung der Apokalypse*).

The consequence of fifteen years of postwar military technology, Schmueckle argued, was the development of "absolute weapons," which made defense impossible. The results, he declared, were, first, that only nuclear armies—with, to be sure, conventional ancillaries—could be taken seriously in Europe; second, that—in implicit contradiction to Taylor and McNamara —nuclear weapons attained their maximal effect against civilian objectives like cities, rather than against selected military targets; and third, that the inevitable result of conflict would be complete national destruction on both sides—destruction, in other words, of the presumable object of defense.

Only nuclear war was conceivable in Europe, Schmueckle contended. Only the inevitable nuclear exchange mattered. As a result, the proponents of conventional forces were, at best, deceiving themselves. By discussing the possibility of conventional war, they were making it more likely. "With their secret lust for war, they fall victim to the most remarkable illusions," he wrote. "They juggle in public with concepts like 'nuclear disarmament,' 'nuclear chain of command,' 'pause,' and 'threshold,' and thus undermine actual deterrence to a point where it loses its credibility." What they in fact accomplished, Schmueckle claimed, was to make people take the satellite armies of Eastern Europe more seriously than they deserved and to convince the Russians that they could operate without fear of nuclear retaliation. Such theorists, he observed tartly, could be defended only by old-fashioned army generals who wanted to go on fighting with tanks.

Schmueckle's article, like the study on which it was based, had a mixed reception both inside and outside the Defense Ministry. Lieutenant Colonel Count Johann-Hartwig Bernstorff, instructor in tactics at the war college in Hamburg, resigned his commission in a rage. According to *Time*, Washington was in no doubt about the main target of Schmueckle's attack and was appropriately infuriated too.

Part two of the study was a logical product of part one and an extension of the speculations current among U.S. officers at NATO headquarters in the fall of 1961. If, as part one had concluded, a Soviet attack would wipe out 75 per cent of West Germany's potential, what would happen if the West anticipated it with a pre-emptive strike? According to a method that some of its readers found basically unscientific, part two reported that a pre-emptive strike would reduce losses to 50 per cent.

What worried Martin was less the first part of the study, which Schmueckle had made public, than the second part, which was kept almost entirely secret. The Solicitor General's office later established that the readership of the complete study had been confined to a small circle of high-ranking officers, a very few civil servants, Strauss himself, and the Chancellor. West Germany's allies were not on the list. Martin himself knew the second part of the study only at second hand. It was his impression that not only the allies but the Chancellor had not been informed of it, an error that became a factor in his subsequent actions.

The report's implicit conclusion was that the Bundeswehr must be capable of triggering an automatic nuclear retaliation from its allies in case of attack, even of launching a pre-emptive strike of its own in order to do so. There was no need of a study to convince those already disposed to such a view. Those disinclined to the view were unimpressed by the study. But what was crucial in the long run was less the study itself than the way it was handled. The normal discretion of the German civil servant was reinforced by the peculiar reflexes of the German officer, most of whom had been brought up in the 100,000-man Reichswehr of the Weimar Republic in which practically everything had been a secret because the Versailles treaty declared it illegal. The super-secret treatment given the war study itself produced a reaction. Instead of simply looking through it, filing it, and in all likelihood forgetting it, its readers talked about it. Distortion was inevitable. This was how Martin became aware of it, and also how he got the impression that not even the Chancellor had seen it. Martin was a Hamburger who was skeptical of Bavarians, an army officer who was skeptical of the air force, a man who had been locked up in the peculiar atmosphere of the Defense Ministry long enough to have become infected by it, and also, according to a close friend, "an emotional man." He decided to talk himself.

Since he was an FDP sympathizer, he hoped eventually to talk to an FDP deputy. But he began with a man named Paul Conrad, who was, among other things, Tunisia's honorary consul in the Federal Republic. Conrad represented business interests as well as Tunisians in Bonn and, like Martin, inclined to the FDP. He was also president of a weekly luncheon group called the Economic Policy Club of which Martin was a member.

Conrad had his own grievances against Strauss, who had had his entry to the Defense Ministry barred in November 1960: in reply to a parliamentary question, the ministry had claimed that Conrad was the representative of a producer of tank treads and had earned a commission of DM 492,000 (roughly $123,000). Beginning in March 1962 Conrad undertook legal action to reverse the ministerial decision. The squabble was ultimately to lead to a slander suit against the federal government. Conrad's lawyer was Dr. Josef Augstein of Hanover, Rudolf's brother and the next link in the chain of connections that led to the Fallex story. Impressed by Martin's account of the war report, Conrad introduced him to Josef Augstein. Josef referred him to his brother. Rudolf and Martin met in March 1962.

In its suit before the Federal Constitutional Court, the *Spiegel* later produced four volumes of documentation industriously compiled by its military librarians, Heinz Hoehne and Robert Spiering. The agonizing reappraisal of Western defense, with its implicit critique of Strauss, was not only in the works in late 1961 and 1962, the *Spiegel* demonstrated, it was virtually complete. Far from being an incursion into the innermost filing cabinets of the Defense Ministry, the *Spiegel* argued, the Fallex article could have been put together in any decent library with scissors and paste.

The argument was something of debating point. In point of fact, Martin represented a crucial breakthrough in Augstein's private war with Franz Josef Strauss. After the *Spiegel's* successive barrages against the motorist, the party boss, the parliamentary politician, the friend's friend, and the officers' supreme commander, Strauss the Defense Minister was still standing. Martin could scarcely have appeared at a more opportune time. A delighted Augstein met him halfway, guaranteeing him both the public discussion and the private connections he was after. In fulfillment of the bargain, Augstein sought out the SPD's Gustav Heinemann, once Adenauer's Interior Minister and in early 1962 one of the grand inquisitors in the Fibag investigation. He also brought Martin together with Conrad Ahlers. An extensive conversation in Oberammergau in April 1962 resulted in the "*exposé*," the transcription of Ahlers' notes, that was to be a basic source of the Fallex story six months later. Between the end of March and the end of September, they met at least seven times.

Ahlers had distinguished himself as a very young airborne officer during the war and studied law before taking up journalism, which he temporarily deserted for government service.

Between 1951 and 1954 he was a ranking official of the Federal Information Office (Bundespresseamt), then transferred to the embryo Defense Ministry in 1954 as Theodor Blank's press officer. In late 1955 he joined the Bonn bureau of the *Spiegel*, but was mentioned as a candidate for the Defense Ministry's press office—under Strauss—in November 1957. He wrote the automobile story of September 1958 that opened the *Spiegel's* anti-Strauss campaign, but he was later quoted by a commercial newsletter as saying that he could no longer reconcile *Spiegel* practice with his journalistic conscience.

In late 1959 he was mentioned as a possible press attaché for the German embassy in Ottawa. Instead he went to the left-liberal, FDP-oriented *Frankfurter Rundschau* as its domestic political expert. A little more than two years later, he returned to the *Spiegel*. Symptomatically, conversations with ranking U.S. officers in Frankfurt and then-Assistant Secretary of Defense Paul Nitze in Hamburg followed shortly after Ahlers' return.

In June 1962 came an article headlined "*Stärker als 1939?*" ("Stronger than in 1939?"). The news peg was Adenauer's impending visit to Paris and then-NATO Commander Norstad's demand for at least six more conventionally armed Bundeswehr brigades—the 20,000 men needed to meet the twelve-division planning quota set for the end of 1963. NATO's planning paper MC 70, the basis of West Germany's nuclear armament, was to expire in 1963. Its successor MC 96, which foresaw U.S. sale of Polaris rockets to NATO and the distribution of nuclear grenade throwers down to battalion level, was under fire from the Kennedy administration, which favored strengthening conventional forces and opposed nuclear weapons at battalion level. The budgetary situation added to the political an economic dilemma, the *Spiegel* pointed out. The Federal Republic could have troops or rockets, but not both.

The conflict, the article continued, was mirrored in the Bundeswehr. Strauss preferred to invest in Pershing rockets, with a 375-mile range, for the air force. Should Washington make Pershings unavailable, he was reportedly prepared to invest in a share of the latest French alternative. The *Führungsstab der Bundeswehr*, the general planning staff, supported him; the army opposed him. It argued in favor of less air and more ground forces to implement the Federal Republic's "forward defense"—that is, defense at the zonal boundary rather than from behind the Rhine—without any direct affront to the Russians and endorsed the accelerated conventional armament envisaged by Washington: maintenance of the tactical nuclear weapon program at its present level without the addition of intermediate range rockets and the creation of a tactical air force to support ground troops. It also opposed purchase of new destroyers for the navy.

The Solicitor General's office, in its professional capacity, was unmoved by the article. The Defense Ministry later testified that, although it was taken aback by the article, it preferred to keep silence rather than run the risk of making things worse by authorizing an investigation of the story's sources.

External circumstances governed the progression from "Stronger than in 1939?" to the Fallex article in October. The *Spiegel* had been considering a general survey of the strategic debate. It first thought of a profile of the Bundeswehr's Inspector General, Friedrich Foertsch, who had taken office in April 1961, as a likely peg to hang it on. Then "Fallex 62," the NATO exercise scheduled for September 21–28, whose basic premises seemed to coincide with the apocalyptic premises of the war study, provided a specific news angle.

Ahlers was assigned to the story with Schmelz of the Bonn bureau to assist him. Individual soldiers proved willing to be interviewed, but the Ministry of Defense was uncooperative. Schmelz approached Schmueckle for an appointment with Foertsch in early September. The request was turned down. In the meanwhile Ahlers had sent Schmelz a draft manuscript. Schmelz added a report on the reaction to Schmueckle's *Christ und Welt* article by the *Frankfurter Allgemeine*'s Adelbert Weinstein, and a biographical sketch of Foertsch, and returned the draft. In the course of checking his story Ahlers consulted Major Juergen Brandt of the Bundeswehr staff college in Hamburg on the atomic chain of command. Brandt found an error. It was corrected. Ahlers also took the precaution of showing his draft to Helmut Schmidt, once a fellow student at the University of Hamburg and now Hamburg's Social Democratic Minister of the Interior, who had been among the spectators at the Fallex exercise and was the author of Germany's only serious book on the problems of contemporary military strategy, *Verteidigung oder Vergeltung* (published in the United States as *Defense or Retaliation*).

Schmidt accommodatingly read through the manuscript and indicated the points he suspected might cause trouble with the official-secrets paragraphs. Ahlers again revised his manuscript. In its issue of September 19, the *Spiegel* announced Ahlers' article as the coming week's cover story.

It was at this point that Strauss decided to remain in Bonn, and the *"Onkel Aloys"* article was run instead. At about the same time a Bundeswehr colonel named Adolf Wicht entered the picture. Wicht was a one-time journalism student and career officer who, in the early 1950s had produced a newsletter on East European affairs before he returned to the army. His army status was in fact nominal; he was assigned to Gehlen's foreign intelligence service, the BND. The newsletter too appears to have been a front; its main subscriber was the Bonn government, which cheerfully bought up the unsold edition—technically accessible to anyone willing to pay DM 30 (about $7.50) a month for it—and salvaged the pulp.

Becker, the *Spiegel's* business manager, had been the first West German reporter to make effective contact with Gehlen, in 1954, and they had maintained loose contacts ever since, trading courtesies, Christmas cards, and occasionally material. The courtesies, according to Becker, consisted at this point of two lunches and a secondhand copy of Moltke's memoirs, inscribed by Gehlen. He regarded Gehlen's efforts to recruit *Spiegel* staffers on at least two occasions for part-time work for the BND as a discourtesy.

It was in connection with material that Wicht now approached

Becker. Becker surmised that the announcement of the Fallex story had caught Gehlen's interest. Ahlers had already discussed with Becker the possibility of a BND check of certain portions of his manuscript. Wicht's appearance facilitated the contact. Although he had no intention of showing the BND the manuscript before publication, Becker had little difficulty persuading Wicht to have Ahlers' questions checked. With the circumspection that had earned him the intra-office nickname of "Confucius," Ahlers took until October 1 to produce them. He then turned in two lists with a total of thirteen questions—one of facts to be checked, the other of requested information. Wicht returned the answers four days later.

With them, Ahlers told Becker, was a judicious dose of doctored information that Gehlen, with a professional interest in covering at least some of the Federal Republic's more vulnerable tracks, hoped to see built into Ahlers' article. He had recommended removal of only one of the facts Ahlers had asked to be checked—one that, as it happened, Ahlers had already dropped from his story. The same fact appeared two weeks later in the *Welt* without visible legal consequences.

Next the *Spiegel*'s editors-in-chief, Engel and Jacobi, went over the manuscript. For the sake of coherence, Jacobi took Foertsch out of the main article and ran a sidebar on him. At the last minute, a couple of specific details on the Fallex exercise were tucked into the lead. The story, now a double story, went to the composing room with *"Onkel Aloys."* Augstein read it only after it was set.

The *Spiegel* was highly sensitive to the risks of premature publicity. The Schmeisser article in 1951 and, more recently, the English translation of the Strauss cover story of 1961 had been stopped by court injunctions. As a matter of policy, potentially risky material like *"Onkel Aloys"* was held back as long as possible—until Thursday when half the edition was set. (Technical bottlenecks delayed the second half until Friday night.) But in the case of the Fallex story there seemed to be no reason for particular caution. Type and proofs stood around for a week before publication. After what amounted to something like eight months' work, the story finally appeared on October 8.

Like all *Spiegel* cover stories, it was very detailed, very pointed, and very long. Even without the Foertsch biography, it ran to nearly ten thousand words; an average *Time* cover story is four thousand. It contained, sandwiched between the account of the Fallex exercises, a résumé of the current NATO situation; a survey of Soviet and satellite military potential in Central Europe; a short history of the nuclear-conventional-arms debate in West Germany summarizing its practical consequences to date; a description of current U.S. and NATO nuclear strategy and its development since the beginning of the Kennedy administration; a synopsis of Strauss's views and reservations and the consequent controversy in the Defense Ministry, with an oblique reference to the 1961 war study; a theoretical discussion of the problems of "forward defense"; an analysis of the Bundeswehr's manpower and budgetary situation; a report of the conflicts arising from Strauss's efforts to increase Germany's rocket strength, and an understated but emphatic conclusion. On July 17, Ahlers reported, Strauss and Foertsch had been to see Adenauer. The Chancellor, who was particularly susceptible to their budgetary arguments, had supported their plan to fill existing manpower holes with rockets while delaying the expansion of the Bundeswehr despite current NATO planning goals. "The supreme commander Strauss and his inspector general marched off satisfied," the article ended. "The results of Fallex 62 were not yet available. They report: With rockets in place of brigades and atomic mortars in place of soldiers, forward defense by the Bundeswehr is impossible and effective deterrence remains questionable."

There had been nothing quite like this, in Germany or elsewhere. The dimensions of the *Spiegel* documentation were evidence that Schmelz and Ahlers had collected a remarkable amount of material, perhaps more than many thousands of *Spiegel* readers really wanted to know. But their thesis was unremarkable; it was little more than an extension of "Stronger than in 1939?" published four months before. The article's extra-military intention was, however, obvious. It was one thing to accuse Strauss of speaking loudly and carrying a small stick, of deliberately deceiving his allies. It was quite another to report that he had kept his generals waiting an hour and a half, and withdrawn to a Riviera beach during the Fallex maneuver while McNamara himself packed two days in Germany into a crowded schedule. As it happened, the Federal High Court was later to write off the article's polemic intention to the *Spiegel*'s credit. There was no need to take the article seriously, the court argued in effect, because it was not a very serious article. Defendants can seldom be choosers of the grounds for their acquittal. Under the circumstances, the argument was as good as any other. But it was not exactly a Pulitzer prize for the article concerned.

The results of the Fallex exercise had been reported elsewhere and earlier. Strauss's confidant, Adelbert Weinstein, had reacted to them in the same way that the CDU had reacted to the Berlin crisis a little over a year before. Rather than deny or evade them, he maintained in a *Frankfurter Allgemeine* editorial that they only proved the Federal Republic's current policy right. If retaliation had failed, that was because it had not been massive enough. Conventional defense was utopian. There was no alternative to nuclear deterrence. In any case, "politics, not weapons, is the decisive factor," he wrote. The *Deutsche Zeitung*, also friendly to the government, was still more pointed. To emphasize the need for immediate passage of a comprehensive program of emergency legislation under fire at the time from the SPD and the unions, it enumerated the results of the exercise in even greater detail than the *Spiegel*.

The rest of the *Spiegel* story was unique—at least in the remainder of the West German press whose limited space, limited libraries, limited initiative, or limited motivation all precluded comparable detail, comparable extensiveness, or a comparable tone. But this was no guarantee that the critique would have any direct effect. It was not even certain that a direct effect was intended. Previous experience had long since induced a healthy skepticism. "Because illusions are unjustified, direct influence is neither intended nor will it be checked *post facto,*" the *Spiegel* staff had agreed in 1960. "No article is to be written because it promises a specific effect, for instance via direct personal attacks in particular situations." Ahlers' later statement that the Fallex piece was an article like any other, Jacobi's claim that it was a cover story like the year's fifty-one other cover stories, may have been colored by resignation or even a certain cynicism. But in principle it was probably true.

The lack of general excitement about the piece among the rest of the staff was confirmed by the lack of precautions taken with it. "There are good cover stories," said a senior editor, "but this was not one of them, and nobody thought it was. Except for Martin, it was a matter of scissors and paste. The few coherent paragraphs in the thing were written into it by Schmelz. If Augstein took it seriously at all, it was only because he thought it might hurt Strauss. He didn't even read the piece. He just checked it over to make sure it was anti-Strauss."

The great debate on West German defense policy conceivably intended by Augstein and certainly intended by Martin never did take place, either before the affair or after. Despite Augstein's visit to Heinemann, the Social Democratic opposition obviously preferred to bury the issue. The Bundestag's later debates on the Starfighter in 1965 and 1966 were characteristically limited to the use and maintenance of the plane, not the strategic assumptions that had led to its purchase in the first place.

"Oddly enough, no one seemed concerned over the substance of *Der Spiegel's* exposé," the New York *Times's* Sydney Gruson noted on November 7, 1962, "—that despite all the money spent on defense, the armed forces were in bad shape and would crumble quickly under a Communist attack. No official even bothered to deny this."

An indeterminate number of readers, probably a small minority considering the military indifference of most postwar Germans, were at least better informed than they had been before. A still smaller minority of readers with a professional interest in strategy and politics, among them Amherst's emeritus political scientist

Karl Loewenstein and Colonel Bogislaw von Bonin, one of the German army's reorganizers between 1952 and 1955, reported publicly that they saw nothing remarkable about the article except the furor that it created.

A very specialized group of readers, those who had witnessed the Fallex maneuver and were committed in writing to maintain secrecy about it, were less bitter about the publication per se than they were about the violation of the secrecy they had all been sworn to.

Schmueckle, the Federal Constitutional Court later reported, had hinted to journalists before the article appeared that Helmut Schmidt, who had seen reporters in the course of the maneuver, might have something to do with the leaks. He apparently did not suggest any direct connection between Schmidt and Ahlers. However, newspaper accounts of Schmueckle's hint prompted Schmidt to call Volkmar Hopf, Strauss's undersecretary, at the Defense Ministry. Hopf recalled later that Schmidt was very angry. Otherwise the course of the conversation and even its date—most probably October 9—was a matter of controversy. According to Schmidt, he referred specifically to the review of the maneuver in the *Deutsche Zeitung*. If the ministry was looking for the source of leaks, he suggested, this and not Hamburg was the place to start. Hopf, Schmidt said, replied that he had seen the piece in the *Deutsche Zeitung* but not taken it seriously; the *Spiegel* piece was much worse. In Hopf's version of the conversation, it was Schmidt who brought up the *Spiegel*. The Defense Ministry would now try to make him responsible for the *Spiegel* piece too, Schmidt is supposed to have said. Hopf said Schmidt added that he knew the *Spiegel* people. They had had no need for Schmidt in writing their article; their sources were in the Defense Ministry. Hopf, who claimed that up to now he had seen neither the *Deutsche Zeitung* nor the *Spiegel* article, called for copies. A *Spiegel* version of the Schmidt-Hopf conversation added yet another detail. According to the *Spiegel*, Schmidt called Augstein the same afternoon. "Augstein," he was reported to have said balefully, "there were secrets in that article."

According to the *Spiegel* later, a small group of readers in the Defense Ministry read Ahlers' article with horror. But at the suggestion of their chief security officer, General Gerhard Wessel, they decided to do nothing about it. Wessel, as it happened, was a confidant of Gehlen's. Only one reader took direct action. This was Baron Friedrich August von der Heydte, professor of law at the University of Würzburg and, since June 1962, the Bundeswehr's only reserve general.

Von der Heydte had joined the army as a career officer in 1935. Hitler himself had awarded him the oak leaf complement to his Knight's Cross, Germany's highest military decoration, on October 18, 1944, and on demobilization in 1945, he was an airborne lieutenant colonel. He later claimed to have had a part in the July 1944 anti-Hitler conspiracy.

His subsequent civilian career was distinguished by a weakness for groups like the *Abendländische Akademie*—roughly the "Western Academy" but western in the sense of Spengler's *Decline of the West*—an ultramontane organization with a distaste for parliamentary democracy and a weakness for Francisco Franco. He also published regularly in the *Deutsche Tagespost*, which, notwithstanding its name, appeared only three times a week and whose circulation of twenty thousand rather qualified its claim to be the "leading journal of opinion" for West Germany's twenty-five million Catholics. A journal of opinion it nevertheless was, particularly of pro-Strauss, pro-CSU opinion, of which von der Heydte was an enthusiastic spokesman.

As might be imagined, he was no friend of the *Spiegel*. In the summer of 1962, he had accused it both of lies and deliberate brinkmanship with the official secrets paragraphs—in effect, with treason. The *Spiegel* had replied with an injunction. Von der Heydte countered with a formal charge of the sort potentially open to every citizen. In a letter to the Solicitor General's office on October 1, 1962, he charged that the *Spiegel* had violated the official secrets statutes. Since Schmelz and Ahlers were themselves ex-officers, capable of recognizing a military secret when they saw one, he concluded that they had probably acted deliberately. His charge specifically implicated four articles, one of them "Stronger than in 1939?". A subsequent letter added a fifth, the Fallex story.

During the pandemonium of the following weeks, von der Heydte became famous. The *Spiegel* honored him with a cover story. Not given to false modesty, he did his bit to let it be known that he had performed his patriotic duty, first by leaking the news to the press, then by a personal article in the *Rheinische Merkur*. Questioned on his motives in an interview with a CSU-subsidized student journal, he replied with simple dignity, "Love of my German fatherland."

IV.

THE ACTION

The action began in Karlsruhe, a pleasant city of 250,000 at the north end of the Black Forest, founded by a Duke of Baden in 1715. An attractive classical château with a formidable cupola testifies to the city's origins. On the edge of its grounds, the Institute of Technology (Technische Hochschule) houses one of the Federal Republic's main nuclear research centers.

Around the two symbolic poles, palace and accelerator, are the monuments of the nineteenth century, witnesses to Napoleon and Bismarck, to 1848 when Karlsruhe climbed the democratic barricades, and to 1871 when it acquiesced to blood and iron. A neo-baroque post office, with "Deutsche Reichspost" still inscribed above its front entrance, dominates the main intersection. Before it stands an obelisk commemorating the remarkable range of causes for which the city's inhabitants have fought and died. Perhaps Karlsruhe was destined for lost causes.

In 1949 it became the seat of the Federal Republic's highest judiciary organs, which were housed in the reconstructed Victorian palaces of Baden's royal family. Like the buildings they occupied and the penal code they represented, the federal attorneys retained something of the nineteenth century. The distance between the Pressehaus in Hamburg and the archducal Schlösser in Karlsruhe could be measured not only in kilometers but in decades. There was something fundamentally old-fashioned about Kuhn's reaction to the Fallex article. The law, to which he and his colleagues were dedicated, demanded an investigation. In the nature of things, he turned to the Defense Ministry for corroboration.

Dr. Heinrich Wunder, thirty-eight, of the ministry's legal department was the man responsible for providing it. Wunder had himself been a public prosecutor, had served three years in Karlsruhe, and was well regarded by his former colleagues. He turned to the ministry for technical assistance in checking Kuhn's suspicions, and was given full support. At his request, an air force colonel, Hans-Joachim Hopffgarten, officially responsible for defense policy, strategic planning, and NATO affairs, and a fervent admirer of Strauss, was named his chief consultant. The ministerial library was charged with checking pre-publication of Ahlers' material. On his own, Wunder also consulted a number of other ministerial officials. But neither the vastly more comprehensive government information agency, the Bundespresseamt, nor the Gehlen organization was consulted.

Both Hopf, the ministerial undersecretary, and Schmueckle, the press officer, were informed of Karlsruhe's concern early on in the proceedings. When he was questioned about this later by the Federal Constitutional Court, Hopf failed to remember details. He did recall starting to read the Fallex piece the day after Helmut Schmidt's call, on the morning of October 10, as the Bundeswehr's top security officer came in to report before leaving for the United States. "Wessel," he had said, "please have someone look at this in your department. There's something funny about it." But that was all. Then there was something about a reminder concerning a *Gutachten*, an official brief, requested by the Solicitor General's office. And then one day several people turned up in his office with a *Gutachten*. "Not my affair," Hopf says he told them, but they thought he ought to look at it. Naturally, Hopf recalled, he first checked to be sure that it had already been signed.

On October 12 a memo was prepared for Strauss, who was still on vacation, informing him of the inquiry from Karlsruhe and the steps taken to satisfy it. On October 13 Wunder himself appeared in Karlsruhe—where he still lived—and confirmed Kuhn's suspicions that important secrets were involved. The federal attorney accordingly demanded a comprehensive written *Gutachten* as a basis for the investigation. Wunder later testified that the atmosphere of impending crisis had played a part in his decisions. For safety's sake, he showed his *Gutachten* to a ministerial intelligence officer before closing it. He said he had been reassured that the intelligence officer regarded things as he did.

What had meanwhile grown to a committee presented its work to Hopf on the afternoon of Strauss's return, October 15, the day after a U-2 flight over Cuba established the presence of Soviet rockets. The next day, the day the results of the U-2 flight were reported to President Kennedy, all ten committee members reported directly to Strauss, who leafed through their paper. The pressure of events demanded speedy action, Strauss is reported to have said. Something had to be done about ministerial leaks. On October 17 Wunder finished his report. The day after, he added a summary of Fallex and the strategic publications submitted by the library to his work. On October 18, with military alarm orders out and MPs standing in the ministerial corridors because of the Cuban crisis, the report was officially closed, typed on official stationery, and signed by Wunder alone. The qualification *im Auftrag* (on behalf of the ministry) supplemented the signature. The same evening Strauss notified Adenauer of the anticipated action against the *Spiegel* and kept him informed of its progress in the week that followed. An official government report indicated that Adenauer encouraged him—it was unclear how specifically—to take appropriate steps.

In the course of the affair, the ministry replied indignantly to the charge of collective responsibility. All ministerial correspondence, it was declared, was conducted on ministerial stationery. All ministerial correspondence, whether it was a memo from the undersecretary or an order for paper clips, was signed *im Auftrag;*

the minister himself was the only exception. Wunder was free to write any *Gutachten* he saw fit. By virtue of his office, the responsibility was his, not Schmueckle's, Hopf's, or Strauss's. He had gone about the job alone, however loyally he may have reported to his superiors. Considering that the source of the suspected dereliction presumably lay beneath the ministry roof, and the ministry could expect to be approached for official assistance (*Amtshilfe*), his report to them was a matter of prudence. But there was no evidence that either Hopf or Strauss had made any direct effort to influence him.

This was all reasonably true. A man only just removed from the midst of the federal attorneys, Wunder inclined to see things as they did. He turned to the sources they meant to consult, and he was prepared to believe those sources. But the participation of others relativized his own responsibility, as he himself was candid enough to admit. Wunder was coordinator and scribe. But his material came *ex officio* from an inadequate library and from the supporters of a controversial minister and his controversial policy, who reported that the Fallex piece contained forty-one secrets within the legal definition, and that only twenty-four of them had been published in one form or another elsewhere. This was the message Wunder personally took to Karlsruhe on October 19 and presented to Kuhn. But, as he had six days before, Wunder again emphasized that the work was provisional. Later he intended to go over several points with both the Bundespresseamt and Gehlen's BND. A passage in the *Gutachten* explicitly distinguished his own opinion from the opinion of his military consultants and the bibliographical summary. Wunder also tried to avoid the strictly legal concept of "official secret," preferring to stick instead to secret in the sense of the ministry's security classification.

Kuhn had no such reservations. He had seen a lot of *Gutachten* in his time, he later told the Federal Constitutional Court, and he could tell a good one from a bad one. Wunder, he was convinced, was both reliable and experienced. He contended with awesome plausibility that he was scarcely aware that the ministry was a party to the controversy the *Spiegel* reported. Like his colleagues, he knew only vaguely that there was a strategic controversy in progress at all, let alone that the Fallex article was meant as a part of it. In any case, Kuhn had already made up his mind. A journalist can get his hands on a single secret without realizing it, Kuhn maintained, but no reporter could publish fifteen or forty-one of them without being aware of the risk. The question of previous publication was the ministry's affair. The law required the Solicitor General's office to investigate where suspicion was justified. The *Gutachten* was at most a confirmation of objective suspicion. Logic alone, he argued, confirmed the suspicion of subjective intent. The next day, a Saturday, he brought a copy of the article, along with Wunder and the *Gutachten*, to his superior, Walter Wagner, deputy to the office's acting chief. For the first time, Wagner started to read the article.

At this point Hopf appeared. In his later testimony, he was again uncertain of the details. Yes, he was passing through on business. Yes, he wanted the federal attorneys to know they had the full support of the ministry: no limits, let the investigation lead where it might. Should they have any problems, the ministry was prepared to make Bundeswehr cars available, for instance.

Wagner, a round, bright-eyed little man in his sixties, on the other hand, remembered the morning of October 20 very well. He said that Hopf was indeed passing through. He had left his wife in a café before coming to see Kuhn and Wagner, and, according to Wagner, he emphasized at the start that the *Spiegel* had published a number of very important secrets; that Robert McNamara had been so shaken he had complained to the Bonn government; that the reliability of the Federal Republic was in question and something had to be done. He denied having seen Wunder's *Gutachten*. He declared he wanted to make all this clear on his own authority.

Wagner was inclined to believe him. He asked whether Hopf was requesting police measures to close the leak in the Defense Ministry. He said that Hopf had replied, "Not exactly," but indicated that he had no very good idea how to go about stopping the leaks himself, and was in favor of the *ultima ratio*.

Wagner recalled that he had reminded Hopf of the potential risks. The war in progress between Strauss and the *Spiegel* was not the happiest premise for an investigation. Hopf, Wagner said, had replied that Strauss had not seen Wunder's *Gutachten* and did not know that Hopf had gone to Karlsruhe. Wagner, according to his later testimony, had agreed that the investigation would proceed according to the *Legalitätsprinzip*, the principle of prosecution irrespective of political expediency.

According to Wagner, Hopf offered full assistance—cars, the Bundeswehr's telegraphic facilities, and the services of the ministry's security agency, the *militärische Abschirmdienst* (abbreviated MAD). This would probably not be necessary, Wagner had replied, and might make the wrong impression. Hopf had agreed that all press and security matters were to remain in the hands of the Solicitor General's office. Wagner had indicated that the investigation would necessarily proceed against "X and others," against the military sources as well as the authors of the article. He neither requested aid nor discussed intended measures with Hopf, he said. But he took Hopf's appearance seriously. He saw it as a confirmation of the *Gutachten*, particularly in view of Hopf's reference to U.S. concern with the Fallex story. It also seemed to be a confirmation of the offense against the official secrets statutes, and further indirect evidence of the urgency of the case. The leaks in the ministry had evidently existed for some time.

Before Hopf left, Wagner scheduled a meeting for Monday with the ministry's top security officers; Wunder; Kuhn; a representative of the *Bundeskriminalamt*, West Germany's only federal police force; and a judge of the Federal High Court who would be responsible for the necessary search and arrest warrants. Hopf, Wagner said, promised to inform the Ministry of Justice of the intended action.

In Washington the next day President Kennedy resolved to blockade Cuba and informed Britain's Ambassador David Ormsby-Gore of his decision. On Monday U.S. embassies were briefed and

other allies informed. The same day the executives of the forthcoming *Spiegel* action met in Karlsruhe. Gehlen's BND was explicitly excluded from the meeting, although Strauss himself let
Gehlen in on the story three days later. Hopf had also asked that
local police be excluded from the action to reduce the number of
participants. But the participation of the *Bundeskriminalamt* was
unavoidable, and with it the Federal Ministry of the Interior to
which it was responsible. Federal Attorney Buback, appointed by
Kuhn to supervise the action in Hamburg, was apparently the first
to appreciate the implications of this: that local authorities would
have to be notified, as the law required, before the *Bundeskriminalamt* went into action within their jurisdiction.

The main problem facing the Monday meeting was one of
dimensions. It was agreed that Ahlers' responsibility was self-
evident. Augstein's responsibility for the editorial contents of his
magazine was presumably established by a well-timed reference to
his decision to postpone the Fallex piece in favor of *"Onkel
Aloys."*

German law permits the arrest of suspects without formal indictment. The suspect can then be held pending investigation.
The law requires only that he be kept separate from persons already convicted. Arrest presupposes a warrant issued by a judge
on the application of the public prosecutor. The judge naturally
has the option of rejecting the application. Under special circumstances, a suspect can be held by police without a warrant.
But he must be brought before a judge within twenty-four
hours for consideration of formal arrest.

Once under arrest, the suspect is entitled to request a judicial
review at any time. An automatic review is required every three
months in cases where the suspect has not himself requested it.
But theoretically, he can be held indefinitely as long as the judge
finds that arrest is still justified by the danger of escape or collusion. A practical example was the case of a sixty-four-year-old
man in Cologne in 1966. Suspected of murder during the Nazi
era, he had been held for investigation without formal indictment
and trial for nearly seven years.

It was now decided to search the *Spiegel* offices for relevant evidence and to arrest Augstein and Ahlers for investigation. Considering the problems involved if large numbers of people were on the premises during an action, it was agreed that a weekend would probably be best for the search and arrests. On weekends it could also be assumed that the suspects would be home from any business trips. Late October weather presumably precluded the possibility of family excursions. The self-confessed failure of Strauss's security officers to locate suspects in the ministry made a simultaneous operation in Bonn desirable. This was assigned to Federal Attorney Oberle. It was originally intended that the investigation should be confined to the ministry. Its extension to the Bonn *Spiegel* bureau occurred to Oberle later.

Next came the question of charges. It was Kuhn's own idea to supplement the treason charge with bribery, although Wunder, he later told the Federal Constitutional Court, supported his reasoning. Questioned by the court about the motivation of the bribery charge, Kuhn replied, with what was meant to be a shrewd wink, "*Lebenserfahrung* (I wasn't born yesterday)." Since it was obvious that any officer caught passing on secrets must expect the ultimate consequences, material gain must have been the motive.

With the experience of years of espionage investigation behind them, the Karlsruhe staff settled back for a quick and efficient operation. "All we had to do was find the material," Kuhn explained. Then there was to be an interrogation of the editors involved and the arrest of the main suspects, and the whole matter would be over in a couple of days. "But it all came out differently than the way we planned it," he added ruefully.

The next day, as Dean Acheson arrived in Bonn to inform Adenauer of Kennedy's intentions, Buback appeared in Wagner's office with comprehensive search warrants and warrants for the arrest of Augstein, Ahlers, and Hans Dieter Jaene of the Bonn bureau. Bribery was written into the Hamburg search warrant. All warrants were qualified for execution at night, although, with the published article already two weeks old, it was hard to see the possibility of catching the suspects *in flagranti* as the law demanded in such cases. Wagner nonetheless had no objections, though he rejected the idea of arresting Jaene and reminded Buback again of the problems to be faced: the proof of Augstein's specific responsibility, the need for a judge to supervise the search, and the strong possibility of difficulties with evidence. Wagner testified later that Buback was to find *the*, or at most several, documents; that he had informed Wunder that written confirmation of the intended action would follow directly, and had asked for appropriate caution in the ministry to avoid any premature suspicion among the yet-undiscovered suspects.

On October 24 Adenauer informed his cabinet of Acheson's visit and the Cuban crisis, which seemed likely to affect Berlin. He had not slept so badly in years, he observed gloomily. In the course of the day, Westram, the acting Solicitor General, was informed of the impending investigation. He emphasized the need to keep the Ministry of Justice informed. Hopf called Karlsruhe the same day to report that he had reached Stammberger's undersecretary, Walter Strauss. It was assumed that this would suffice.

It did not suffice from Stammberger's point of view. Stammberger's only source of information to date had been the carbon copy of an inquiry about the progress of the Wunder *Gutachten* that had inadvertently come to his attention. At a meeting at the Defense Ministry the afternoon of October 24, Hopf and Franz Josef Strauss informed Walter Strauss of the conversations in Karlsruhe the preceding Saturday and enjoined him to make an official of his ministry available on short notice for consultation —weekends included. But they also instructed him not to inform his minister any further until the action was under way. This official government report on the affair indicated that Strauss had intimated this was on orders from the Chancellor.

A day earlier, Buback and Oberle had left for their respective missions. Oberle went directly into a huddle with the Defense Ministry's security officers and set to work analyzing the Fallex article for possible clues. Attention centered on the army general staff, the *Führungsstab des Heeres*, but this still left something like a hundred suspects. "Stronger than in 1939?" brought to his attention on Thursday, seemed an easier place to begin. Oberle later recalled he had cursed the reluctance of the army investigators to take action in June when the circle of potential suspects could have been limited to half a dozen. The reference nonetheless redirected his attention to Jaene and the Bonn bureau where the story had, in part, originated.

Meanwhile Buback and the federal police assigned to him, with the tacit aid of the MAD-men made available in Schleswig-Holstein, began organizing the action in Hamburg. The five police officers arrived half-briefed on the nature of the case. Their leader, Karl Schuetz, had read them the Fallex article on the way. In Karlsruhe testimony later, he conceded that the group traveling in a second car had not heard the story. Buback continued the briefing. The police were to put Ahlers, Augstein, and the editors-in-chief, Jacobi and Engel, under observation. He then indicated what was to be done, but not when. Timing was to be decided when all suspects had been definitely located. Buback also emphasized the potential difficulties involved in searching editorial offices whose contents and operation were protected by law.

On Friday the suspects had still not been found. Buback's thoughts turned to the possibilities of weekend recreation in Hamburg. Schuetz allowed himself and his men the luxury of a long lunch. By chance, they found a private room at a Hamburg restaurant where Schuetz reports he briefed them again on the legal niceties of their mission. He even read them relevant passages from the standard constitutional commentary. He also encouraged them to buy copies of the incriminated *Spiegel*.

The *Spiegel* was aware of the investigation but not the details. Helmut Schmidt's conversation with Augstein on October 9 had been a first warning. Ahlers, warned independently of unusual activity in the Defense Ministry, had suggested to Becker that he might like to approach Wicht for confirmation. Becker spoke with Wicht at a meeting on October 16. "Nice article," Wicht remarked with an allusion to his own participation. "Not the story I heard," Becker says he replied. "What's this about an investigation?" Wicht promised to look into the matter. He returned two days later to confirm that what Ahlers had heard was true. "Don't put the blame on us," he told Becker, although he agreed to accept responsibility for the BND's help with Ahlers' questions. Ahlers' tip and Wicht's confirmation made it clear that the Fallex article was involved. At this point Becker consulted Armin Sellheim, the *Spiegel* lawyer. "What could they charge us with?" he asked. "Treason," Sellheim answered. Ahlers was informed in writing that he could make use of his right to protect his sources. Becker, Jacobi, Engel, and Ahlers got together to discuss what to do. They concluded optimistically that the Strauss-Augstein squabble precluded any substantial action. Ahlers nonetheless removed his notes and expense account records from his office before leaving for a Spanish vacation on October 19, turning them over to his secretary who took them home.

"The ideal situation would have been this," Buback later declared. "We would have got all the suspects at one blow, gone into the office, found the material we were looking for, and left." But the situation was the very opposite of ideal. To begin with, the suspects couldn't be found. By Friday, only Engel and Jacobi had been located. Although Augstein had been in his office every day since Wednesday when the police arrived in Hamburg, they had somehow failed to notice him. For three days they had also stood in front of the wrong house, waiting in vain for Ahlers to emerge. They failed to discover that he was on vacation at all.

A routine check of the public registry had meanwhile produced the discovery of Augstein's 1957 campaign address, extending the search to Düsseldorf. On Friday afternoon the federal police learned that a large and impressive Mercedes with a Hamburg license had been seen in front of the *Spiegel*'s Düsseldorf bureau. It was assumed that Augstein was in it. The voice of reason, in the person of an incredulous police official who had seen Augstein on TV within the past few weeks, was drowned out in the din that followed. At 6:30 P.M., as the suspect reappeared with a Sunday duck wrapped up under his arm and the evident intention of driving away, he was stopped and taken to the next police station. A burly man of fifty-three with a pear-shaped face, he reportedly had some difficulty taking the whole thing seriously. He was not Augstein, he repeated; and indeed he was not. He was Erich Fischer, one of the *Spiegel's* advertising salesmen. With considerable reluctance, they let him go. "God knows what was going on in their heads," Becker observed a few years later. "Only *their* boss drives that kind of car. Maybe that's what they thought." When it was later self-consciously presented to the public as a quasi-excuse for the historic Friday night action, the episode seemed too ridiculous to believe. It was even interpreted as a specimen of particularly subtle Machiavellianism. But it was all quite true. In any case, it had to be reported to the administrative center of the operation, the Federal Police Office in Bad Godesberg.

The report had its effect. "I was beside myself," Oberle recalls. Foremost in everyone's mind was the potential danger. What if Fischer were to notify Augstein and the others? It was resolved to carry on. Not North Rhine-Westphalia's FDP interior minister, Willy Weyer, but his CDU undersecretary, Ludwig Adenauer, a nephew of the Chancellor's, was informed shortly after 8 P.M. of an impending action within his jurisdiction. A representative of the Federal Ministry of the Interior, dispatched to Hamburg to notify Helmut Schmidt, reached him at home about the same time. Around 9 P.M. Buback went into action. Since the *Spiegel* went to press on Friday night, they found a full house to greet them.

Buback asked for Augstein's office and was directed to the back of the building. Augstein had left at eight, but Jacobi was in the office next door. He told the visitors that he was the only responsible editor in the house. He was thereupon asked to clear the offices. Aware that this would delay or prevent publication, he refused. Buback dispatched Schuetz to get rid of the sixty-odd remaining staff members who by now, as the official report later observed fastidiously, were "indicating with exclamations of displeasure that they refused to leave the premises." Buback called the Hamburg riot squad. They arrived and looked on skeptically as Buback exhorted them to render aid and assistance. They finally agreed to provide "protection" while Buback and his men conducted the actual investigation. Staff members agreed to withdraw to the editorial conference room until the search was finished. Jacobi was taken into custody. The next day he was formally arrested. Sometime after nine, Engel was stopped as he approached the Pressehaus and also taken into custody.

Augstein was notified indirectly of the police activity by Josef Klessinger, a staff reporter, and Leo Brawand, the *Spiegel*'s economics editor, before the telephones, teletypes, and the house intercom were cut off. Klessinger resourcefully called dpa, the German wire service, and asked them to get in touch with Josef Augstein. Brawand had already reached him via a call to his wife. Josef Augstein passed the message on to his brother and Becker at a party. They had just opened a 1959 Mosel, Becker later recalled, and were at first reluctant to believe the story. Josef Augstein, who had no similar doubts, hung up and drove off to Hamburg at one hundred miles an hour. He arrived at the Pressehaus around 4 A.M.

Brawand had meanwhile called Jacobi on the intercom while the police stood in Jacobi's office. On the correct assumption that the police would not understand, he delivered the message in English. "Very good," Jacobi replied. With police audibly headed in his direction, Brawand tucked himself into his coat closet until the search had gone past, then cut the seal of his door and prepared to go home. He was challenged at the main entrance by police astonished that they had missed him. "I was sitting in my closet," he answered truthfully. "In your closet?" the policeman echoed. "I always sit in my closet when I have a difficult problem to think about," Brawand said.

The visit of the police was documented with some success by a staff photographer, Frank Mueller-May, who followed them around until they lost patience and threatened to take his camera away. The first roll of film was tucked into the pocket of a darkroom assistant who subsequently smuggled it out of the building in her brassière. The pictures appeared the following week. A later roll was confiscated and not returned.

While the police made their way through the building, sealing offices and clearing out the balance of the staff, Jacobi delegated a rump group of ten to close the edition. They were escorted by eleven policemen. Since refusal to permit work to continue would have prevented the appearance of the next issue, Buback's acquiescence cleared a potential constitutional hurdle. Another turned up in the course of the evening when police tried to seize a set of proofs. Johannes Matthiesen, the makeup editor, refused to hand them over. Schuetz had to intervene. The proofs were confiscated, sealed in an envelope, and brought to Buback, who was to pass them on to the judge assigned to supervise the search. The seizure was ordered explicitly to prevent an extension of the original "treasonable" publication, for instance, an "epilogue" to the Fallex article. But such an "epilogue" would have appeared in any case in Monday morning's Spiegel. That the proofs contained evidence directly relevant to the Fallex article was in any case implausible. Under the circumstances, the confiscation seemed a direct attempt to prevent further treasonable publication, or, as the Spiegel saw it, to exercise censorship. The judge who looked through the proofs permitted publication as usual. By this time, it was 4:45 A.M.

Although Jacobi and Engel had been arrested, the search for them continued well into the evening. Reporters from the Hamburg papers monitoring the police radio first realized something was in progress when a squad car was sent in pursuit of a car alleged to contain a Herr Augustin (sic), as well as a Herr Jacobi and a Herr Engel. The car belonged, in fact, to a plasterer named Werner Dolata who had been working in the Pressehaus cafeteria. He had attracted the attention of the police by running to his car, partly because it was cold and he had no coat, partly because he was hungry and eager to get home. Police pursued the bewildered Dolata to the door of his house, stopped him, established their error, and fined him five marks for speeding.

A further search for Jacobi led to the apartment of the *Spiegel*'s Ernst Hess, who writes under the name of Peter Bruegge. The doorbell called Hess from the bathtub. His suspicions were awakened by the alacrity with which one of the policemen put his foot into the door. He waited for them to leave, then called police headquarters to report the incident. There were men poking around his apartment, he said, who claimed to be police officers. Another car was dispatched to look into the matter.

The entire episode might have been written for the Keystone Kops.

Engel and Jacobi, by this time in firm custody, were taken to their homes where the police proceeded to search their houses, confiscating, among other things, a private postcard of Engel's and the business card of a Hamburg créche. The search of Engel's office the next morning produced a correspondence with a photo archive in Moscow and an exchange of letters with the Bavarian Radio concerning a radio play about J. Robert Oppenheimer. At Jacobi's the search extended even to the children's beds—from which the children were temporarily removed—and the straw of the pony's stall. A soap carton of private correspondence and manuscripts, a tape with family recordings on it, and a notebook with sketches by Jacobi's son were carried away as evidence. As the law required, everything was neatly itemized on a receipt before being taken away.

In Augstein's absence, his house was searched in the presence of his wife and John Jahr. Here the police carried off a mass of private papers, including letters going back to the war and a book of school essays. Ahlers' home was searched in the presence of Frau Ahlers' aunt, Fräulein Wildhagen, the Ahlers children, and a maid. Because she could not negotiate stairs, Fräulein Wildhagen was carried to the basement to witness the investigation there as the law demanded. In the evidence seized was an airline prospectus confirming what Fräulein Wildhagen had already volunteered: that Ahlers and his wife, at the moment, were in

Torremolinos near Málaga. Frau Ahlers, she added, had called during the day to announce that they were planning an excursion to Tangier the next day to visit an old school friend. They then planned to return to Torremolinos and to arrive home on November 8.

Around midnight, the information on Ahlers' whereabouts was relayed to the Federal Police Office in Bad Godesberg, where three representatives of the Defense Ministry were observing the proceedings. One of them was Wunder, a second was from the MAD. The third was Councillor Schnell, who was responsible for investigating corruption in the ministry. He was present at Strauss's specific request.

Schnell ("swift") was the possessor of one of the allegorical names that somehow turned up in the affair with remarkable frequency. Other examples were Wunder ("wonder") and Wicht ("villain"), Becker's contact man from the cloak-and-dagger BND. Although not altogether appropriate to his role in the affair, there was also Dickopf ("fathead"), the director of the Federal Police Office. A bit further removed was Kleinknecht ("hired hand") of the Ministry of Justice, and even Strauss himself. Strauss's defense policy had already inspired innumerable puns on Vogelstrauss ("ostrich"). His single-minded pugnacity now recalled Strauss—"skirmish" or "squabble."

Schnell shared Schmueckle's telephone line. As a result, he was one large step ahead of the police. They established Ahlers' whereabouts only around midnight on October 26. Schnell had known for days where Ahlers was. One of Ahlers' surviving contacts from his Blank Office days in the early fifties was Colonel Achim Oster, the son of Major General Hans Oster, Admiral Canaris' chief of staff of wartime counter-espionage, who had notified the Dutch of the impending invasion of their country in 1940 and was later executed after the failure of the anti-Hitler plot of July 1944. Achim had been a founding member of the CSU and was thus an old acquaintance of Strauss's. He was now military attaché at the German embassy in Madrid. Before leaving for Spain, Ahlers had written to suggest they get together. Oster had called Schmueckle to inquire what to do. The ministry had no objections. Schnell monitored the call. Late in the evening on October 26, Schnell called Hopf.

Between eleven and midnight, Hopf called back to inquire about the possibility of extradition. Brueckner, the deputy director of the Federal Police Office, was skeptical. He recommended three alternative courses: the Foreign Ministry, the Justice Ministry, and the West German Interpol headquarters in Wiesbaden. But he doubted that anything was likely to come from any of them. The international convention on extradition limits it to criminal offenses. Political offenses are specifically excluded. Hopf replied darkly that the Defense Ministry had another course of its own. After he hung up, Brueckner mentioned the call, and Hopf's oracular reference. He then called his chief in Wiesbaden, Paul Dickopf, to tell him to expect a call from Hopf. As he was to accompany Federal President Lübke the next day on a tour of the Far East, Brueckner authorized a member of the Godesberg group, Theo Saevecke, to take his place in the direction of the *Spiegel* action, and went home.

Hopf remained at the telephone. He first talked to Dickopf, then to Dr. Kleinknecht, an official of the Ministry of Justice ordered to be available for consultation during the action. Kleinknecht confirmed what Brueckner had already told Hopf. He was altogether out of sympathy with Hopf's proposal that "wanted" notices be posted. So was Kuhn, whom Kleinknecht called next. A round of calls between Kuhn, Kleinknecht, Dickopf, and Saevecke followed. All of them agreed that the case was beyond the prerogatives of Interpol.

The subsequent investigation by the Bonn district attorney's office established that Hopf now went his own way, to the ministry and Strauss, who had returned there from an evening engagement. After an intensive conversation, Strauss had his adjutant call Madrid sometime after midnight. He was connected with an embassy clerk named Reif. Oster was to call him on an extremely urgent matter within half an hour, he announced to the startled clerk, then asked if he knew whether

Oster had booked a hotel room for a *Spiegel* reporter in southern Spain. No, Reif replied. "Do you know whether a *Spiegel* reporter named Ahlers is presently in Spain?" Strauss asked. Yes, Reif replied. "Knowledge of his whereabouts is enormously important in connection with the Cuban crisis," Strauss retorted. "I hereby enjoin you to mention this conversation to no one but Colonel Oster. This is an order. I am acting at the moment in the name of the Chancellor and the Foreign Minister." The validity of the first claim was later a matter of controversy. The latter, however, was a straightforward misrepresentation. The authority of the Defense Minister does not extend to diplomatic personnel. In any case, there had been no contact whatsoever with the Foreign Ministry. Reif, however, asked no questions.

Shortly afterward, Hopf called Dickopf again to report that he had heard that Ahlers was in Spain and that highest government sources were intensely concerned that the action be led to a successful conclusion. Dickopf repeated that he had no authority to order an arrest abroad—in Spain or anywhere else. Hopf replied that he would contact Oster.

According to the Bonn district attorney's report, about a quarter of an hour after Strauss's call, Reif reached Oster, who drove directly to the embassy and reached the Defense Ministry around 1:30 A.M. Strauss asked him if he knew of Ahlers' presence. Oster replied that he had neither arranged the trip, nor found a hotel for him, but had seen him the week before as he passed through in the direction of Torremolinos. Strauss announced that a number of *Spiegel* editors had been arrested on suspicion of treason, and that a warrant had been issued against Ahlers on suspicion of bribery as well. This, like the reference to the Foreign Ministry, was untrue. Unfortunately, Strauss continued, the investigation also extended to a number of officers. He indicated that proceedings were under way against about a dozen. All this, he emphasized, was a severe blow to the security of the Federal Republic in the midst of an international crisis.

At this point, Strauss switched from the intimate pronoun, with which the conversation had thus far been conducted, and addressed Oster with portentous formality. "Colonel Oster," he said, "I have just come from the Chancellor and what I now have to say is an order, not only in my name but in the name of the Chancellor." This again was not true. It was a matter of decisive significance, Strauss said, that Ahlers be arrested as quickly as possible.

A particularly vivid aberration followed. Ahlers had telephoned Jacobi from Málaga the day before to ask how the *Spiegel* was going to deal with the Cuban crisis. "Should I pack my bags?" he asked. "Not necessary," Jacobi replied. "Rudolf has taken care of it already."[1] Both later recalled that it had been a particularly bad connection—probably, Ahlers surmised, because the MAD was tapping the line. He assumed it was they who heard the word Cuba. Strauss apparently further embroidered their report. It was particularly important that Ahlers be located, Strauss de-

---

[1] He took care of it with a blistering attack on U.S. policy.

"The American public—with its European allies in tow—made a decision fateful for Europe and particularly for Berlin when it established the Kennedy doctrine without exhausting the existing possibilities. This was the doctrine that a world power need accept no essential threat to its interests on its own borders. The connection between Berlin and Cuba was in Kennedy's mind two months ago when he rejected the proposal of a Cuban intervention with reference to West Berlin.

"It is hard to see how so self-evident a calculation can have changed and why the administration in Washington has now come to the view, according to the New York *Times*, that the Cuban blockade has interrupted well-planned Soviet efforts to achieve a Berlin settlement humiliating to the West.

"On the contrary, it has exercised a might-is-right philosophy that makes any limitation of the risks in the conflict between the respective power blocs impossible. . . . The world will skid into World War III as it slid into World War I, on a slide of uncalculated risks and liberating, 'now or never' determination. To be sure, there are the gravest reasons to doubt whether any historians will be left to bemoan the slide."

In the introduction to a later published collection of his editorials, Augstein admitted that he had misjudged Kennedy's sense of proportion. "The error was terrific," he wrote. "Khrushchev's decision to back down the next day might well have saved mankind. It certainly saved the *Spiegel.*"

clared to Oster, because Augstein was already in Cuba. The leak in the Defense Ministry had to be stopped. It was oppressive to think, he said, that he might have to take action in defense of Berlin the next day with the additional hazard of disloyalty in his own ranks.

To Oster's objection that he lacked any basis for such an action, Strauss replied that the arrest warrant was under way via Interpol. He told Oster to notify the Spanish authorities of Ahlers' whereabouts and to support their efforts to take him in custody. Oster told the Bonn district attorney's office later that he had the impression in the course of the conversation that Hopf was within earshot, an issue that was later to be of considerable importance. Whether he was physically present, however, or on another line was something Oster was unable to establish. Like Reif, he asked no questions.

Instead he went directly to Dr. Feit, the director of the embassy's consular section, and told him the whole story. As Feit later testified, it had improved in the meantime. As he understood it, Oster told Feit—according to Feit's later testimony —that the *Spiegel* editors had all committed treason, betrayed NATO plans, and committed bribery. The entire *Spiegel* office had been seized by police.

By now it was 2 A.M. Feit asked Oster if he were sure that the arrest warrant was under way. Yes, said Oster. Was he also sure that Strauss had referred to Schroeder? Yes, said Oster.

Feit recommended that they see the consular secretary, Kunz, who was in permanent contact with the Spanish police. Kunz called the director of the Spanish Interpol office, Pozo Gonzáles, who agreed to receive them. Oster reported the whole story with reference to a "criminal dereliction" (meaning bribery), "Communist organization," "danger of war," and "flight of the *Spiegel*'s publisher to Cuba," it was later recalled. Pozo Gonzáles interpreted this as a request for provisional custody of Ahlers pending extradition. He took Oster's word that the warrant was on the way. Considering the somewhat unusual circumstances, he agreed to act immediately and ordered the police authorities in

Málaga to advance on Ahlers' hotel in Torremolinos. Ahlers' request to be called at 6 A.M. so that he could make the plane for Morocco played a role in his decision, the Spaniard later reported.

At 3 A.M. Ahlers and his wife were awakened by the police. Linguistic barriers prevented a serious exchange of views. The police turned away modestly while Frau Ahlers dressed. Then, because their orders left some doubt about the situation, they locked up both of them at the local police commissariat. Frau Ahlers was released with apologies later in the morning. At 5:30 A.M. Feit was notified. He notified Oster who called Strauss.

The Bonn district attorney's office reported that in the absence of the ambassador, who was on vacation, the embassy's chargé d'affaires, Breuer, was meanwhile screaming for the promised warrant. At 7 A.M. Oster called Strauss's adjutant, at nine he repeated his story once again to Breuer. Breuer observed that he could act only on the orders of the Foreign Ministry. Oster called Hopf, informed him of Breuer's position, and asked for intervention at the Foreign Ministry. Hopf replied that he had called Schroeder's undersecretary, Karl Carstens, a quarter of an hour before, and that Carstens had called Breuer. Breuer later testified that Carstens had informed him of the urgency of Ahlers' arrest. At this point, Carstens learned from Breuer that the matter had already been taken care of. Unfortunately he neglected to pass the information on to Schroeder until it had become an international incident.

As Saevecke returned to the Federal Police Office in Bad Godesberg at nine on Saturday morning, one of the observers from the Defense Ministry met him with the request that the arrest warrant be sent on immediately to Oster at the embassy in Madrid. Assuming that the embassy wanted the warrant for its own information, Saevecke agreed. Since he had no direct teletype connection to Madrid, he passed the request on to headquarters in Wiesbaden. Wiesbaden, the Federal Republic's Interpol center, forwarded the message to Madrid.

Breuer meanwhile visited the Spanish Foreign Ministry, which informed him it would consider an extradition request, but was not prepared to guarantee its success. A second possibility was that Ahlers might be declared *persona non grata* and requested to leave. But he could not be asked to fly directly to the Federal Republic against his will. The third possibility was voluntary agreement to return home. Both the embassy and the Spanish Foreign Ministry agreed that the last suggestion was the most promising.

The plane was scheduled for 3:20 P.M. Feit, who, as it turned out, had studied with Ahlers at the University of Hamburg, accompanied him to the airport. "I never was much of a law student," Ahlers recalled telling him, "so maybe you could answer a theoretical question for me. If I hadn't agreed to leave voluntarily, could I be extradited?" It was unclear, Ahlers said, whether Feit couldn't answer the question or whether he wouldn't. Before departure, Ahlers remembered, Feit had observed with simple patriotic pride, "I think it's just wonderful that our government is still capable of delivering such a punch." To prevent any possible suicide attempt, Ahlers' toilet articles were confiscated as he boarded the plane and deposited with the pilot, who thought they were important diplomatic documents. At 7:15 P.M. Sunday evening, Ahlers arrived at Frankfurt airport and was immediately arrested. By this time, Augstein had long since turned himself in and Engel had been released.

The remainder of the Bonn action was anticlimactic by comparison. Friday night, as Buback advanced on the Pressehaus, Oberle and his group headed for the bureau in Bonn. They found it closed. Reporter Hans-Roderich Schneider, who had been the last man to leave the office, was brought back to open it. He was enjoined to bring along "the papers" he had taken home with him as he left. They turned out to be the day's newspapers. Schneider reiterated that not he but Jaene was the man responsible for the bureau. Finally he was believed. Around 9 P.M. Jaene was called away from the family TV by the appearance of the police. In the meanwhile, the remaining detectives passed the time of night with Schneider, an economics specialist. They talked about cars, Schneider later reported. One police official asked him with evident concern what he should do with his Volkswagen shares. The office copy machine seems to have made a particular impression. They wished they had such a new one, one of the policemen observed.

Shortly before ten, Jaene arrived and Oberle read him the search warrant, requesting his assistance. The search went on for several hours. "What would happen if I decided to leave?" Jaene asked hypothetically. He would be taken into custody and jailed, was the reply. Jaene, an officer's son from Potsdam who had already been locked up in the Soviet occupation zone for illegal political activity as a teenager, decided against leaving. Instead, he was taken home to pick up pajamas and toilet articles and kept for the night at the Federal Police Office in Bad Godesberg. At eleven the next morning he was brought back to the bureau, where the remaining offices were searched and the files confiscated. Two photocopied transcripts of sessions of the Bundestag's defense committee were found among Schmelz's papers. They concerned the air force lieutenant colonel, Barth, who had been transferred from his command by Strauss in 1961. Saturday night Jaene was released.

Sunday the search resumed at Schmelz's house. Schmelz himself was in Budapest. Frau Schmelz was witness. It was military material that was sought, and military material that was found— but military in the widest conceivable sense, such as material on the Reichswehr of the twenties and the so-called Röhm putsch of 1934. Material on Strauss was also collected, as well as information on the conduct of political justice in the Federal Republic. A private phone book of Frau Schmelz's was confiscated and the family bank book was examined with interest.

Schmelz himself was informed of the action only on Monday by the press secretary of the Hungarian Foreign Ministry who had read it in a Reuters report. Rather than wait for a postponed interview with Hungary's Deputy Premier Kallai, he proceeded to Vienna, where he met Josef Augstein. Toward midnight on October 30, he called Bonn for confirmation of the situation.

With his colleague Ferdinand Simoneit, he then drove directly home and turned himself in. Dpa reported that he had been offered asylum by the Hungarian government. "Asylum," however, turned out to be a rescheduled interview with Kallai.

All the while the search was under way in Hamburg, accompanied by endless difficulties. "The atmosphere was nightmarish," Buback recalled. He was regularly interrupted by phone calls, some anonymously threatening, some sophomorically prankish. "This is Augstein," said one caller. "I'm at my friend Strauss's, and we've made up again, so you can stop and go home." Having just laboriously given up cigarettes, Buback started to smoke again.

At noon on Saturday, Augstein turned himself in in a blaze of publicity. The valet tagging behind him with his suitcase attracted particular notice. The publicity included a story in Bucerius' *Die Zeit* and Nannen's *Der Stern* in November 1962, which pictured the federal police who made the arrest, although it did not name them. The three, Schuetz, Siegfried Heider, and Heinz Luebke, thereupon sued for DM 10,000 damages plus 4 per cent interest dating from November 11, 1962. They claimed that foreign intelligence agents had thereby learned their identity with resulting risk for their personal safety.

Their suit was rejected in the first instance, and an appeal was later rejected in Hamburg. A third plea, presented as a civil suit in Düsseldorf in 1966, was turned down again. The Düsseldorf judges distinguished between "absolute" and "relative" historical actors. The plaintiffs, they declared, belonged to the latter group. The arrest of October 27, 1962, was a significant historical event, they argued. The plaintiffs, "relative" historical actors all, had no say in the matter, they were just there. It was a kind of occupational hazard. The plaintiffs were ordered to pay court costs.

With his brother's encouragement, Augstein agreed on his arrest to support the investigation that until then had been going on in Becker's presence. On Sunday, Augstein was taken to the office to confront a Buback already worn out by the preliminary efforts to find a hypothetical needle in a large field of haystacks. Ahlers had cleared his office before leaving for Spain.

The fact that nothing was found there only confirmed Buback's suspicions. Augstein's office yielded more. At Buback's suggestion, they began with the safe. At the top of the pile inside it was an envelope addressed to Augstein personally. In it was Ahlers' "*exposé*," the transcript of his first conversation with Martin. Both of them stood there shocked, Buback recalls. He speculates that Augstein had forgotten, since May, that it was there.

In fact, Augstein had not forgotten it. On the contrary, he remembered it only too well and had tried, without success, to slip it into a pile of papers Buback had already searched. "It is quite true that I could not completely suppress my dismay when the "*exposé*" turned up," Augstein later wrote an acquaintance. "It was clear to me what it meant at this point in the proceedings . . . , and Buback himself then ran over to my safe and took custody of the pistol that was lying in it."

In the course of the afternoon, Bucerius, the publisher of *Die Zeit*, stopped by to see how the investigation was progressing. He found Buback sweating with exhaustion. "I'm here all alone," Buback sighed, "and have to look through all these things myself." "You can't do it like that," Bucerius replied. "When you take on a job like this you need a general staff plan. You can't come around with one man. You need at least a dozen. There must be at least that many public prosecutors in Germany." Bucerius called Karlsruhe, where his message was received with evident surprise. Karlsruhe agreed to send more men.

Meanwhile Oberle was up to his ears in the investigation of the Defense Ministry, although no arrests followed immediately. Taking a reference to the "Davy Crockett" in the Fallex piece as his point of departure, he began with the relatively small group from the Bundeswehr who had been to Washington to investigate it. But the lead was a dead end. From here on the search grew ever wider. Taking Hopf at his word, he spared no one. The Bundeswehr's finest, Maizière, Baudissin, Trettner, Steinhoff, finally the entire *Führungsstab des Heeres*, were systematically interrogated without result. Martin's participation was clear from the moment Ahlers' notes were found, but there was no proof that the assumed conspiracy began and ended with him. For safety's sake, Colonel Fritz Beermann, a personal friend and private correspondent of Schmelz's, was called back from Washington and held for two weeks under house arrest in Bonn's Stern Hotel before his innocence was established.

The locked-out *Spiegel* meanwhile regrouped to resume publication as usual. Hamburg's press came solidly to its rescue. Jahr put offices at its disposal, Bucerius and the *Abendecho* next door offered library, teletypes, and telephones. Even Springer offered assistance, although the offer was gracefully rejected. On Monday morning, Becker rounded up over a hundred employes at the main entrance and rallied them in the composing room for the first shop meeting in the *Spiegel's* history. The TV eyes of the nation, even of the world, were upon him. Despite two and a half days of exertion, he was witty, spirited, and effective. "Don't go home," he told the staff. "There's enough for everyone to do." The police had agreed to release necessary material on request. He asked that requests be kept short to facilitate the investigation. Improvisation was the order of the day, he said. He confirmed the offers from the rest of the Hamburg press. "I can't resist mentioning such an offer from a man who not long ago left a party because his hosts hadn't told him I would be there too," he added. "Just remember," he concluded, "you're not employed by Al Capone. You're working for Herr Augstein."

Not until Wednesday were the telephone switchboard and the first editorial offices again cleared for use. Elsewhere the search went on and on through a hundred additional rooms and something like 32,600 square feet, including one of the world's finest newspaper libraries. Buback, increasingly desperate, pursued more complicated chains of association in his search for *the* clue, seizing material until he had accumulated something like a short history of the *Spiegel*.

Particularly conspicuous was material on Strauss: Strauss and the Fibag project, Strauss and "Uncle Aloys," Strauss and Kapfinger, the Passau publisher, Strauss and his father-in-law Zwicknagl, Strauss and the German Automobile Club. Material on the Schmeisser case was taken too, and on the Epstein leak. A map with certain routes marked in red was seized for its possible military significance. It turned out to be Willy Brandt's 1961 campaign route. Even the manuscript of the *Spiegel*'s report of Hemingway's suicide was taken. It began with the sentence "The shot went off at 7:30 in the morning." "Under the circumstances, a certain, if remote, connection to military affairs cannot be denied," Horst Ehmke, the *Spiegel*'s attorney, later observed dryly. The bookkeeping department was also searched.

Well aware of what would be found in his office, Becker managed to hold off the searchers until the end of the week in order to help keep the magazine running. Since nothing was ever thrown away and everything methodically made its way into the files, a memo of Becker's contact with Wicht turned up as soon as Buback reached his office. This revelation of the *Spiegel*'s awareness of the impending investigation confirmed Buback's suspicions yet again. Copies of a talk held some time before by the former Solicitor General, Max Güde, on German press law and the journalist's right to protect his sources were naturally viewed as evidence of concrete preparations. Becker and Wicht were arrested on November 2. As he arrived to be booked, Becker listened to a radio report of the arrests. It was only then, he mused, that he believed Wicht's name was really Wicht.

The search went on until November 26. While it was in progress, Augstein was held in Hamburg, where he spent nights in jail and days in his office. The law permitted him to go on writing. He continued even after the search had ended and he had been transferred to Koblenz. What he turned out was a curious mixture of aggressive jubilation and introspective shock.

"Must the state be ruined so that one man gets what he wants?" he wrote in mid-November. "This is a question I will not cease to ask."

The Old Testament, a week later, turned his thoughts to the administration of justice. Arbitrary, patriarchal, vengeful justice,

"justice à la Adenauer," he observed. The editorial antagonized West Germany's Protestant establishment and was followed by a flood of correspondence from theologian-readers. "I experience my present situation as a Christian," Augstein wrote. "I feel my imprisonment as a deputation, as the setback of one who has always been excessively favored by luck." A few years later, he conceded to an interviewer that this had been a bit exhibitionistic. It was nonetheless a faithful reflection of his state of mind at the time, he said. He really had been miserable, although less about being arrested as such than about the search through his most intimate papers and affairs.

In his contact with his interrogators, he was considerably more subdued, poised, and rational. Buback later recalled to an interviewer that Augstein lost his temper only once. "Let's face it," Buback challenged him one day. "You were so determined to get Strauss that you were prepared to commit treason to do it." At this point, Buback observed with awe, he had the feeling that if Augstein had had a beer bottle, he would have hit him with it.

Ahlers was no less cooperative, despite his initial reluctance to turn in his notes or draft manuscript, which, in the meanwhile, had made their adventurous way through a number of hands to Josef Augstein. Martin's arrest on November 29 changed this. Confronted with Martin's arrest and testimony, Ahlers asked Josef Augstein to surrender his material. On the basis of it proceedings were later introduced against Helmut Schmidt and Major Brandt. On December 4 Josef Augstein and Conrad were arrested. By this time Jacobi had been out of jail again for nearly three weeks. Becker was released two days later.

Josef Augstein was released on December 10, Conrad on December 14, Wicht on December 21, Ahlers on December 22, Martin on December 29. At year's end, only Augstein and Schmelz remained. Schmelz was released on January 20, full of discreet praise for his jailers, who had permitted his wife to cook for him and, contrary to all rules, had even allowed him a nightly beer or schnaps. Augstein, with the eyes of at least some of the nation still upon him, consoled himself with the games, home-made cakes, Christmas wreaths and candles, cigarettes, hand-knit socks, winter underwear, pictures, books, and telegraphed greetings on all the special forms in the Bundespost catalogue, that were forwarded to his cell in Koblenz. Three well-wishers sent him recordings of the current hit *"Junge, Komm bald wieder, bald wieder nach Haus"* (roughly: "Son, Come Home Soon"). He was finally released on February 7 after 103 days under arrest. Schmelz had been held 81 days, Ahlers 56, Wicht 49, Becker 34, Martin 30, Jacobi 18, Conrad 12, Josef Augstein 6, and Jaene and Engel one day each. Since his arrest, Augstein had lost fifteen pounds, but on this account, at least, he did not regret the experience.

V.

THE POLITICAL AFFAIR

Political consequences were inevitable, although no one could have predicted where they would lead. The government dug in behind the claim that the action was an affair of the sovereign judiciary. But this was no defense, and would have been none even if the government's role, i.e., the role of Strauss and Hopf, had been as disinterested as was claimed.

The courts were in fact sovereign. The 1949 Basic Law guaranteed their parity with the legislative and executive branches for the first time in German constitutional history. But this applied only in part to the Solicitor General's office where the action began. Its official designation is *Generalbundesanwalt beim Bundesgerichtshof*—Solicitor General at the Federal High Court—and as an ostensible demonstration of its status the Solicitor General's office occupies a corner of the High Court building. But both the Solicitor General and his staff are named by the Federal Minister of Justice and operate to some extent under ministerial supervision. To what extent, unfortunately, is largely unclear. "The government charged reporters with constitutional illiteracy," UPI's Wilfried Saliger noted in mid-December in an annual report to the service's subscribers. "But none of its lawyers seemed able to explain where and when the Solicitor General's office was subordinate to ministerial control."

The question was bound to be raised, and not only by the press. Since, under West German law, only the Chancellor is ultimately responsible to parliament, the question necessarily implicated not only the Minister of Justice but, potentially, the entire government.

The crucial weakness in the government's position, however, was psychological. The Friday night police action had summoned up the entire register of national traumas. The night raid alone would have been enough. It was followed by children pulled out of their beds; a treason charge the day after Strauss's parliamentary whitewash and his remarkable performance in Brühl and three weeks after the publication of the article in question; and, finally, an army of investigators snooping through the files and accounting department of the country's most prominent opposition journal.

The first call reached the Solicitor General's office at eleven-forty Friday night from an elderly Karlsruhe stringer seeking confirmation of the arrest of Herr Augenstein (sic). From then on the phone rang continuously. The official reaction was ambivalent, half institutional pride in the flutter of public interest, half inveterate suspicion of the press. The office's position was further complicated by its ignorance of some of the affair's most interesting aspects, including the arrest of Ahlers. Not surprisingly, Karlsruhe's spokesmen put their feet in their mouths every time they picked up the receiver.

"The German public is a *Spiegel* affair richer," Federal Attorney Antonius Berard announced portentously. "No one can say where it will end." By way of explanation, he added that it was a matter of treason and bribery, of "publications that dealt with national defense in a way that endangered the existence of the Federal Republic as well as the freedom and security of the German people." The initiative had not come from Strauss, he said, which was true. He also said that the Solicitor General's office had acted independently after a "routine check of the press," which was less true. "Routine check" suggested that federal attorneys made a systematic practice of reading the papers. This was not the case, nor was it supposed to be. Quite apart from the problem of censorship, there were only eight federal attorneys and ten public prosecutors delegated to Karlsruhe by the supreme prosecuting agencies of the respective states, eleven additional lawyers delegated from the respective ministries of justice, and forty-six clerks. Had they made it their mission to comb the press, they would have had scarcely any time left for anything else.

Political spokesmen were no more successful than the federal attorneys in explaining the affair. The first more or less official statement from the government side, made by Josef Hermann Dufhues, the CDU's executive secretary, set the pace. "This is not an affair of the press," he said, "it is an affair of the *Spiegel*"—thereby immediately recalling Goebbels' famous 1933 pronouncement, "This is not an affair of the parties, it is an affair of the SPD," made as the Nazis forced the SPD out of the Reichstag as the first step in the dissolution of all other parties. Each successive official statement only made things worse. But so did silence. "When once a problem reaches a stage at which contrary developments are apt to produce equally unfavorable results," Sir Lewis Namier has written, "it is doubtful whether any man can save the situation." In this case, none could.

The first SPD statement came from Herbert Wehner. In its general caution, it would have done credit to Jean Jaurès, who was convinced at the outbreak of the Dreyfus affair that France's Socialists had nothing to do with a squabble among the bourgeoisie. The authorities had to see to it, Wehner said, that the suspected informants in the Defense Ministry got the same speedy and severe treatment as the journalists already arrested. Only then did he add the discreet hope that the action was not a mere matter of domestic political tactics. It was an inauspicious beginning.

Other Social Democrats were more direct. Ulrich Lohmar, a member of the Bundestag's Press, Education, and Culture Committee, demanded that the committee convene immediately to consider the matter. Gerhard Jahn and Adolf Arndt, the SPD's legal experts, demanded a special session of the Judiciary Committee. Both requests were refused. House rules, it was claimed, allowed no question to be discussed in committee that had not been referred there by the plenum. This guaranteed that the matter would turn up in the plenum in full view of the press, radio, and TV. Meanwhile Fritz Saenger, once editor-in-chief of dpa and now an SPD deputy, demanded a special session of the largely decorative German Press Council.

The crucial reaction—or perhaps nonreaction—came from the FDP. Stammberger learned of the action on Saturday morning in Munich from the newspapers. Willy Weyer's protest followed shortly. The apparent coincidence was hard to overlook. At this point the *Spiegel* crisis became a coalition crisis. The FDP's Oswald Kohut demanded that Stammberger suspend the officials in his ministry associated with the action. Stammberger hesitated. They had only done their duty, he said. It took him another three days to reach the conclusion that he had been left out on purpose.

The return of Ahlers added yet another ingredient to the explosive brew. Spain, still redolent of barely repressed associations with the Legion Condor, was among the leading national taboos. SPD press statements mused publicly about its unusual alacrity in extraditing—if this were the case—a democratic journalist, considering its more familiar protection of wanted Nazis. Once again, official statements only increased the general confusion and made it more and more obvious that there was something to hide.

At the first official press conference, Heinrich Thiesmeyer, official spokesman for the Ministry of Justice, denied that Interpol was involved in Ahlers' arrest. Under heavy questioning, he suggested that Ahlers might not have been arrested at all. But Frau Ahlers declared that he had. Strauss's spokesman, Schmueckle, added fuel to the fire two days later. The security agency of the Defense Ministry was not involved, he announced, and refused to answer further questions. "We are among those who might be affected in this matter," he said, before lapsing into silence. With Ahlers behind bars, the dilemma remained.

Anticipating where this situation was likely to lead, Schmueckle denied strenuously that the action had anything to do with revenge. He also denied that Strauss had threatened anyone at the Brühl reception. Karl-Günther von Hase, speaking for the government, denied that Strauss had seen the *Gutachten* on which the action had been based. Strauss himself carried on from there with the first in a long line of interviews. "I have anything but an interest in fouling my own nest, if you will permit a vulgar expression," Strauss told the *Frankfurt Abendpost*, "and I want to say that neither I nor the leading officials in my ministry had anything to do with starting this affair." Questioned on the incident in Brühl, Strauss declared his innocence once again. "I had no idea of the form, extent, or objective of the Solicitor General's action," he said.

The SPD had meanwhile half resolved to back down. On Monday, Jaene appeared in Jahn's office to report that the Bonn investigation had turned up the minutes of the Bundestag defense committee that Jahn had passed on to Schmelz the preceding summer. An appalled Jahn, who had entirely forgotten the incident, went directly to Fritz Erler, his parliamentary floor leader, and confessed. As one of the party's parliamentary whips, he indicated his willingness to accept the consequences of the oversight. The fact that Schmelz was an SPD member made the situation even more unpleasant. The problem was discussed in the party executive, which agreed to cover Jahn and play on—quietly—by ear. In an effort to keep the story under control, Franz Barsig, the SPD press secretary, passed it on confidentially to a few reporter acquaintances. Unfortunately one of them was drunk. The next day it was public knowledge that Jahn was involved in the affair.

Suspicion also extended to the FDP's Wolfgang Döring. Whether this was by accident or deliberate, and if the latter, on whose part was hard to say. The FDP, by this time, was in any case up to its ears in the affair. The allegation of Döring's complicity went out on the dpa wire during the meeting of the party executive. An infuriated Döring immediately threatened to sue dpa. The meeting continued around him.

Of all the parties to the affair, the FDP was in the most ambiguous position. Buttressed by ignorance, CDU supporters rallied without second thought behind their leaders. With the Cuban crisis vivid in everybody's mind, Adenauer had no difficulty underlining the urgency of the situation. Cuba was the only official point of discussion at a special cabinet session on Monday morning. The *Spiegel* affair came up outside the regular agenda. Security was security, Adenauer told the cabinet. "The whole house is rocking," he said. Bundeswehr officers, too, were involved in the investigation, he reminded them, not to mention officials of other ministries. This last was not true, but it was a revealing reflection both of Adenauer's general disposition at the moment and his sources of information on the action in progress. Even Stammberger murmured acquiescently that freedom of the press had its limits. The cabinet agreed in principle to broad special powers for Strauss should NATO declare them necessary.

For the SPD, the situation was equally simple. Despite the complications afforded by Jahn and Schmelz, the SPD, the parliamentary opposition, had, for once, an unambiguous mandate to oppose.

For the FDP, things were harder. Neither government nor opposition, it was at the same time both. Irrespective of the evident affront to Stammberger, the affair mobilized the party's most atavistic liberal instincts. Many of its deputies, Döring foremost among them, knew Augstein and Ahlers. The charges against them stretched their credulity to the breaking point. The action taken left them momentarily speechless. But even here there were differences of opinion. One of his parliamentary colleagues had the impression that Erich Mende, the party chairman, took the treason charge more seriously than many other FDP deputies. Yet the affront to Stammberger demanded, as even Mende had to admit, that the party do something.

The immediate solution was to find the responsible parties

or at least a satisfactory scapegoat. Stammberger threatened to resign. The CDU only made it easier for the FDP to be tough. Von Hase, speaking for the government, defended the responsible undersecretaries, Hopf and Walter Strauss. Their offices bound them to top secrecy, he said. It was understandably asked in reply whether undersecretaries, mere political civil servants, had somehow become the government. Meanwhile, in the absence of the FDP, the rump government added insult to injury by passing a series of social welfare bills that the FDP opposed.

Hopf now appeared to help the FDP out of its trouble. Walter Strauss had incriminated him, and the FDP's Thomas Dehler, most liberal of German Liberals, suggested he be called to answer the charge. Hopf arrived by way of the Chancellery. His appearance astonished reporters waiting in the Bundestag lobby. He then proceeded to astonish the FDP with a declaration of responsibility for the unfortunate incident. This was the first official acknowledgment that the Defense Ministry was involved. Hopf offered to resign. The FDP was amenable. There could hardly have been an easier or more elegant way out of the crisis than the slaughter of so willing a scapegoat.

In a new interview with the 8-Uhr-Blatt in Nuremberg, Franz Josef Strauss did his best to help. "This was not an act of vengeance on my part," he declared once again. "I have nothing to do with the matter, in the truest sense of the word nothing to do with it." He had come back from vacation to discover that the Solicitor General wanted a Gutachten, he said. Naturally he had guaranteed full official assistance. He had nonetheless delegated the matter to two officially designated ministerial experts—meaning Wunder and Hopffgarten—and given Hopf full official responsibility. In effect, Strauss declared, Hopf had been acting as minister.

The affair was now a week old. The FDP was resolved to end it, at least politically, with an ultimatum. Adenauer was given until the following Monday to release the nominal culprits, Hopf and Walter Strauss from their positions. In a particularly strenuous session of the government's generally placid official press conference Friday afternoon, Hase agreed that Stammberger, strictly speaking, should have been informed of what was, after all, going on under his authority. But Ahlers' arrest continued to cause difficulties. "Would that it were night," Hase sighed under pressure, "or that Herr Blank would return." Blank, Strauss's predecessor as Defense Minister and now Minister of Labor, was to report on the government's recently approved welfare program. The paraphrase of the Duke of Wellington ("Would that it were night or the Prussians would arrive") made an instant hit. "Just what is it that Herr Blank should return *to?*" a reporter inquired amid general hilarity.

The Bavarian election campaign had now got under way. Mende took advantage of this to make a speech in Schweinfurt. Treason was a bad thing, he informed his listeners; freedom of the press ends where treason begins. He added that his party was anxious to avoid a government crisis. The resolutely pro-government *Deutsche Zeitung* stood behind him, reminding its resolutely pro-government readers that only the SPD stood to gain from a split. Wehner replied saturninely for the SPD that the thought of his party's intervention was absurd. The SPD was not prepared to climb into the fire to rescue the government's chestnuts, he said.

Saturday was marked by conferences. Adenauer, whose scheduled visit to Washington had been postponed because of the Cuban crisis, conferred instead in Bonn. His weekend appearance at the Chancellery was interpreted as at least as eloquent a reflection of the gravity of the situation as his proverbial reminders. In the course of the day he conferred with Federal President Lübke, who also conferred with Mende and with the FDP's venerable Reinhold Maier, who appeared out of retirement as a de facto mediator between Döring, whose position was fixed, and Mende, whose authority was under fire, to assure the Chancellor that the FDP meant business. *Die Welt* reported that the CDU had considered the possibility of continuing as a minority government, but had dropped the idea, agreeing instead to consider disciplinary action against Hopf and Walter

Strauss and to authorize its Minister of the Interior, Hermann Höcherl, to apologize to Willy Weyer. Adenauer criticized what were now known as the "accompanying circumstances" of the affair and commiserated with Stammberger. He then conferred on undisclosed matters with his most intimate confidantes, his former parliamentary floor leader, Heinrich Krone, and his undersecretary, Hans Globke.

Franz Josef Strauss reappeared on the scene with another interview. Stammberger had been informed of the impending action, he said. In any case, he saw no reason why he should have been informed. Judiciary branch is judiciary branch, he concluded.

On Monday, Hopf and Walter Strauss were provisionally removed from office with appropriate expressions of regret. Walter Strauss was suspended, no great inconvenience since he was already scheduled for transfer to Luxembourg in early 1963 as the West German representative on the High Court of the European Coal and Steel Community. Hopf was sent on vacation. Since he had undergone gall bladder surgery in July, it was a matter of a well-deserved convalescence, Franz Josef Strauss explained in an interview on the Hessian Radio.

Indeterminate voices in the CDU/CSU squeaked and grunted at the apparent capitulation. Addressing party faithful in Augsburg, Baden-Württemberg's Minister-President, the later Chancellor Kurt Georg Kiesinger, declared that "the question these days is not one of the freedom of the individual vis-à-vis the state, but vice versa, a question of how to defend the authority of the state against an unbridled, anarchic freedom." The audience cheered. At a rally in Munich, Economics Minister Erhard warned his audience against indulging in the luxury of excessive preoccupation with the *Spiegel* while the world burned. The FDP backed down. Mende announced in a TV interview that the crisis was resolved. An official party spokesman assured the press that Adenauer had satisfied FDP demands. Stammberger withdrew his resignation and agreed to stay. There was no fur-

ther need for an investigation of his ministry, he said; the necessary steps had been taken.

For the government, Hase announced that settlement had been
reached on the following conditions: Adenauer had confirmed
Stammberger's right to information on matters concerning him
and had authorized him to investigate any remaining questions;
Walter Strauss and Hopf had been suspended from office; and
the coalition parties had agreed that treason was the basic issue
in the affair. Hase gave the last point particular emphasis. It was,
after all, the gravest such case in the history of the Federal
Republic, he said.

There was still the problem of Ahlers. At the government
press conference following the strenuous weekend, Hase refused
to answer further questions about it. With a hopeful show of
self-confidence, he instead denounced allegedly tendentious TV
treatment of the government position. Further questions were
explicitly deferred pending the Bundestag session two days later.
Stammberger, as responsible minister, announced that he was in
the process of preparing answers. Hase, altogether in the dark,
addressed himself privately and tactfully to Adenauer. He had
officially protested the North German Radio's televised "Panorama" report on the affair, he indicated. He considered it one-
sided, hostile, and prejudicial to both state and government. He
nonetheless had the impression, he said, that most CDU politicians, not to mention government supporters in the press, would
have more confidence in the government position if the government would report what had in fact gone on. Adenauer returned
Hase's letter with a laconic handwritten note in the margin.
"Questions will be answered during question period on Wednesday," (signed) A.

Meanwhile the answers from Bonn were anticipated by answers from Madrid. There, too, questions had been accumulating
ever since Ahlers' mysterious return to Germany. By November 1
they had reverberated to Oster. He had nothing to hide, but
also no further comment, he told interested German correspondents. A Bavarian SPD deputy, Alois Strohmayr, who had once

had an architectural office in Barcelona, sat down and wrote a personal letter to Franco.

A few days later the *Stuttgarter Zeitung*'s Robert Held pointedly referred to British treatment of an apparently similar case in the recent past. George Blake, suspected of espionage, had been summoned home from the Middle East by telegram in 1962, not arrested. He had returned voluntarily, was tried, convicted, and sentenced to forty years. (Blake subsequently escaped to Prague in 1966.) Held also recalled that the Spaniards were ordinarily not keen on extradition. They had in fact jailed three Israelis who had tried to abduct Léon Degrelle, once Belgium's leading Nazi, from his Spanish refuge. There was, Held wrote, a curious German assumption of common interests with Spain going back to the prewar cloak-and-dagger days of Admiral Canaris. It struck him as a curious form of international cooperation to make Spain responsible for the arrest of Ahlers as Bonn seemed resolved to do.

But was Spain indeed responsible? The German idiom, "there's something Spanish [i.e., odd] about this," was enjoying record currency. The Spaniards, indignant about unfavorable publicity, charges of malicious collaboration, and Bonn's unbroken silence, finally took the initiative themselves on November 6. At a large press conference, Manuel Fraga Iribarne, the Minister of Information, reported the entire series of exchanges with Wiesbaden. As his trump card, he produced the telegram of October 27 and Ahlers' declaration of willingness to return home.

With implausible but quite legitimate innocence, Antonius Berard, the spokesman for Karlsruhe, denied all knowledge of the matter. Dr. Reinhard Dullien, the director of the Federal Police Office in Wiesbaden where the telegram originated, replied to reporters' queries, "Surely a very interesting case," he replied to reporters' queries. "There are more things in heaven and earth than your philosophy dreams of," he added.

What Berard said, dated November 6, appeared in the official government *Bulletin* the next day as an advance barrage for the government's planned parliamentary counterattack. Berard confirmed that Augstein and the other suspects had known of the impending investigation since October 18 at the latest. The investigation had nonetheless proved to be its own justification, he declared, citing Ahlers' "*exposé*" with other, less plausible evidence.

One such piece of evidence was the report of a *Spiegel* correspondent who had visited a Bundeswehr training center in the United States and been encouraged by its American instructors to follow the trainees' progress on his return home. The Bundeswehr, considerably less enthusiastic than its American counterparts, declared the group and its activities secret. The reporter, supported by his editors, continued his efforts, although the story was finally canceled. Berard interpreted the situation as a matter of intent: despite official notification of secrecy, the *Spiegel* had encouraged its reporter to violate security.

Kuhn supplied the CDU/CSU parliamentary delegation with an exhaustive memo—four feet of teletype, which included a list of the contents of Augstein's safe—on the same theme. Adenauer presented it in the party caucus on the morning of November 7 where it had the effect of removing any remaining hesitation about full solidarity in the Bundestag session that directly followed. The normal tendency of parliamentary groups, like wagon trains, to draw together under fire from outside was reinforced for those with memories of Weimar by the ghost of an intriguing, politically ambitious Reichswehr, a presumable "colonels' conspiracy" in Strauss's Defense Ministry.

Stammberger, thrust to the center of the stage by the pressure of events, broke down in his efforts to explain them. Minutes before his scheduled appearance in the Bundestag on November 7, his secretary turned up to report that he had suffered a circulatory collapse the night before and was too sick to come. Not malicious intent but the rules of order prescribed Strauss's fellow Bavarian, Höcherl, as substitute for the missing Minister of Justice. But under the circumstances it was something like sending Polonius onto the stage in the role of Hamlet. Höcherl advanced, bright-eyed and indefatigable, into one of the most remarkable sessions in the Bundestag's history to answer the opposition's questions. Strauss, the man who knew the answers, sat by in silence on the government bench.

It was never clear how much Höcherl really knew. *Ex officio*, he knew little enough, which was a genuine advantage. Peppered with questions on the delayed notification of competent authorities in Hamburg and Düsseldorf, on the delayed notification of Stammberger, on the preparation of the *Gutachten* against the *Spiegel*, the apparent three-week delay in the action, and the dimensions of the search, Höcherl answered with sophistic but unmistakable skill.

With three exceptions, all questions came from the SPD. The FDP intervened only twice, both times in the person of Oswald Kohut, an outsider even in a party of outsiders. Gerhard Stoltenberg intervened once for the CDU with a set-up question so obvious that it might have been rehearsed. Did the minister not feel that it was a dubious matter to interfere so radically with a judicial investigation while it was in progress, he asked. The answer was self-evident.

Now the defender of the state in its hour of danger, now the defender of the independent judiciary, now the hail fellow well met, now the innocent abroad, Höcherl received cheers from the government deputies as he answered, but even more protesting roars from the opposition. Rather than turning away wrath, his soft answers provoked it.

Neither a minister nor an undersecretary was involved in preparing the *Gutachten*, he declared, although he admitted that Hopf had had a hand in sending it off. He denied that Defense Minister Strauss had discussed the matter with Hopf and Walter Strauss in Stammberger's absence; but there was no proof that he knew the contrary to be true. He insisted, perhaps overgenerously, that he had met his obligations in informing Hamburg and North Rhine-Westphalia of the impending action. Despite the hasty onset of the action, the warrants had, after all, been issued on October 23. His interpretation of the Hamburg police measures was a palpable misrepresentation. He denied that the

Spiegel's office facilities had been confiscated and claimed that their use had been merely restricted.

Neither the Ministry of Justice nor the Solicitor General's office nor Interpol had ordered Spanish authorities to arrest Ahlers, Höcherl replied to a series of questions on the events in Spain. This, at least, was true. The Spanish impression that Interpol was involved was a confusion, he said, based on the ambiguous source of the telegram from Wiesbaden, which was the headquarters of both the Federal Police Office and the West German Interpol. When the telegram arrived, the Spaniards had considered the possibility of declaring Ahlers *persona non grata.* Ahlers had returned voluntarily to the Federal Republic. Strictly speaking, this was no answer. But it was also no lie. At the end of the hour question period, Höcherl and the government were ahead on points. Bundestag Speaker Gerstenmaier had every reason to congratulate Höcherl on his performance. Pending the next day's session, the house resumed its debate of the coming year's budget.

The debate was interrupted in midafternoon by old Heinrich Ritzel of the SPD, one of the thirteen deputies whose parliamentary careers went back to the pre-Nazi Reichstag. Ritzel had been a member of the SPD deputation that voted alone against Hitler's Enabling Law in 1933. For him it was suddenly 1933 all over again. The trigger was a taunt from the CDU whip, Will Rasner. "SPD," Rasner trumpeted. "That means 'Spiegel Partei Deutschlands' (German *Spiegel* Party)." Ritzel rose to read a personal statement into the record. He resented implications that the SPD was involved in the affair, he said. It was concerned rather with the legality of ministerial action and with the rule of law.

A furious Adenauer went to the rostrum for the first time to reply. He resented the implication that citizens of the Federal Republic had to be defended against their judicial authorities, he said, and he felt impelled to express his personal thanks and respect to those authorities. Government deputies cheered, the SPD jeered. "There has been an act of treason," Adenauer continued. "This is practically certain—treason by a man with power, journalistic power in his hands. I say that the more journalistic power a man has in his hands, the greater is his responsibility to keep within the limits that patriotism—"

At this point Gerstenmaier had to intervene to silence the roar of SPD protests. "*Spiegel* party," shouted Otto Schmidt, a CDU deputy. "Neo-fascist party," the SPD bellowed in reply. Adenauer continued, "Ladies and gentlemen, is it not appalling" —"Hear, hear" and applause from the SPD—"is it not appalling" —"Yes" from the SPD—"that a colonel of the Bundeswehr, after hearing that an investigation has been launched against Augstein and the editors of the *Spiegel*, goes and tells them so that they can hide the evidence?"

This time it was Erler who rose to reply. "A parliament that earns a reputation for failing to control a treason investigation, with the result that law and constitution fall to pieces, has neglected its control function," he proclaimed to the cheers of his party. "This is the question today. This and nothing else." Adenauer returned to the rostrum. "In a constitutional state," he announced, "the foremost duty is to avoid intervention in judicial proceedings." The government deputies cheered. In the face of uninterrupted heckling from the SPD, Adenauer reaffirmed once more his confidence in the judicial authorities. "Now, ladies and gentlemen"—shouts from the SPD—"we have"—continued shouts—"an abyss of treason in this country. Think of it, ladies and gentlemen, when a magazine appears in an edition of a half million and systematically commits treason just to earn money"—shouts, whistling, and cries of "*Pfui*," the absolute limit of public disapproval.

A CSU deputy, Gerhard Wacher, followed Adenauer. "Please excuse me," he said in the direction of the SPD, "if I have the impression that you take the marginal aspects of this case more seriously than treason itself"—applause from the CDU/CSU, more shouts of "*Pfui*" from the SPD. "Since you express suspicions, you have to accept the fact that we suspect you when you permit the impression to arise that you seem to be making a par-

ticularly strenuous effort on behalf of your arrested Comrade
Schmelz. You make yourselves suspect by so strenuously taking the *Spiegel*'s part. Under the circumstances, you can hardly
be surprised to be characterized as '*Spiegel* party.'"

Erler again replied for the SPD, first with a reference to the
tone the Bavarian campaign seemed likely to take, then with a
predictably violent reaction to the all-but-explicit equation of
SPD with treason, an equation guaranteed to reawake party traumas going back to the "Stab in the Back" legend of the Weimar
Republic, which had held the SPD responsible for sabotaging
the German war effort in 1918. Erler finally returned to the
still inexplicable arrest of Ahlers, to the inadequate protection
and instruction of the press, which had conceivably led to the
present situation, and finally to the rule of law. The SPD and
even some FDP deputies cheered. Adenauer, more provoked
than ever, returned to the rostrum to defend the state he more
than any one else had created.

Again he defended the judicial and police authorities, expressed his rage that a Bundeswehr colonel—Wicht—had warned
the *Spiegel* of the impending investigation. "The person of Augstein involves two considerations," he declared. "On the one
hand, he earns money from treason and I find that contemptible."

"Is that proven?" "Hear, hear," and "Unbelievable," roared the
SPD.

"And second," Adenauer continued, "he earns money from
the general persecution of the coalition parties and you like that,
as you won't deny"—cheers and laughter from the CDU/CSU,
shouts of "Infamy" from the SPD. "By the way, I would like to
remark that I ordinarily don't read the *Spiegel*, I have better
things to do"—laughter and applause from the CDU/CSU.

"My God, what does Augstein mean to me?" Adenauer asked.
"The man earns money in his way. There are those who helped
him at it by subscribing to the *Spiegel* and advertising in it. I
have very little respect for such people."

With another indication of respect for the judiciary, he came
to Ahlers' arrest: "And now Málaga. The responsible agency also

issued a warrant for Ahlers' arrest on the assumption that he had committed a crime and a particularly despicable crime at that, namely treason. It was the Federal High Court that issued it. Now, he happened to be in Málaga. I only just learned that there was also talk of Tangier. You try to get somebody out of Tangier. I don't know how you would do that"—laughter. "If Herr Ahlers had been in Germany and been arrested, no one would say a word"—jeers from the SPD. "By coincidence, he was in Spain and there he suffered the same misfortune"—more jeers from the SPD. "Now we want to see whether any legal provisions have been violated . . . But whether the man, against whom the High Court issues an arrest warrant on suspicion of so grave a crime, is arrested in Málaga or Hamburg is something I refuse to get upset about"—cheers from the CDU/CSU.

At this point the Chancellor took a curious turn toward conciliation. "Now I have a request for you, ladies and gentlemen, particularly for the opposition. Next Tuesday I am to fly to Washington on President Kennedy's invitation." Under the circumstances, he said, he found it particularly unpleasant that the impression should arise that the Federal Republic was using Gestapo methods. "Gentlemen," he declared, "I know what Gestapo methods are like"—"We too," shouted the SPD deputy Peter Blachstein—"I was arrested twice myself"—"We too, Herr Bundeskanzler," Blachstein shouted again. "I almost feel inclined to say I'm glad we have the experience in common," Adenauer countered to applause from the government deputies.

If procedural errors had been committed, they would be investigated, Adenauer continued. He assured the SPD of its role in postwar Germany, its interest in preventing the impression from gaining currency that the Federal Republic was a land of Gestapo methods. It was not such a land, he said with pathos, to the applause of the CDU/CSU. If there had been error, it would be looked into, he went on to shouts from the SPD. But, he concluded, "let us not, in this case where men have been arrested on gravest suspicion of a crime on the basis of evidence before the Federal High Court, let us not raise the question 'Error, error,

error, procedural error.' We damage the German cause in the whole world." He sat down to an ovation from the CDU/CSU and deputies of the FDP.

The FDP's Döring rose to answer him in the most remarkable speech of a remarkable day. He began with an oracular but effective debating point. "The Chancellor has said that arrest of this man or that man is itself a proof for this or that," Döring began. "I personally think, Herr Bundeskanzler, that it would be well worth the effort in this investigation to establish which of our intelligence agencies found it expedient to work with the *Spiegel*, and which of them found it expedient to work against it." The SPD cheered.

But the burden of the speech was moral. "Herr Bundeskanzler," Döring continued. "I find it particularly hard to say what I now feel obliged to say. I think I scarcely need to say that I have been friends with Augstein for many years. I think I also scarcely need say that no one would regret it more than I if treason, as the law defines it, were to be proven in this case.

"But I owe it not only to my friend Augstein but to Augstein the citizen, and all the others, to protest that you say here that Herr Augstein earns money on treason. By doing so, you make yourself the first to pronounce a verdict that only a court has the right to pronounce." The SPD and some but not all deputies of the FDP cheered.

"Herr Bundeskanzler, I know what I say. I am not prepared— and this is no question of coalition policy—to accept without contradiction that people may be convicted by a certain kind of influence, irrespective of whose it may be, before they even enter a courtroom.

"As little as I am prepared to stand in the way of a legal conviction of my friend Augstein or his editors, so far do I feel obliged to say publicly, as a member of this coalition, what many people felt on the day the suspicion arose, or seemed justified—that not everything in this affair has gone the way the law requires. Among these people is the person closest to me, my wife, who lost twenty-two of twenty-six members of her family in German concentration camps, a woman who found it hard to return to Germany, on whose account I struggled for weeks and months to explain that all the cares and doubts she might have in this or that case were unjustified, a woman who now asks me: Is it possible, where suspicions arise that things have not gone according to the law, that inhibitions exist about clarifying them?

"Ladies and gentlemen, I appeal to my fellow members of the coalition: let us not permit the impression to be given that this is a question of the coalition, a question of power. Read the foreign press! We all have a common interest in seeing to it that not a trace of suspicion remains clinging to us." The SPD cheered and cheered. The FDP cheered. Mende was not among those cheering his rival for the party leadership. It was noted that instead he took Döring aside in a visible state of excitement and presumably of disapproval. Of all Döring's colleagues, only Oswald Kohut shook his hand as he descended from the rostrum. "Döring acts as if the *Spiegel* action were another Reichstag fire," a CDU deputy was heard to say.

The last significant contribution came from the SPD's Adolf Arndt who earned the day's biggest laugh with a pointed rebuttal of the Chancellor. "The Chancellor has again sought to create the impression that this is a matter of the courts and that somebody was trying to prejudice a judicial investigation," Arndt observed. "The only such intervention is that Augstein is already being treated as a convicted traitor and that *Spiegel* advertisers are being publicly insulted. The Chancellor seems to have overlooked the fact that the Bundeswehr always advertises in the *Spiegel*."

The three-and-a-half-hour debate—marked by scarcely controllable passions, nightmarish historical reminiscences, obsessive reference to the foreign press, and a demonstration of the principle governing parties, unshakable and apparently unquestioning solidarity with their leadership that would have done credit to the Supreme Soviet:—it was the Federal Republic's moment of truth. The question of Ahlers' arrest was still unanswered.

The next morning, November 8, the SPD tried again to find the answer. Höcherl was again at the rostrum for the government. His reaction proved that the previous day's excitement had left its mark on the government position. He referred the question to Strauss, who rose white-faced and unusually soft-spoken.

The German military attaché in Madrid had been requested to approach the Spanish authorities, Strauss confirmed. "Hear, hear," roared the SPD. The initiative passed back to Höcherl. The SPD demanded that it return to Strauss. This time Strauss backed into an answer. The federal police had failed to find Ahlers, he noted. Ahlers had once been press officer of the Defense Ministry and was author of the article in question. The military attaché in Madrid was aware of his address in Spain. Under the circumstances, Strauss said, the Defense Ministry would have been derelict in its duties had it neglected to come to the aid of the police. He sat down and turned the floor back to Höcherl. What exactly was the legal basis of the government's intervention in Spain, an SPD deputy asked. The question inspired Höcherl to a dubious analogy and an answer that was to become proverbial.

A provincial high school teacher named Zind had been convicted a few years earlier of anti-Semitic statements. The case had, in fact, first been reported in the *Spiegel*. Höcherl recalled that the man had fled the country, and that the Federal Republic had asked both the Austrian and the Italian government for aid. Zind had been arrested in Italy, but an Italian court had established six weeks later that the extradition application was invalid. Nevertheless there had been no German protests then that the extradition attempt, like the current one, was "somewhat beyond the limits of legality." Considering that Zind, unlike Ahlers, had been tried and convicted at the time of the attempted extradition, the analogy was as questionable as the rhetoric. Höcherl was interrupted by jeers and shouts from the SPD. Strauss was laboriously called back to the rostrum.

He now produced an analogy of his own. Only a few days

before, he recalled, Britain's Prime Minister Harold Macmillan had come under heavy fire from the House of Commons, not because he had tried with all available means to solve an espionage case in the Admiralty, but because he had not. (He was referring to the case of an admiralty employe named William Vassall, who was discovered to have passed on documents to the Russians over a period of years. The London satirical magazine *Private Eye* took up this reference a few days later. A montage photo showed Macmillan meeting Adenauer at the airport. "This *Der Spiegel* business could never happen in my country, old man," Macmillan is saying. "No, because you've got no official secrets left to reveal," Adenauer replies.)

Strauss again sat down, returning the floor to Höcherl. Did Oster request the arrest of Ahlers, the SPD's Ludwig Metzger asked. "Is the question directed at me?" Höcherl asked innocently. "At the government," Metzger replied. "How should anybody know who of you is responsible?" Wehner bellowed from the floor. "Herr Wehner," Höcherl retorted with a scarcely veiled hint at Jahn's—however peripheral—association in the affair, "can't you see what a difficult situation you get yourself into with all these questions? Don't you see that?" The question period ended with the question of Strauss's role still unanswered.

Official Madrid replied with indignation to the implied effort to put the final blame on Spain, and Schroeder for the first time demanded a report from the German ambassador there on what had transpired in his embassy.

The next day, November 9, the SPD tried again and this time produced the information that Strauss had been kept informed of the impending proceedings since his return to office October 16. He had then made Hopf responsible for the ministry's share in the action, Höcherl repeated. Was it Hopf himself or someone else who called Oster to request Ahlers' arrest, Erler wanted to know. Between 1 and 2 A.M. on October 27, Strauss himself answered, the police office in Bad Godesberg had notified the Defense Ministry of its failure to find Ahlers. The ministry, he said, had called Oster, who had demanded to speak to the minister himself. He had complied, Strauss said. What had he said, the SPD's Friedrich Schaefer asked. That it was the duty of an official person to aid the policy, Strauss replied, and that the arrest warrant was under way. Had he ordered Oster to see the Spanish authorities, Schaefer demanded. Strauss plunged in deeper.

"After Oster had been named by the central police office in Bad Godesberg, the occasion arose to preclude any suspicion of collusion in the Defense Ministry by sending Herr Oster to the Spanish authorities to report the situation," he explained. "Had I done anything else, you would have every reason to charge me with dereliction, but a different kind of dereliction from that which you are now charging." Happy for an occasion to applaud, the CDU/CSU deputies applauded.

Was Strauss still prepared to stand by his story that he had nothing to do with the affair, the SPD's Karl Mommer asked pointedly. He was, Strauss answered. He was informed of the investigation on October 16, then informed after midnight on October 27 that Oster knew of Ahlers' whereabouts. Wasn't this a contradiction, Ritzel inquired. No, Strauss replied. He had been asked whether he had been involved in instigating the action, and whether he had had a say in the executive organization of the investigation. He had not, he said, and "it would have been a violation of the division of powers had it been otherwise." There were more cheers from the CDU/CSU.

Had nothing happened between October 16 and 26, Erler asked. He had naturally been kept informed of developments, Strauss said, but he denied any further participation. Adenauer took the rostrum in a spectacular effort to save the day. He had noticed that his telephone was being tapped, he announced to the startled house.

Telephone tapping, as most Germans learned with a shock a year later in the course of a full-scale phone-tapping affair, was a prerogative in principle reserved to the former occupation powers when the Federal Republic regained—or almost regained —its sovereignty in 1955. In practice it was delegated to the third of the Federal Republic's intelligence services, the Office for the Protection of the Constitution (*Verfassungsschutz*), a dependency of the Ministry of the Interior. But the possibility was not exploited "before November 1962," Höcherl declared later.

That the possibility existed and was being exploited seems to have been one of the implications in Döring's oracular reference two days before to the mysterious practices of the intelligence services. It appeared that Döring himself was one of its victims. A close friend and FDP colleague was approached mysteriously in the matter by an agent of the *Verfassungsschutz* in the week following the question periods. To his shock, he discovered that Döring, who was on close terms with the BND, had evidently been denounced to the *Verfassungsschutz* by a fellow FDP deputy for alleged Communist contacts, and that Döring had for some time been under official observation.

Little if any of this was known at the time, which had immediate consequences for the Chancellor. Adenauer's reference was probably intended both as a shocker and a diversion. He may have meant to imply that one or more of the occupation powers was involved in the affair. In any case the British embassy in Bonn caught this implication and quickly denied any use of phone-tapping. But the reference was evidently missed both in the Bundestag and in the press. "Then we're companions in suffering," Wehner shouted back at Adenauer from the floor. "That's just it," Adenauer answered to a general roar of laughter. For the moment, that was the end of the story.

The *Spiegel* affair had now become a Strauss affair. Brentano, who had expressed his fundamental disapproval of the entire parliamentary fuss two days before—"This isn't a *Spiegel* parliament," he said—now expressed a preference for question periods *à l'anglaise* with questions that could be answered only with yes or no.

The Spaniards were again quick to answer questions Strauss and Höcherl had neglected. At a press conference in Madrid, Fraga Iribarne reported that it was indeed Oster who had intervened with the Spanish police, using the danger of Ahlers' escape to North Africa and the imminent arrival of a warrant from Wiesbaden as persuasion. As the German ambassador arrived in Bonn to explain the situation to an indignant Schroeder, the SPD observed that it was symptomatic that more information came from Spain than from the German government. Strauss's CSU grouped in its chief's defense. He was only rendering official assistance, it declared. Schmueckle denied misleading the press by his silence in the preceding weeks. Orders from above, he said.

The CDU lapsed abruptly from confidence to consternation. "Like Weimar," a CDU deputy from Berlin was quoted as saying. "I'd like to give up my mandate here and now," a North German colleague added. "We're knocking the state *kaputt*. Why did he have to deny what he did?"

It was suddenly the war of all against all. On the eve of the Hessian state elections, the Hessian CDU, optimistic for the first time since the war, gave up every hope of the victory it had dreamed of only a week before. Even CDU ministers, it was reported, were reluctant to trust their CDU undersecretaries. The *Welt*'s Georg Schroeder quoted one of the suspended undersecretaries in the Bundestag lobby Friday evening. He wanted to retire to write and lecture, he said, to reawake his countrymen's historic loyalty to their state. "It's nineteen thirty-two," he said. "What Hitler destroyed has not recovered. The state is Business, Inc., a pork barrel, that's the cause of all we've experienced this week." The reporter was impressed. "And each word was in bitter earnest," he emphasized.

While Stammberger defended himself against mounting charges of inadequacy in office, accounts of telephone manipulation accumulated in the newspapers. A friend of Ahlers had called Ahlers' mother, it was reported, to ask where to send greetings on Ahlers' fortieth birthday. Ahlers was locked up at the moment in Euskirchen in the Rhineland, he was told; Jacobi was in the little town of Düren; and—click. An editor of Die Zeit reported being interrupted in midcall by unfamiliar noises on the line. "If you have to tap this conversation, you might at least be a little more discreet about it," he sneered into the receiver. "I'll be damned if I'm going to let you tell me what to do," an indignant voice replied. "I'll cut into your conversation again."

On Sunday, November 11, Hessen went to the polls, the Solicitor General's office went on television, and the American reporters in Bonn came to Adenauer. The confrontations dominated the news in Bonn on Monday. On the eve of his departure for his delayed visit to Washington, Adenauer told his guests he intended to return Hopf to office. Under massive pressure to produce results somehow commensurate with the mounting turmoil, Federal Attorney Joachim Loesdau presented a nationwide TV audience with a report that the investigation was making good progress.

Suspicions were only intensified by the evidence discovered, he declared confidently. The bribery charge? "We're busy trying to clarify it, but are having problems due to the code names on certain payments." Naturally the suspects were still being held. Danger of collusion, Loesdau said. They all agreed on the same story, and one of them even admitted destroying evidence. This was presumably Ahlers, who had claimed to have burned his notes and manuscripts but in fact had only hidden them. Becker's contacts with Wicht were the grand finale. "And I can tell you more," Loesdau announced, his voice rising in a joyful crescendo. "We have a memo of a conversation between the suspects indicating that they expect to get off with a warning 'because otherwise the connection with the Strauss campaign would be too obvious.'"

At the same time, the Hessians presented the CDU with a beating.

	1962	1958	1961 (Bundestag)
SPD	50.9%	46.9%	42.9%
CDU	28.8%	32.0%	34.9%
FDP	11.4%	9.5%	15.2%

The FDP reacted to both Adenauer and the qualified success of the election returns with fire in its eyes. Mende denied that Hopf would return to office—not so much as a statement of fact, it would seem, but as a threat. Elsewhere in the FDP there was support for qualified reconciliation: Hopf's return to office if matched by Strauss's departure. Hase, as government speaker, had no comment. The SPD, which had won every Hessian election since the end of World War II, denied any connection between the *Spiegel* affair and its victory at the polls. The other parties drew their own conclusions. The FDP resolved to be tough. Increasing numbers of CDU deputies decided not to be. Like the Hessian CDU, Adenauer ascribed the defeat entirely to the *Spiegel* affair in his interview with U.S. reporters and added philosophically that more of the same could presumably be expected in Bavaria two weeks later. Radio and TV had an "appalling influence" on public opinion, he sighed. It was unclear whether he meant performances like Loesdau's, broadcast interpretations like "Panorama," or the preceding week's Bundestag sessions as broadcast news per se.

It scarcely mattered. The broadcasting media, as Adenauer was inclined to view the situation, were the least of his problems. With his undersecretary Globke on a recuperative holiday in Switzerland—he had left Bonn on November 7—and Strauss promoted to *primus inter pares* among the Chancellor's advisers, there was no one in reach to tell him otherwise. For him, the connection between the *Spiegel*, Schmelz, and the SPD was already evidence of a conspiracy. The connection between the *Spiegel* and the FDP was axiomatic. The discovery of the *Spiegel*'s contacts with the BND only seemed to show how far the conspiracy had gone. The combination of the BND's American origins,[1] with the assumption that it had been Ahlers' source as well as Becker's protector, led the presumed conspiracy all the way to Washington. Characteristically, Adenauer called Walter Dowling, the U. S. Ambassador, to the Chancellery to com-

[1] Cf. p. 38.

plain retroactively that the United States had saddled him with Gehlen.

Gehlen's cordial relationship with the MAD's General Wessel, who had advised against a *Spiegel* action altogether,[2] led in turn to the Defense Ministry where the line met neatly with Martin and, presumably, yet another round of conspiracy. Ahlers later reported that he had the impression during his interrogations that not only treason but sedition charges were being considered.

Attempts to defend Gehlen, like Foreign Minister Schroeder's at a session of the cabinet shortly after the arrest of Wicht, seemed to make things worse. A witness recalled that Adenauer had listened red-faced with anger. Döring's efforts to exculpate Gehlen in a private clarification of his Bundestag reference to the intelligence services seemed rather to incriminate Döring, although it was reported that Globke himself had intervened in both Gehlen's and Döring's behalf. Under the circumstances, the trivial coincidence that Döring's wife had for a short time been Randolph Churchill's secretary appeared to extend the conspiracy to Britain.

This particular spark of inspiration was fanned by Strauss himself. At the beginning of the affair, Chaloner and Bohrer, the *Spiegel's* fathers, had returned to the scene in Chaloner's Rolls-Royce to offer their support to the embattled staff. Chaloner, who was now a London publisher's representative, had gone on from Hamburg to Munich to see business connections there and to solicit aid for publication of the *Spiegel* abroad if necessary. The MAD trailed him on his way. For Strauss, the presence of Chaloner and Bohrer was yet another aspect of what now seemed to be a conspiracy virtually without limit. "What about what you said in the Bundestag?" he was asked by the *Daily Telegraph's* Reginald Peck in the course of the Bavarian campaign. "What about Bohrer and Chaloner?" Strauss roared in reply; and he later repeated the question in an off-the-cuff interview with the Minneapolis *Tribune's* Graham Hovey.

[2] Cf. p. 64.

On November 12, as Ahlers later reported in the *Spiegel*, bizarre premises led to appropriately bizarre consequences. Stammberger was in Karlsruhe conferring with Kuhn on the progress of the investigation when a call from Bonn ordered him and Kuhn to proceed immediately to the Chancellor's office. They caught the next train and came direct from the station to find two officials of the Ministry of Justice waiting there already. Adenauer came directly to the point. "Herr Stammberger," he said, "you have to arrest Herr Gehlen. He's sitting in the next room. You can get him right away."

Stammberger, whose presence of mind was continually being questioned during these weeks, seems, in this case at least, to have risen to the occasion. "Herr Bundeskanzler," he replied, "it's not that easy. I need a warrant. Why should I arrest Herr Gehlen anyway?" Because, Adenauer replied, Gehlen had told Wicht of the preparations for the action, and Wicht had passed this information on to the *Spiegel*.

"But, Herr Bundeskanzler," Stammberger answered, "unless we have some substantial evidence in our hands, we're not going to find a judge prepared to issue a warrant." Adenauer, indignant, turned to Kuhn. "What do you say to that?" he asked. Kuhn agreed with Stammberger. "I was once a public prosecutor myself," Adenauer replied with disappointment. "In those days everything was different."

They settled instead on the alternative that Kuhn question Gehlen in the next room. Gehlen revealed that he had learned of the impending action from Strauss himself and passed on the story to two of his subordinates on his return to Munich. He had not informed Wicht, let alone the *Spiegel*. Kuhn appeared satisfied, Adenauer resigned. Gehlen returned to Munich. The affair went on.

"Is it true that the Chancellor tried to arrest General Gehlen?" an interviewer asked Globke several years later. "The Chancellor denies it," Globke replied.[3]

[3] Interview with the author February 1, 1966.

November 12 was also a day for press conferences. In the course of the day, the Solicitor General's office publicly confirmed Wicht's connections with the BND. Schmueckle tried without success to suggest the Foreign Ministry's connection with Ahlers' arrest. He was immediately contradicted by the speaker for the Foreign Ministry. Will Rasner, the party whip, strenuously denied any intention on the part of the CDU to capitulate to FDP pressure on Strauss. As a result, he hinted, the affair was likely to go on for some time.

The SPD announced for the first time that it would demand Strauss's dismissal and a full investigation of Ahlers' arrest. Adenauer got there first. As a farewell gesture before leaving for Washington, he commissioned a joint report from the Ministries of Justice, Interior, Defense, and Foreign Affairs. Höcherl let it be known that the report could be expected within the week. The next day this was amended slightly. The first meeting was scheduled to take place within the week, and it was estimated that it would take another week to complete the report.

Speaking for the government, Hase's assistant declared a moratorium on official information pending the report. At the last minute, Adenauer removed Krone, whose loyalty he could depend on, from the Washington delegation and left him in Bonn to mind the shop. Stammberger denied that he had any intention of resigning, and the German Trade Union Federation proposed a grand coalition—without the FDP and with the SPD—as the answer to the Federal Republic's problems.

Adenauer, whose hands were already full with the problems of saving Strauss, his government, and indeed himself, now faced the additional problem of saving the good name of the Federal Republic in Washington. Schroeder's conspicuous good humor contrasted oddly with the late autumnal atmosphere—both real and metaphorical. There had been not one but two Strauss-Oster phone conversations, he cheerfully informed the German press corps on his arrival in Washington, and he had no doubt that more surprises were in store. He, Schroeder, did not take the situation lightly, he added, and turned the stage over to Adenauer.

For a last time on American soil, Adenauer rose to the occasion, but the occasion was unmistakably elegiac. The picture
of America's youngest President at the airport, coatless in a sharp
November wind, on the day after an historic victory, and the
old Cold Warrior beside him, bundled up more conventionally
as the season demanded, struck witnesses as symbolic. In a private session with German reporters, Adenauer reasserted his opinion that Khrushchev after Cuba was likely to be even more
dangerous than before. It was another variation of "the situation
has never been so grave." But it was no longer the same.

A tired patriarch, he posed publicly at the White House with
John F. Kennedy, Jr., and listened patiently to the citation that
called him "a visionary, a great statesman." In private, he swallowed U.S. administration demands for an increased West German defense effort and more conventionally armed troops to
support the Berlin contingents in the West in the event of a
Soviet thrust.

In his reply to a Kennedy toast, Adenauer himself took on
the *Spiegel* affair, at least from the flank. His toast was published in the Bonn government's official *Bulletin* the next day.
Germany had learned from the past, Adenauer assured his hosts
and fellow guests; he faced his meeting with the National Press
Club without apprehension. The press could be exasperating, he
observed, but the press was in no danger in Germany. He added
an anecdote from his years as Mayor of Cologne. He had once
had a squabble with the newspapers, he recalled. The same evening he had dinner with the dramatist Max Halbe and complained about it. Halbe commiserated with Olympian irony. "My
friend," he wrote on the menu, "when you have trouble with
the press, don't worry about it. There will be another paper
tomorrow."

Before a packed house at the National Press Club, Adenauer
faced the affair head-on. George Cullen, the president, collected
the *Spiegel* questions submitted from the floor in a single omnibus query and presented it last. The Chancellor answered at
majestic length, and there were no further questions. The action

was fully legal, he declared. The responsibility lay with the Solicitor General's office. It had been supported by the Federal Police Office. The search and arrest warrants came from the Federal High Court. All were justified. He took particular offense at references to Gestapo methods. "I know how the Gestapo worked," he said. "I was arrested by it twice myself." It was important to find out who had informed the *Spiegel*. He refused to see any threat to the freedom of the German press. As evidence, he cited the boom in *Spiegel* circulation since the start of the affair and Augstein's unhampered and uninhibited anti-Strauss editorials from his jail cell.

The audience viewed the performance as the last stand of an old fighter who refused to go down, observed the *Süddeutsche Zeitung's* Hans-Ulrich Kempski. The Los Angeles *Times* commended Adenauer's wit and stamina. In an unusual gesture of esteem, President Cullen presented Adenauer with a silver beer mug on behalf of the club. The Washington *Post* was more skeptical. "Dr. Adenauer's whole tone seemed to suggest that the *Spiegel* was a police court matter and not a major political dispute," it said the next day. "To say that an editor is 'free' because he can write an editorial from jail is to offer a curious concept of free expression. The Chancellor is no dictator, and he may be right about dismissing the excited charges of Gestapo tactics. But this was not one of his happiest moments; the *Spiegel* affair is still very much alive."

By way of indirect confirmation, the New York *Herald Tribune* reported that Adenauer called Krone the same day to ask him to try to keep the lid on things until his return to Bonn two days later. His conversations in Washington ended, he left Friday evening eight hours ahead of schedule and arrived in Bonn to find the affair approaching a new climax.

Krone, anything but inactive in the Chancellor's absence, had presented a new *Gutachten* and seen to it that it was distributed to all CDU, CSU, and FDP deputies. Ostensibly the work of prominent lawyers, the new *Gutachten* reached the thumping conclusion that Strauss was entitled to intervene in the search for Ahlers, that he would, in fact, have been derelict in his duties had he failed to do so. It suggested that the approval of the Foreign Ministry could be assumed, and was in fact granted *ex post facto* the next day, and that the federal government was justified in requesting the aid of foreign states. At least one CDU deputy inquired of Krone how it was that none of the prominent lawyers nominally responsible for this effort chose to sign their names to it. Krone replied with tired resignation. "You're altogether right," he wrote, "but that's how things are *bei uns.*" And, said the skeptical deputy, "*he* was right."

The other parties were prepared to go some distance to ease Adenauer's way out of the crisis. According to the *Stuttgarter Zeitung*, Wehner was not prepared to replace the FDP in a new government but would consider an all-party government as he had a year before. The FDP was prepared to sell out Stammberger and its controversial Finance Minister, Heinz Starke, for the sake of peace.

At the same time, SOS's were resounding from Bavaria where a regular state election appeared to be turning into a fight for Strauss's political life. Mid-October polls had predicted an absolute majority for the CSU, but nobody believed them any more. The Bavarian Party, a sectional secession group from the CSU, expected to take 10 per cent of the vote at the expense of the CSU. Bavaria's traditionally embattled SPD counted on increasing its share from 30 to 35 per cent.

Adenauer's return coincided with a one-man counteroffensive. In a campaign speech in Fürth, Strauss emphatically denied any intention of resigning. In a widely published interview, he declared that the SPD demand for his resignation was nothing more than a new edition of its anti-atomic weapons campaign of 1958, and that Jahn and Heinemann were in fact collaborating with the *Spiegel.*

The SPD, he intimated, was making a fuss only to cover the tracks leading to Schmelz. Questioned on his own role in the affair, he was the picture of injured innocence. "I never said I knew nothing about the matter," he protested. "I only said that neither the Defense Ministry nor I myself had anything to do with introducing charges." In a speech in Straubing, such self-defense reappeared as the best offense. Strauss the campaigner took his cue from Strauss the Defense Minister. "Nehru released his Defense Minister," Strauss proclaimed with reference to Krishna Menon's departure in the wake of the apparently irresistible Chinese surge across the Himalayas, "because he hadn't done enough. Here at home a Defense Minister is supposed to be released because he did too much." It was all Communist propaganda, he cried. He had been facing it for six years.

In an interview with a CSU-sponsored student magazine, he modestly denied any ambition to become Foreign Minister. On the contrary, he protested, Schroeder had his full respect. Did he aspire to become Chancellor, he was asked. Whatever he replied was likely to lead to conjecture, he answered with a diffident wave of his hand; he had no alternative but silence. He was prepared to support Erhard, however, or any other qualified candidate. Erhard, according to dpa, returned the compliment a few days later with support in the cabinet for Strauss's further tenure in office.

Adenauer, his misgivings carefully repressed, upheld Strauss in nine hours of negotiations with the FDP following his return home. The FDP held firm in the face of repeated allusions to the difficult international situation. Either Strauss went, it declared, or it would vote with the SPD against the government. For the CDU, the situation was a dilemma of classical simplicity. If Strauss went, the CSU would leave the government. If he did not, the FDP would. With the Bavarian election impending, the CDU appeared prepared to brazen it out. "Strauss is no longer the question for the CDU," the *Welt* reported on November 19. "For the CDU the main question is whether it can concede to one coalition partner the right to issue demands that affect the chairman of another."

In an interview for the Sunday edition of the *Welt*, the *Welt am Sonntag*, Strauss announced with satisfaction, "I expect to remain Defense Minister. I am unable to foresee any other development. I am pleased to establish that the Chancellor's judgment of this situation coincides with my own."

The next day the FDP put its own and the Chancellor's resolution to the crucial test at a meeting of the party executive and the Bundestag delegation in Nuremberg. It was noted that the hotel room in which they convened was decorated with Nibelungen motifs—Siegfried vs. the dragon, but also Siegfried being murdered by Hagen. Outside demonstrators brandished placards admonishing the party this time—with reference to the debacle of the previous autumn—not to back down. It responded happily to the challenge. The five FDP ministers resigned collectively from the government. For the sake of tact, their statement did not refer to Strauss and indicated a conciliatory willingness to return to a new government "as consistent with the mandate of the electorate."

The same evening Strauss appeared in the Bavarian village of Weilheim, the center of his parliamentary constituency. Although nearly two hours late, he was received by a full and wildly enthusiastic house. For the sake of order, the meeting, originally scheduled for an auditorium of twenty-five hundred, was moved to a five-hundred-seat hall. With an analogy of India's situation with the SPD's he had the audience in his hands. "He gave the impression," the *Süddeutsche Zeitung's* Josef Riedmiller wrote the next day, "of a man determined, despite the obstacles of the most sinister domestic forces supported by the Communist bloc, to save the nation from destruction. Like Laocoön wrestling with serpents, he feels himself enmeshed in the coils of his political opponents, who themselves are less concerned with his personal downfall than with the paralysis of the Federal Republic—in complete unawareness of the danger from the East."

The same themes reverberated in CSU campaign ads. "A conspiracy against our security is the end of freedom," was the *leitmotif* of an urban version. "Support for treason endangers security and freedom," was the rural variation; "Treason or Security: CSU." CSU speakers were instructed to answer criticism of Strauss by declaring it a threat to democracy—because it implied that legitimate official assistance was a form of revenge. "Khrushchev, Ulbricht, Mende, and Wehner extend their hands to one another," the CSU announced in an election broadcast on the Bavarian Radio.

A full page of fine type in a number of Bavarian papers on November 22 showed a photograph of Strauss with his British opposite number, Peter Thorneycroft. It was flanked by *Time*'s Strauss cover of December 19, 1960, and the most recent equivalent *Spiegel* cover. For *Time*, the ad proclaimed, Strauss was a statesman. (*Time*'s cover story was, in fact, anything but friendly, but what the reader didn't know, it was apparently felt, wouldn't hurt him.) For the *Spiegel* he was "The target of the will to destruction and self-destruction of Germany's 'lost generation.'" While the FDP and SPD applied themselves to the task of engineering Strauss's fall in the midst of an international crisis, it declared, while they sought to execute the order of the FDP's Augstein, on trial for treason, Strauss was negotiating with his international colleagues. Who was to represent the Federal Republic at the coming Paris NATO meeting if not Strauss, the man with ten years (sic) of experience, the man who symbolized Germany's reliability in the Western alliance and who had been the object of Communist attacks for the past decade? The SPD immediately sought an injunction. It was rejected. In private conversations, CSU functionaries reckoned with the loss of urban votes.

On November 22 Erhard announced in Munich that Strauss had proposed the collective resignation of the CDU/CSU ministers from the government. In response to popular demand, he might have added. Berlin's CDU executive publicly demanded a reorganization of the cabinet, and Dufhues, the national executive secretary, personally intervened. The CDU ministers announced their willingness to march out of office behind a five-point statement.

Between 1949 and 1961 the Federal Republic had enjoyed stable government, the statement began. Since 1961 the FDP had made this impossible. The FDP was solely responsible for the crisis. The CDU retained complete confidence in Adenauer; he was authorized to do what he thought necessary. The resignation was the idea of Dufhues and Strauss. All ministers had willingly agreed to surrender their offices. A new coalition with the FDP would be considered only after relevant questions of form and policy had been clarified.

Strauss gave another interview. Was the collective resignation a gesture of solidarity with him, he was asked. It was a suggestion of Dufhues' and himself, Strauss replied. It seemed the easiest way to facilitate necessary changes. Actually, he himself was only a pretext for the FDP; they were really after Adenauer. An unfortunate tactic, he murmured darkly, considering their association with Augstein. As he viewed the situation, the coalition was void, and with it Adenauer's obligation to resign in midterm. He himself made no specific claim to a seat in the new government as chairman of the CSU, but he would naturally claim the same number of seats for his party in the new government as it already held. The entire crisis was artificial, he said.

Speaking for the FDP in his home town, Coburg, Stammberger was at least as conciliatory in his way. Franz Josef Strauss alone was guilty, he declared. Hopf and Walter Strauss were fully rehabilitated.

The government's official *Bulletin* echoed momentarily in the void with a prediction that the evidence against Augstein and Ahlers would suffice to support indictment and justify a trial. "How do they know?" asked an SPD speaker. The controversy was drowned out in the climactic barrage from Munich. A new CSU ad identified the *Spiegel* with the SPD, and the SPD with its one-time deputy Frenzel, who had been convicted of espionage for Czechoslovakia. Filled with violent hate for the Federal Republic, it declared, they had now succeeded in reawakening foreign antipathy for Germany. They had not protested the foreign arrests of Zind, the Lower Saxon schoolteacher,[4] or the

4 Cf. p. 116.

abduction of Eichmann, or the American effort to extradite the convicted Dr. Robert Soblen.

The international scene was fraught with danger, it continued. America was obsessed with peaceful coexistence; Britain with complexes, injured national vanity, and envy of German competition; France with anti-Gaullism which was equated with anti-Germanism; Italy was under pressure from the left: a sell-out of Germany was the necessary condition for the Italian Christian Democrats' "Opening to the Left." All of this focused on Strauss, not as a person but as a policy. *Time*, the *Neue Zürcher Zeitung* and the *Corriere della Sera* appreciated the danger, the nihilism of left and right. Perhaps it was the Bavarian election that had mobilized this formidable anti-German coalition; perhaps it was a collective effort to corrupt the common sense of the Bavarian voter.

Somewhat different noises came from the north. In the course of a meeting of the CDU executive in Berlin, Adenauer told an estimated twelve thousand hearers that the crisis was the result of "altogether superfluous squabbles." To whistling hecklers, he remarked patriarchally that as a boy he had always wanted to learn to whistle with two fingers himself. He sought refuge in court decisions against the release of the *Spiegel* suspects, drawing a protest from a federal judge the next day, and turned again to the TV cameras.

Infuriated by what they expected to be an effort to swing the Bavarian election, the FDP and SPD canceled their respective five minutes of answering time. But the TV speech was a curious dud. A legal exposition rather like his National Press Club statement in Washington, it made listeners wonder whether he were aware that there was a crisis in progress. *Christ und Welt* in Stuttgart, close to Bundestag Speaker Gerstenmaier, saw no recourse but a grand coalition of CDU/CSU and SPD with Helmut Schmidt as the new Defense Minister.

Erhard, at the convention of the Hamburg CDU, declared that he had favored laying the cards on the table from the beginning. He was not one to deny that mistakes had been made, he said, nor that democracy in Germany had taken a beating. Erik Blumenfeld, chairman of the Hamburg CDU, left no doubt about his opinion that Strauss should have talked, and indeed that the government should have made him.

Strauss replied with a new blockbuster. In an interview with the sympathetic *Münchner Merkur*, he let it be known that he had acted only in accordance with the Chancellor. From here on, the stakes were all or nothing. The FDP, its head on the block, reacted violently. Intransigently anti-Adenauer for the past decade, it suddenly found itself defending him. It was Strauss who had told Walter Strauss to bypass Stammberger, Döring announced. Strauss had claimed Adenauer's authority. But the Chancellor himself had sworn to FDP deputies that he had never had it to claim. At a press conference in Ansbach, Stammberger resolutely pursued the same line.

Packed houses in Munich heard Strauss repeat his statement the next day in greater and still more emotional detail. With symptomatic ambivalence, the CSU staged its final rally twice, in the mammoth auditorium of the Deutsches Museum and the cavernous Löwenbräukeller. Contrary to all previous practice, it also issued tickets to make sure that the right audience appeared. A handful of hecklers stood around outside. A still smaller group, which had made it through the doors, was easily silenced by the partisans within. The odds were against the hecklers anyway. Heckling Strauss was like heckling a tornado. Sweating profusely, roaring with the fervor of a revivalist and the confidence of a home-town boy at home, he overcame resistance in minutes, then spoke—thundered, bellowed, trumpeted—for two hours before refueling and repeating the performance.

His party and even the government heralded him on his way. Stammberger, the CSU howled, was insupportable, totally disqualified by his inept treatment of the affair. Strauss, the government added indirectly through the mouth of a law professor from Kiel, was not insupportable because Ahlers' arrest was consistent with the latest legal opinion. Modern legal interpretation, Professor Hellmut Mayer announced in the official government *Bul-*

letin, tended more and more to the position that all judiciaries are one. Common defense interests, he contended, went hand in hand with common extradition of traitors. Foreign arrest was valid if it met German requirements.

On November 25, while Bavarians finally went to the polls, Dufhues, the CDU's executive secretary, announced on television that, if necessary, the purge would extend even to Adenauer, Erhard, or Schroeder. The suggestion was pursued by the *Süddeutsche Zeitung* to its ostensible origin in *Christ und Welt's* proposal of a "grand coalition," meaning a government minus Adenauer, Strauss, and Stammberger, under the leadership of Chancellor Gerstenmaier. What was meant as public reassurance was, seen this way, almost a declaration of war of all against all.

So, as it soon turned out, were the Bavarian returns. To the surprise of most observers, they made two if not all sides happy.

	1962	1958
CSU	47.5%	45.6%
SPD	35.3%	30.8%
FDP	5.9%	5.6%

But happiest of all was the CSU, and happiest of the CSU was Strauss. Reproduced by the complicated mechanics of the Bavarian election law, the returns meant 108 of 204 seats in the Landtag, the CSU's first absolute majority since the creation of the Federal Republic.

In a conversation with the Minneapolis *Tribune's* Graham Hovey, Strauss was cagey about the implications of what he considered his victory. Naturally he couldn't speak for the Chancellor, he said, and wouldn't think of doing so. But there was no way around the Bavarian returns, he believed. Bavarians had answered those who were trying to keep "us" from "defending the Federal Republic."

In effect, Hovey noted, he had the impression of Strauss standing at the East German frontier, holding back the onrushing tide of Red Bolshevism with one hand, while with the other he pulled out the knives stuck in his back by—though no names were mentioned—Augstein, Erler, McNamara, various unnamed operatives in Whitehall and the CDU, not to mention Arthur Schlesinger, Walt Rostow, and just possibly McGeorge Bundy.

Whether the triumph was real was another question. The clearest single result was the FDP loss, despite the nominal 0.3 per cent gain. In Middle Franconia, the center of FDP strength in Bavaria, the party had in fact lost 0.9 per cent, declining from 12.1 to 11.2 per cent. Statistically the biggest winner was not the CSU at all, but the SPD. And while the CSU had undeniably won, it was hard to prove that the victory was Strauss's.

If, as he argued, the returns were a personal vindication on an issue of national importance, the appropriate standard of comparison was the national election of 1961 in which the CSU had won 54.9 per cent. In this perspective, his victory was relative at best. Under normal circumstances, it is hard to call a loss of 7.4 per cent a victory. If, on the other hand, the Landtag election of 1958 was to be the standard of comparison, then the victory was the Bavarian CSU government's, not Strauss's. What mattered in the days that followed was less the debatable point that Strauss had won a victory than that he said he had, and that after the racket of the preceding weeks, there were people prepared to believe him. It was as important that the FDP, at least in porportion to its efforts, had lost.

Bonn was covered by a heavy fog on the morning of November 26 as Strauss reappeared and vanished for a two-hour session with the Chancellor. Hase was once again left to do the dirty work. The prediction of indictments against Ahlers and Augstein was only a prediction, he declared accommodatingly in the face of evident indignation. The CSU campaign ads were not a statement of government policy, he added in the face of still more of it. Then he innocently announced that the official *Spiegel* report was ready, pending only the signatures of the four ministers.

This was confirmed the next day by Stammberger. At the

same time, his co-signatories made themselves formally unavailable by going through with the resignation offer of the previous week. As the CDU/CSU ministers put their offices on the block, the parliamentary delegation authorized Adenauer to negotiate "with all sides," although it was reported that anti-SPD forces still had the upper hand. According to the *Süddeutsche Zeitung*, Erich Ollenhauer, the SPD chairman, replied in kind. The SPD was not prepared to blackmail the FDP, he said. He denied that a grand coalition was in the making, but added that his party was not prepared to support a minority government. Did this mean that the SPD was for an all-party government or that it was prepared to try to form a government with the FDP?

"Many things are possible," the SPD's Erler announced oracularly. Only Strauss was out of the game, his "victory" notwithstanding. Strauss later contended that either a minority government or a coalition with the SPD could have saved him. But the former could have saved him only at the cost of the government itself, while the latter was conceivable only at the cost of Strauss. Beyond this, however, virtually any combination was conceivable.

The CDU showed interest in committing Adenauer to retirement plans and demonstratively applauded Erhard. There was general agreement that Brentano, a fighting issue for the FDP, should not get a post in the new government. Speaking for the Catholic, trade-unionist, left wing of the party, Hans Katzer speculated on a coalition with the SPD, committed to an electoral reform that would increase the directly elected share of the Bundestag from 50 to 70 per cent and thus, inevitably, weaken the FDP, which last won a constituency directly in 1953 and whose deputies had since come only from the 247 members of the Bundestag elected proportionally.

The *Frankfurter Allgemeine* reported that the SPD was interested in a genuinely radical reform, the so-called constructive vote of no confidence, which would bring down Adenauer in favor of a provisional SPD-FDP coalition, to be followed by dissolution of the Bundestag and new elections. The alternative, of course, was the grand coalition. But this was problematic. Reluctant to write it off—with good reason, as it turned out a few days later—the SPD was also reluctant to risk antagonizing its voters by saving Adenauer, the man who for the past thirteen years had announced that the SPD was roughly equivalent to Germany's destruction.

Not three but four parties were on collision courses, and the question was as much whether Strauss would be made to go as whether Adenauer would manage to stay. It was a strenuous week. Strauss, even the civil servants confided, had run amok, beginning with threats to break up the affiliation of CDU and CSU that had prevailed since the parties' creation. On Tuesday he had delivered an interminable self-defense in the party caucus, while Adenauer sat by, to the exasperation of CDU deputies, in stony silence.

But by Wednesday, even Strauss seemed to have agreed on an "honorable departure." The rest was a rear-guard action. Pleading illness, Strauss boycotted a cabinet session while Adenauer presided, then turned up at a meeting of the CDU/CSU parliamentary executive and proceeded to denounce Adenauer for two hours. Adenauer had given him a blank check on October 18, he maintained, and he had not been drunk on October 25. While his colleagues sat by appalled and embarrassed, he recalled how years before he had personally had to help Adenauer and the CSU's ex-Finance Minister Fritz Schäffer home from meetings with the occupation high commissioners on the Petersburg, opposite Bonn.

Adenauer appeared on Wednesday afternoon to announce that he had given Strauss the sack. For the sake of form, Strauss was elected to the negotiating committee scheduled to meet the next day to compose a compromise statement on his departure.

On November 29 a four-hour conference discussed a graceful exit for the Defense Minister. In the evening, CDU leaders convened with the FDP on the premise that Strauss was through. It was understood that Stammberger's official *Spiegel* report had been Adenauer's decisive weapon. It was conceivable that, having done its duty, the report would not be seen again. It also appeared that there was considerable feeling in the FDP about undoing the ignominy of 1961 and getting Adenauer too, a threat that, by its nature, mobilized every self-protective instinct in the CDU. At a press conference, Brentano indicated delicately that it was unlikely that "certain people" would be in the next government, though official confirmation, let alone more specific information, was deferred until after a meeting of the CSU executive in Munich. The CSU's Werner Dollinger meanwhile let it be known that "the pressure was relieved."

A sociable peace conference had been scheduled for the evening of November 29 on Krone's invitation. He had assured the FDP that Strauss would not be at the Chancellery. Schmueckle announced the contrary, however, in midafternoon, and Brentano confirmed Schmueckle's report half an hour before the scheduled dinner. Strauss had apparently invited himself. The peace dinner for the FDP turned into a preliminary farewell dinner for Strauss. The FDP remained in its offices and ate sandwiches. On its arrival at the Chancellery later in the evening, it was in anything but a conciliatory mood. "Do you mean to be Chancellor until 1972?" Döring is supposed to have asked Adenauer. The question had long since become the source of popular jokes. "What's the difference between Adenauer and the German plumber?" was a typical example. "Adenauer never goes, the German plumber never comes," was the answer.

The Munich conference confirmed Strauss's withdrawal. A party statement thanked the Bavarian electorate for its vote of confidence. It declared once again that Strauss had delivered official assistance as his conscience dictated, that he regretted eventual errors of form, and emphasized that, when in doubt, security comes first. It deplored the exploitation of the situation by the SPD and FDP that forced Strauss to leave office, thanked him for his selfless service, announced its awareness that the crisis provoked by the FDP must be resolved and that the party was prepared to help, confirmed Strauss's resignation from office while noting that the FDP had taken a well-deserved beating in the previous Sunday's election, and commended Strauss again for his services and sense of duty.

In a valedictory statement on Bavarian TV, Strauss announced that his future plans included getting a decent night's sleep and an extensive vacation, devoting more time to his family, and seeing to it that his policy, particularly his defense policy, was maintained in his absence.

The bombshell exploded on December 2 in the vacant spaces of Germany's underdeveloped Sunday press. *Der Tag* in Berlin, which had connections with the CDU, was first with the story. The reverberations were felt in Bonn in all their magnitude on Monday, an overture to what one commentator was to call without exaggeration the most interesting week of domestic politics in the history of the Federal Republic to date.

Behind the fog on November 26, Paul Luecke, the CDU Minister of Housing, had established contact with Wehner. Supporting him was his colleague, Baron Karl Theodor von Guttenberg from the CSU. Preoccupied with Strauss, everybody had been too busy to watch the Ministry of Housing where Wehner and Luecke had conferred from 7 P.M. to 10:45 P.M. Wehner's step-daughter had in fact been spotted there, waiting patiently at the ministerial reception desk. But the clue was brushed aside by the press corps. Wehner, it was reasoned, was also interested in housing.

The conference, like its consequences, was a model of complementary interests. Luecke was worried about the future of his party and, beyond that, about the future of the Federal Republic. A Catholic and a member of his party's labor-oriented left wing, he was particularly worried about the problems of further liaison with the FDP.

Wehner, the engineer of the great political change of heart of 1960 and something of a Moses seeking a way for his following out of the desert of opposition, was, for his part, prepared to pay a price for access to the promised land, to put up with Adenauer and the risks of majority voting, which, whatever else it might do, was guaranteed to finish off the FDP. With provisional agreement on these terms, Luecke reported to Adenauer. The Chancellor, indignant about FDP intransigence, authorized him to carry on. Not only was it a possible way to save himself and outflank the FDP, it was also a way of eliminating Erhard from the succession to the chancellorship.

A convenient opportunity for further negotiation presented itself the next day. Wehner and Guttenberg found themselves together in Berlin on business. They met and agreed on comprehensive terms. Adenauer and majority voting were already settled. Maintenance of present policy in foreign, defense, economic and social matters, support for an integrated European nuclear force, and exclusion of the controversial issues of school and educational policy from any eventual government program were added to the list.

Satisfied with the terms, Adenauer let successively larger numbers of party leaders in on the secret. On December 1, the day after the CSU had folded Strauss's tent in the face of what it assumed to be unqualified and unilateral FDP demands, a six-hour meeting of CDU and CSU delegates again authorized further negotiations. The CSU's Werner Dollinger was among the negotiators, as was Strauss. The final decision was referred to the full 251-man parliamentary group. Adenauer's sincerity was later questioned. But the deliberate confrontation of his party's executive and then of its parliamentary rank and file with the problem seems, in retrospect, convincing evidence of his good faith.

With panic reinforced by spite, CDU deputies took to the idea with startling enthusiasm. Almost overnight a hard core of support turned into something like general euphoria. The CDU's labor wing joined hands with the representatives of big business in mutual confidence that they had discovered the answer to all their problems.

The *Frankfurter Rundschau* reported that Gustav Stein, a CDU deputy and executive secretary of the *Bund deutscher Industrie* (BdI), Germany's National Association of Manufacturers, had invited the SPD's Erler, Carlo Schmidt, and Heinrich Deist to his home to emphasize business' interest in an agreement. Fritz Berg, chairman of the BdI, and Hans Günther Sohl, director of the trade association of the German steel industry, now general director of the August-Thyssen-Hütte, Duisberg, concurred. Erhard, they declared, was no reliable bulwark against the upward wage-price spiral. If the SPD were prepared to lean on the unions, they were prepared to support the SPD.

Erhard, the CDU's deputy floor leader Kurt Schmuecker, Blank, and Strauss were against the arrangement. Schmuecker, a diligent representative of small business interests, was later to be Erhard's successor as Minister of Economics. Blank foresaw the loss of not only his program but his seat in the cabinet if the SPD joined the government. Strauss could more easily envisage his return to an Erhard cabinet than to any other. They were, however, a minority among the two dozen speakers at a meeting of the parliamentary group on the evening of December 3, and they found themselves in increasing isolation.

The next day Adenauer received Ollenhauer, Wehner, and Erler and laid out the conditions of negotiation. He was prepared to draw up an agreement on the spot. The Wehner-Guttenberg program remained the basis of the CDU position. In return, Adenauer was prepared to offer at least parity in the new cabinet, including access to the Ministries of Defense, Justice, and the Interior with their implicit potentialities for carrying the *Spiegel* affair to an appropriate, from an SPD point of view, conclusion, i.e., total defeat for Strauss.

Ollenhauer, Erler, and Wehner withdrew to report the terms to their executive; at the end of the evening the SPD leadership came out with a pyrrhic victory by a vote of 23–13. The scars of thirteen years were not to be operated away in two hours. "It was a madhouse," said a participant later. For a party with proportional representation in its bones, majority voting was hard to accept. There were also inhibitions about complicity in the murder of the FDP without notice and an adequate transitional period. Finally, for a party bullied, badgered, and finally beaten four times by Adenauer, the Chancellor himself was an issue.

Coalition with Adenauer was moral capitulation, a minority protested.

The voting issue was a conditional obstacle, as it turned out. An SPD deputy, on his way back to his office late that evening, happened on the CDU's Rainer Barzel in the Bundestag corridor. Discreetly indicating his party's reservations, he inquired just how far the CDU meant to go on electoral reform. Perhaps from 50–50 to 70–30, Barzel replied candidly. The matter could presumably be worked out later. Majority voting also had its risks for them, the CDU deputies had discovered, particularly for the eighty-nine Protestant deputies. There was little consolation in the calculable advantages of a different voting system, they felt, if all those who were to benefit from it were Catholics.

But the Adenauer issue was absolute, as Adenauer himself was quick to grasp even before the entire SPD parliamentary group had convened the next morning to discuss the matter. Seven hours of debate finally produced a compromise resolution, but not before the dynamism of the party's leadership had smashed on the reefs of incomprehension. For a vast majority of the parliamentary rank and file, majority voting meant nothing more or less than the loss of their seats and very likely a CDU majority for all eternity. Coalition with Adenauer struck them as a kind of political black mass. Wehner, Hamburg's ex-Mayor Max Brauer, and Schumacher's former secretary Annemarie Renger argued with passionate conviction that Adenauer in office with the SPD would finish himself; but their arguments failed.

In the end, only twelve deputies opposed and four abstained from the compromise: "The SPD parliamentary delegation resolves in conjunction with its executive to continue negotiations with the CDU with the provision that all questions of persons and policies necessary to the formation of a government be submitted to negotiation." But the compromise, reinforced by the interpretation of Franz Barsig, the SPD speaker, sufficed to bring things to an end.

The resolution meant, Barsig explained, that the party had reservations about Adenauer and majority voting. He specifically asked not to be quoted, but was again[5] tripped up. At 7:28 P.M. Barsig's statement went out on the dpa wire and was noted in the Palais Schaumburg a few blocks away, the seat of the Chancellery. It confirmed Adenauer's doubts and further chilled the cold feet of the CDU parliamentarians. "Now we'll have to look for a new bogey man to replace Wehner," a CDU deputy observed in the course of a meeting the same afternoon.

As it happened, Döring was with the Chancellor when the dpa report arrived. He had arranged a meeting with the SPD for 6 P.M. Delayed at the Chancellery, he turned up instead at nine-thirty, unaware of the dogged resistance to majority voting in the SPD. It was, in any case, too late for a deal. "The idiots," an SPD deputy later observed of the FDP, "they missed their chance." But there had never really been one. The majority would have been precariously thin under the best of circumstances. The FDP's opportunities for pressure vis-à-vis the power-starved SPD would have been even greater than they were vis-à-vis the CDU/CSU. The SPD was resolved—although in vain —to go ahead with the CDU, while the CDU had determined to go ahead without the SPD.

"Having failed to come to terms with the murderer," Stammberger observed, "the CDU has decided to make a deal with the victim." Majority voting was the crucial issue, Brentano declared subsequently. But there had been reservations about this in the CDU as well, and nothing but reservations in the FDP, which was now the only alternative coalition partner. Although no one said so, Adenauer was the primary issue, with intimidation of the FDP not far behind.

The threat had its effect. The FDP, especially Mende, was now prepared to listen to reason, from a CDU point of view. Immobility, Giselher Wirsing of *Christ und Welt* observed, had triumphed over élan. All that remained was to celebrate the exhausted reconciliation with a few appropriate sacrifices. By coincidence, Hopf, whose head was conspicuous among those *not* scheduled to fall, returned to office on December 6.

[5] Cf. p. 101.

CDU, CSU, and FDP negotiators convened again on December 7. At 9:34 A.M., dpa announced Adenauer's confirmation of his resignation promise. The Chancellor's head, as it were, was to be hacked off in installments. The rest of the cabinet list was settled the following week. Berlin's Ernst Lemmer, co-founder of the CDU in 1945, and a cabinet member since 1956, learned that he had been relieved of office at a meeting of the parliamentary group. The CSU's Siegfried Balke, Minister of Atomic Affairs, learned of his dismissal from his secretary, who heard it from the doorman, who heard it on the radio. Balke rushed off to the meeting in progress where the report was confirmed.

The deputies listened in silence to the announcement of their new government. "Herr Bundeskanzler," a CSU deputy declared, "I was once one of your most enthusiastic admirers. This is no longer true. Today you are far from the electorate, far from the parliamentary group, and far from your friends."

The final issue was the Defense Ministry. On December 7, Adenauer persuaded Kai-Uwe von Hassel, Schleswig-Holstein's Minister-President and the organizer of the 1961 campaign, to succeed Strauss. According to Die Zeit, the major opposition came from Strauss, who wanted to see the ministry remain in CSU hands. When Adenauer remained intransigent, Strauss demanded the Finance Ministry. The FDP countered with a demand for retention of the ministries it already held. The resultant compromise was achieved at the expense of the incumbent Starke. Stammberger was also replaced.

It appeared that nearly everyone had lost in the shake-up. The CSU had lost weight in the cabinet; the FDP—henceforth vulnerable at any moment to the threat of a new CDU deal with the SPD—had lost still more of its freedom of motion; Adenauer had unequivocally lost his grip on the Chancellorship.

A few weeks later, Erhard was interviewed by the junketing W. R. Hearst, Jr., Bob Considine, Serge Fliegers, and Frank Conniff. "I'd have done it all a bit differently," he said. He laughed abruptly, they reported, then turned serious again. "I admit," he added, "if I had had the concern, the conviction, serious reason to believe that treason had been committed, I would have gone to the German people the next day and said so, and explained why steps had been taken. Had the government laid its cards on the table, there would have been no *Spiegel* affair and no Strauss affair." It was, he conceded, probably not the end of Strauss. "But," he observed, "one thing is sure. He isn't going to be Adenauer's successor."

The end of the affair took the form of successive acts in a frivolous epilogue. On December 12 it was agreed that the CDU's inoffensive Hans Joachim von Merkatz would represent the Federal Republic at the Paris NATO meeting. Merkatz, until the great shake-up Minister for Federal Affairs, was himself one of the affair's victims. He had been succeeded by the CSU's Alois Niederalt. The same afternoon, the Defense Ministry announced that Merkatz would be its interim minister. Giving way to Strauss's protests, Adenauer agreed he could remain until Hassel took office two days later. A minister as provisional non-minister, two ex-ministers as minister, finally Niederalt as Merkatz's successor: the Federal Republic, one could say, had advanced from its recent embarrassment of vacancy to an embarrassment of ministerial riches. "Evidence of how well-qualified we are," the SPD observed.

On December 17 the CSU took steps to get even with Guttenberg, who, since early December, had been enjoying a far better press than its chairman. Strauss, who had not been exactly a model of loyalty in his relations with Stammberger a short time before, made disloyalty the theme of his attack on Guttenberg. Had the party known of Guttenberg's rendezvous with Wehner, it would have thought twice about throwing Strauss to the wolves on November 30, the CSU executive argued. A party tribunal demanded that Guttenberg practice self-criticism. "Who is Baron von Guttenberg anyway?" roared the CSU's deputy chairman Weiss. "Right you are," Guttenberg replied with a broad ironic smile.

On December 19 Hopf staged a farewell dinner complete with military tattoo for his departing superior at the air force base at Wahn (lunacy, in English) near Cologne. The SPD refused to attend. "I do not regard this as farewell," Adenauer announced. Hopf himself; Foertsch, the Bundeswehr chief of staff; and the CSU's Richard Jaeger were not far behind in their expressions of loyalty. Foertsch presented Strauss with a dagger that had once belonged to Bavaria's King Maximilian II; Jaeger compared him to Scharnhorst, the reformer of the Prussian army.

Other voices were more critical. In an interview with the *Süddeutsche Zeitung*, the CDU's Dufhues indicated that his party had perhaps neglected its contacts with the press and the intellectual community. A rural CSU mayor named Karl Dräxlmaier resigned his post and quit the party, but no one followed.

On January 4 *Christ und Welt* published an interview with Paul Bausch, a CDU deputy since 1949, and a man regarded by his colleagues as an articulate loner. On November 23 Bausch had written Brentano, "Please realize that it is altogether impossible for me to defend the position of the government any longer before the public and my voters. That might be possible in Catholic constituencies. In predominantly Protestant constituencies, it is impossible. The government is no longer credible." Brentano had replied in kind: "There is no reason for you to think that I regard the situation very differently than you do." The reply failed to reach Bausch, but unaccountably turned up a few months later in the *Spiegel*.

Frustrated by seeming indifference to his concern, Bausch finally sought a public forum. He had been pleased with Adenauer's determination to fight on November 7, he told *Christ und Welt*. He had taken offense at some of the Chancellor's formulations, but was nonetheless in sympathy with the general line. He had, however, approached Adenauer with some unnamed "friends" on the same day to urge the Chancellor to apologize for his rhetorical excesses before it was too late. But the Chancellor refused to listen, he said. From here on, Bausch concluded, the battle was lost. In the course of the succeeding week he had seen the government lose the initiative and had himself been sincerely ashamed of its association with Strauss. Wehner, he declared, was a better democrat.

Not surprisingly, Bausch's apparent aspersions on the Federal Republic's Catholic voters offended the CDU's Catholics. The *Spiegel's* publication of his unreceived letter from Brentano offended Bausch. Characteristically the CDU's only public self-criticism ended with a new suit aimed indirectly against the *Spiegel*. The culprit was never found.

The government report on the curious goings-on of late October was still unpublished. Confronted by an SPD threat to produce a report of its own, Will Rasner, the CDU whip, took action. In a phone conversation with his opposite number, the SPD's Karl Mommer, he alluded to Jahn's unfortunate connection with Schmelz and the photocopied minutes of the defense committee. If the SPD would hold off, he suggested delicately, the CDU would do the same. Mommer refused to be intimidated.

The CDU regrouped for a counter-offensive, which opened with a series of appropriately slanted questions by Rasner, Berlin's Ernst Benda, and Hamburg's Erik Blumenfeld. The very sparrows were whistling Jahn's involvement from the roof, Rasner declared. The sparrows, he later indicated in a private interview, were several of Jahn's fellow SPD deputies. With impending elections in Lower Saxony and Rhineland-Palatinatc, the consequence was a full-blown but ultimately fruitless series of hearings that went on until the summer recess. It was supplemented by the announcement that the Solicitor General's office had introduced proceedings against the SPD's Helmut Schmidt. In the course of the hearings, Jahn publicly confessed his role, but by this time it scarcely mattered.

The government report appeared on February 3. The only surprise was that it appeared at all after the prodigious backing and filling that had preceded it. Stammberger's successor, the FDP's Ewald Bucher, earned the lion's share of the credit for its appearance. The original plan, a joint report by all four ministries, had long since disintegrated. Strauss never signed the report at all.

The Defense Ministry's view of the controversial events appeared in a section by itself. Höcherl's Ministry of the Interior added an appendix. Schroeder's account of the events in Madrid was outstanding in its candor.

A month later the SPD stopped its exploitation of the affair with its own long-awaited report, systematically itemizing the weaknesses in the government's official statements. It mattered less how often the government had lied than that it lied at all, the *Süddeutsche Zeitung* observed. The high-quality paper the report was printed on, it added ironically, nonetheless deserved a word of praise. The appearance of the SPD report was, as much as anything, the end of the affair. "What else could we do?" an SPD deputy asked helplessly.

"Tout commence en mystique et finit en politique," Charles Péguy observed more than half a century ago, reflecting on his youthful experience of the Dreyfus affair. If historical parallels were to be established at all, this one was as appropriate as any other.

VI.

THE PUBLIC AFFAIR

"It makes an impression on one to be called up at 1 A.M. on a Friday night by a stranger in Hamburg," Nicholas Benckiser noted in the *Frankfurter Allgemeine* on November 19. The stranger, scarcely articulate, had happened to be a witness to the proceedings at the Pressehaus. He was resolved to sound the alarm. Was it, he demanded finally with a reference to 1933, time to emigrate?

For press and public alike, the call was a symbolic overture to two of the most strenuous months in the history of the Federal Republic. The excitement—and the confusion—reverberated abroad within hours. "It was," a *Newsweek* correspondent later mused nostalgically, "the best story since the war."

"*Gigantesque Scandale de Presse en Allemagne-Ouest*," *France-Soir* announced in appropriate-sized headlines on Sunday. "*Grave Atteinte à la Liberté de la Presse*," the altogether more serious *Le Figaro* echoed on four columns a day later. *France-Soir's* Stéphane Roussel reported that forty journalists had been arrested. The New York Sunday *Times's* Anthony Terry gave the figure as eighteen; the Baltimore *Sun's* Henry Trewhitt as seventeen; London's *Daily Worker* as sixteen, *Le Monde's* Roland Delcour as three, with another six held for questioning.

In East Berlin, Karl-Eduard von Schnitzler, the East German

regime's chief propagandist, and Karl Friedrich Kaul, its best-publicized lawyer, meditated publicly on the significance of the affair at a meeting of the Federation of (East) German Journalists. Schnitzler leaned to the view that the crisis had its origin in NATO differences, somehow reflected in the *Spiegel*'s origin as a creation of the British secret service and its subsequent support by the FDP and the West German monopolists.

Kaul resourcefully distinguished between monopolists. There were monopolies like Krupp that favored conventional war, and monopolies like the chemical industries that favored nuclear war, he noted. It was obviously the *Spiegel*'s option for the former that had precipitated the affair. Both he and Schnitzler agreed that whatever it might be, the affair was, in Schnitzler's words, "not an accident, but a genuine crisis of West Germany's *haute bourgeoisie.*"

Schnitzler developed this line further in his next regular TV appearance. The Federal Republic could no longer support even a fig leaf, he observed, adding that, unlike Carl von Ossietzky, the 1936 Nobel Peace Prize winner, who had declared in 1933 that the enemy was to be found only on the right, Augstein insisted on fighting on two fronts.

East German support for the *Spiegel* in particular and the freedom of the (West) German press in general, inspired Bonn's official spokesman, von Hase, to one of his less fortunate moments when at a regular press conference on November 5 he complained about the government's bad press. It was symptomatic, he declared, that the first criticism of the action had come from East Berlin. The audible displeasure of the reporters present made it advisable to change the subject.

In a private report to Hamburg, the *Spiegel*'s correspondent in Rome reported joy in the German colony there, and consternation among Italian acquaintances, even including Catholics averse to the "Opening to the Left."

The first demonstrators appeared on October 28. A group of twenty young men posted themselves on Stuttgart's Königsstrasse with copies of the *Spiegel* in their hands and adhesive tape over their mouths. In Berlin the political cabarettist Wolfgang Neuss presented his audience with a manifesto of solidarity with Augstein. By coincidence, the *Gruppe 47*, a club of some of postwar Germany's most prominent writers, was meeting in Berlin over the weekend. Neuss claimed forty signatures for his statement.

The sentence, "In a time that has made war unusable as a political method, we consider public information about so-called military secrets a moral obligation," soon turned out to be strong medicine for at least two of the signatories. The actors O. E. Hasse and Curd Juergens signed without reading the statement. They subsequently withdrew their signatures. The next day the *Gruppe 47* issued a new statement indicating that the emphasis was intended to be on "so-called." The qualification failed to prevent seven suspicious citizens from filing charges of incitement to treason with the authorities. In due course the official investigation was suspended.

Typical of the atmosphere was a widely quoted editorial in the *Frankfurter Rundschau* on October 29 by Karl-Hermann Flach, Ahlers' successor on the staff and a former executive secretary of the FDP. "If the doorbell rings early in the morning, we can no longer stretch in the reassuring feeling that it can only be the milkman or the kid with the breakfast rolls," Flach wrote.

"If someone knocks on our door at midnight, we can no longer be sure that it is nothing worse than a messenger with a telegram or a drunken neighbor who confused the doors. We have to reckon with the possibility that it is the political police looking for traitors by night and fog.

"When we hear that children cry because their rooms are combed late at night for incriminating evidence against their parents, that editors' proofs of their own articles are confiscated and brought before the censor, when it is reported that the *Spiegel* offices in Hamburg and Bonn are occupied in one blow by armed police units, and one editor can no longer call up the editor in the next office, then we can no longer be sure that this is a story out of Moscow, Prague, Leipzig, or Berlin in 1944. But we can be reassured. This is all happening in the name of and in the interests of our freedom."

Karl Gerold, the editor-in-chief of the *Rundschau,* appended to Flach's editorial a testimonial to the loyalty and patriotism of his former employe Ahlers.

The same day, the *Internationale der Kriegsdienstgegner,* a pacifist group, demanded the suspension of Strauss and an investigation of the political past of the judges, federal attorneys, and police officers responsible for the action. This and similar queries led to the discovery that several federal attorneys had been party members during the Third Reich. But there was no evidence that they had distinguished themselves as such. Their party membership tended to show that they were conformists rather than that they were, in any serious ideological sense, Nazis. The investigation did have consequences, however, for Inspector Theo Saevecke of the Federal Police Office who turned out to have been in the Gestapo. He was suspended in May 1963 for investigation of reports that he had been involved in war crimes in Italy and Tunisia. But he was cleared and reinstated in November 1964.

On Düsseldorf's Königsallee three demonstrators marched up and down with a poster showing Strauss clad in a butcher's apron and armed with a bloody axe. They were led off by the police while spectators jeered at the officers and let the air out of their squad car tires. The prosecution later asked three-week sentences for two of the demonstrators and four weeks for the third. The two were let off in summer 1964 with fines of DM 300 each for resisting arrest, the third with a fine of DM 400 for insulting the arresting officer.

In the main line of respectable caution was the *Frankfurter Allgemeine,* whose studied liberalism characteristically expressed itself in discreet conservatism. Waving its editorial forefinger, it reminded its readers that Ahlers' piece had surely confirmed at the very least much of what the Russians might know about Western defense. By comparison, George Vine, the *Daily Mail's* correspondent in Bonn, declared on November 2, *"Der Spiegel's* revelations climaxed a whole series of disclosures of Bundeswehr military secrets which were no doubt gratefully lapped up in Moscow and would have got Augstein in hot water anywhere in the world."

Freedom of the press was not enough, Alfred Rapp, the *Frankfurter Allgemeine*'s bureau chief in Bonn, continued. The press must accept its responsibility, and a greater responsibility today than in conventional times of peace. This was "on the one hand." On the other he conceded that there was a tendency in Bonn to make excessive use of the rubber stamp. There was no alternative, he concluded, but to await the outcome of the investigation.

The result was a small revolution, which was all the more remarkable in so unrevolutionary an environment. Younger staff members, reinforced by reports from the circulation department of seven hundred canceled subscriptions, switched the editorial line by main force. Bruno Dechamps' second-day editorial threw "on the one hand, on the other hand" to the winds. Dufhues' distinction between an affair of the press and one of the *Spiegel* was not a reassurance but an affront, Dechamps declared. This time the editorial finger was poked not at the reader but at the Solicitor General's office and the government. Why the long delay, Dechamps asked. Why the unclarity of the official statements? Why the remarkable secrecy about the arrest of Ahlers and the nighttime search of the *Spiegel* offices?

The same day, October 30, there was a critical statement from the International Press Institute in Zurich, which suspected with reason that trouble for the *Spiegel* was one object of the exercise, and a demonstration of 150 university students who marched through downtown Frankfurt with protest placards. There followed a telegram to Adenauer from the West German Federation of Journalists, and critical declarations from the Police Union. The action against the *Spiegel* was not a police action, a union statement protested. It was a judiciary action.

On November 1 two thousand people—some estimates reached four thousand—appeared for a scheduled panel discussion on freedom of the press at the University of Hamburg. Since the capacity of the auditorium was eight hundred, the meeting was postponed. The crowd marched on the local jail where Augstein and Jacobi were held, roaring in chorus "*Spiegel* Dead—Freedom Dead," and "Everybody raise a din/Get Augstein out and get Strauss in." Helmut Schmidt appeared in a police car. From the running board, he denied that Hamburg had been involved in the action and appealed successfully to the crowd's Hanseatic civic spirit to get it to break up and go home.

Within, Augstein was consoled by a sympathetic letter from Kay Sely, the former press licensing officer at British Military Government headquarters. "You needn't have taken so literally," Sely wrote, "what I recommended to you in 1948 in my office in Berlin (British, not Russian—notice for the censor), namely that you should criticize the Allies less and concern yourself with domestic German affairs more. Had you not followed my recommendation, you wouldn't be sitting today where these lines reach you."

It was also reported that Axel Springer, despite his intense rivalry with Augstein, had ordered his *Welt am Sonntag* to defer editorial judgment on the affair over the weekend. His *Bild Zeitung*, Germany's *Daily News*, was, however, allowed to introduce the subject of special treatment for Augstein, who had allegedly got a new washbowl and eating utensils, a chair instead of a stool, a bed instead of a cot, a fresh coat of paint for his cell to cover the most recent layer of graffiti, and a blanket over the window to reduce drafts. The prison administration reacted sharply. All prisoners were entitled to a second blanket, and the cell was due for painting anyway, it announced.

Over the weekend of the second week, Hans Zehrer, a veteran of the "conservative revolution" of the 1920s, reflected on the affair to date in Springer's *Welt*. Kennedy had succeeded, he wrote, because both U.S. leadership and public opinion were up to the tasks they faced during the Cuban crisis. The *Spiegel* affair proved that Bonn was not up to its task. "The entire treatment of the *Spiegel* affair," he observed, "from its beginning to this very day, demonstrates a failure of leadership and an inner insecurity that make obvious a dangerous weakness of the state." But the fault also lay with the public, he declared. Public opinion, according to Zehrer, was in a state of promiscuity, of which the *Gruppe 47* was typical. He traced it all to the "nihilistic" *Spiegel*.

The archdiocese of Baden made clear where it stood by notifying the *Spiegel* that, with the introduction of charges, a scheduled interview on the relations of church and state was indefinitely postponed.

In a radio interview, Vice Admiral Rogge, the former NATO commander in Schleswig-Holstein, observed that the action had made a very bad impression on West Germany's allies. On his return from a visit to London, Willy Brandt reported the same. By way of spontaneous confirmation, two professors at the University of Wisconsin, Ralph Nafziger and Bryan Kearl, declared their solidarity with the German press in a telegram to the Press Council. There was, they wrote, a difference between treason and criticism, which was a journalistic responsibility.

Under the critical eyes of U.S. and German television audiences, the *Spiegel* went to press on November 3 in an edition of 700,000—300,000 more than usual. With 178 pages and 115 ads, it was the biggest *Spiegel* to date. The edition was sold out in a matter of hours. The *Kieler Morgenpost* reported a black market in second-hand copies. The *Frankfurter Rundschau* reported that thirty thousand telegrams of solidarity had reached the *Spiegel* in the course of the preceding week. The *Neue Zürcher Zeitung* noted acrimoniously but accurately that support for the *Spiegel*, or, more appropriately, opposition to the government, extended from East Germany's ruling Socialist Unity Party to the Federal Republic's ultra-right-wing *Deutsche Soldatenzeitung*.

On November 5, Kurt Ziesel, a right-wing journalist with a weakness for libel litigation, filed charges against Hamburg's Mayor Paul Nevermann, Bavaria's former SPD Minister-President Wilhelm Hoegner, the *Gruppe 47*, and Bertrand Russell. Their public criticism of the action, he claimed, threatened the independence of the West German judiciary.

A lawyer in Oldenburg, indignant about the mysterious circumstances of Ahlers' arrest, filed kidnaping charges against "unknown." The deputy chairman of the inconsequential Journalists' Union filed charges against the Hamburg policemen who had seized *Spiegel* proofs the night of October 26. A student of the Technical Institute in Stuttgart filed treason charges against Strauss on the basis of a television report of his own easy-going treatment of official secrets.[1] In Düsseldorf, a man filed charges against Strauss and Stammberger for failing to file treason charges themselves against the *Spiegel* after reading Ahlers' Fallex article. The Oldenburg charge led to a serious investigation and an ambiguous result.[2] The rest had a momentary flutter of publicity and a quiet demise in official filing cabinets.

At a performance of Rossini's *La Pietra del Paragone* at the Hamburg State Opera, the audience applauded thunderously as a journalist character on the stage sang, "It's a matter of freedom of the press." The first in a long line of letters of concern on the state of public morality reached President Lübke. It was from the Boy Scouts.

While all this testified to an unprecedented level of spontaneous public feeling, it was, up to this point, a long way from revolutionary. Baron Franz Ferdinand von Stackelberg, a Wiesbaden lawyer who had recently won damages in a libel suit against the *Spiegel*, now volunteered to represent it. But this was a private gesture, only indirectly political. Despite symptomatic quivers like the momentary backing and filling of the *Frankfurter Allgemeine* or Springer's unexpected offer of aid,[3] the lines of political association, by and large, held firm.

On November 6, the eve of the Bundestag debates, the North German Radio's televised "Panorama" attacked the government with unequivocal savagery. But the attack differed from earlier

[1] Cf. pp. 49–50.
[2] Cf. Chapter VIII.
[3] Cf. p. 92.

"Panorama" efforts only in degree, not in kind. Not treason, but Germany's complicated security legislation, the mystery of Ahlers' arrest, and the form and length of the investigation made up the bulk of the program. Its authors, Gert von Paczensky and Rüdiger Proske, noted *Le Figaro*'s report that Norstad had complained of Weinstein's *Frankfurter Allgemeine* treatment of the Fallex maneuver. They wondered openly whether Weinstein's cordial relations with Strauss might have been a contributory factor to the obvious non-prosecution of the *Frankfurter Allgemeine*.

Dufhues, the CDU secretary, was invited to explain his distinction between an "affair of the press" and an "affair of the *Spiegel*." But he refused to appear. Sebastian Haffner appeared in his place. A one-time Berlin lawyer and former correspondent of the *Observer* in Germany, once a political opponent of Augstein's and a sometime defender of Strauss, Haffner was now a free-lance writer.

Haffner was plainly shocked. The police action had obviously been well prepared, he said. In fact, the contrary was true. But under the circumstances, it was hard to deny the plausibility of the statement. Haffner pointed to the evasion of Stammberger, the failure to find suspects to justify the bribery charge in the search warrant, and the apparent intent to frustrate further publication. Should the government succeed in this, he declared, "then adieu, freedom of the press; adieu, rule of law; adieu, democracy." The program drew von Hase's first and only official protest,[4] and indirectly cost von Paczensky and Proske their jobs the following May.

To no one's surprise the liberal *Frankfurter Rundschau*, the *Süddeutsche Zeitung*, and the *Stuttgarter Zeitung* were also behind the *Spiegel*. The *Süddeutsche* sniffed a combination of anarchy and authoritarianism behind the democratic façade, the *Stuttgarter* speculated about new elections. But, like the "Panorama" critique, this was consistent with general editorial policy.

Equally consistent in their ways were Springer's *Bild*, with its

[4] Cf. p. 106.

egalitarian resentment of Augstein's extra blanket, and his *Welt*, with its basic orientation around a father-image government and a latently juvenile-delinquent public. The *Frankfurter Allgemeine*, although prepared to express its reservations, was not prepared on November 5 to accept the risk of a coalition split and a government crisis on account of them. The alternative was a change of heart, not a change of government. The stalwartly Catholic *Kölner Rundschau* and the business-oriented *Deutsche Zeitung* accepted what the government told them.

For unabashed government support, however, no domestic German paper came close to the *Neue Zürcher Zeitung*. A report from Bonn on October 31 was typical. "The *Spiegel* people, who have developed a skillful technique for performing on the very outer edge of journalistic freedom, are now presented as martyrs of journalistic freedom. The idea is a joke. The suspects seem, by the way, to be enjoying this new and unexpected role and have struck their attitudes on the stage accordingly."

But the Bundestag debates were a turning point. From November 7 on, the lines started to move until Strauss at least, if not the government coalition, was without a single serious journalistic friend.

On November 8 Braun, Inc., in Frankfurt, a regular *Spiegel* advertiser and designer of Germany's best-looking electrical appliances, protested Adenauer's disqualification of *Spiegel* advertisers. Braun was answered hotly the next day by a priest in a little town in the Eifel. "I noted with distaste a reference in the paper today to what seems to me an inappropriate telegram you sent to the Chancellor," he wrote the firm. "In the past I have continuously bought your products. I must now inform you that I intend to buy no more of them in the future if you insist on associating yourselves in this way with the *Spiegel*."

"Chancellor: Treason to Earn Money," was the *Bild* headline on November 8. But by the end of the week it was more careful. "We agreed with *Time* yesterday that the methods with which this action has been conducted are a bad thing too." Ahlers' arrest was a scandal, *Bild* declared. The government must be mindful of foreign opinion. Problem No. 1, it declared in conclusion, was treason. But Problem No. 2 was the methods employed in dealing with it. There might have been some questions about the priorities, but who, in principle, could disagree?

Christ und Welt's Giselher Wirsing, like the *Welt's* Zehrer an alumnus of Weimar's "conservative revolution," lapsed into complete despair. Unable to find a single sympathetic face around him, he reported nothing but villains in his field of vision: the incompetent Machiavellians of the government on the one hand, the nihilists of the *Spiegel* on the other.

Die Zeit's satirical columnist Wolfgang Ebert described a fictitious conversation with an official of the Defense Ministry. "Now look," Ebert says, "let's take the improbable case that the other side rallies its forces and fights back. It even shows gains. In other words, things go wrong. The minister finds himself in a tough spot. Does he resign?

"My friend from the Defense Ministry looked at me in amazement. 'Resign? The Defense Minister? You mean like this Krishna Menon? Man, we're not in India.'"

The *Frankfurter Allgemeine* shifted again. Friedrich Sieburg, one of its founders and an influential conservative critic, pointed to impending catastrophe. The affair, he feared, was likely only to make the unpolitical still more unpolitical while the authorities became more authoritarian. But there was evidence of hope. "A libertarian current is making itself felt in our public life," he wrote. "Until now it has almost always failed to appear when one thought it would be a force. This time it is there. Will it last? That would be a happy result of this otherwise unfortunate affair."

The same day, November 10, the *Frankfurter Allgemeine* carried a reader's letter from Professor Gerhard Ritter of the University of Freiburg, a grand old man of German historiography, who had taken part in the anti-Hitler conspiracy of July 1944. Ritter, like Sieburg, was straightforwardly appalled—but from the opposite direction. The *Spiegel*, he declared, without a trace of doubt, had committed treason. The FDP had turned a trivial question of ministerial prestige into a government crisis. "Is there no longer such a thing as a public conscience," he asked rhetorically, "something so self-evident and immanent in our awareness of responsibility for our state and its external security that, in the name of the common interest (*Staatswohl*) it transcends even the interruption of Spanish vacations?"

Bild was meanwhile indignant again. Why had the government not told the truth about Ahlers' arrest from the start, it wanted to know.

The controversy settled temporarily over the weekend as Bonn society marched off to the annual Press Ball. The Bavarian contingent, preoccupied with the election campaign, was conspicuous by its absence. Colleagues set a symbolic place for the absent Augstein. The hit of the ball was the freshly composed "*Spiegel* Twist":

> Dance the *Spiegel* Twist with me
> Even if a cop you be.
> Happy he
> Whose twist is free
> From memory
> Of the powers that be.[5]

Trude Herr repeated it with equal success the following week before mass audiences in Cologne and Dortmund. The *Frankfurter Allgemeine*'s Walter Henkels observed Heinrich Thiesmeyer, Stammberger's spokesman; Schmueckle, Strauss's spokesman; and von Hase, the government's spokesman, among the Press Ball guests. All three looked as though they had been drinking vinegar instead of champagne, he reported.

> [5] *Tanz mit mir den* Spiegel-*Twist,*
> *Auch wenn du von der Kripo bist.*
> *Glücklich ist,*
> *Wer dann beim Twist*
> *Vergisst,*
> *Was nicht zu ändern ist.*

A record version was released by an RCA subsidiary in mid-November.

The following Monday, the day after the Hessian elections, found *Bild* still quivering with outrage. In a rare signed editorial, its editor-in-chief, Strauss's friend, Peter Boenisch, declared the Minister of Justice a failure, and the Minister of Defense a liar. Under the pressure of the FDP, he continued, the Chancellor had turned out to be—at least politically—a murderer. The cabinet was, without doubt, the worst and weakest since 1949. But it was not Weimar, Boenisch assured his readers. The courts were incorruptible, the constitution exemplary, parliament active, and the press free. "Countrymen," he exhorted his readers, "watch the minor enemies, fight them where they turn up. But never forget the major, the Red danger, on their account. Think of our national anthem. Don't just sing it—live it: Unity and Justice and Freedom for the German Fatherland!"

The next day an estimated thousand students demonstrated in Munich against Strauss and the government. Britain's National Union of Journalists issued a statement of solidarity with the *Spiegel*. Karl Dietrich Bracher, professor of political science at the University of Bonn, replied to Ritter's letter in the *Frankfurter Allgemeine*.

"Professor Gerhard Ritter's letter on the *Spiegel* affair is an appalling document," Bracher wrote. "Both language and argumentation carry all the marks of a public philosophy that tolerates political initiative only from above and grants practically unconditional priority over civil rights and the rule of law to a foreign policy-oriented *raison d'état*.

"Perhaps," he continued, "the parliamentary discussion of the past week has meanwhile demonstrated to him too that a tactic of silence, cover-ups, and *faits accomplis* means precisely the scandal that leads to a genuine political crisis (*Staatskrise*). A Chancellor who dismisses an illegal arrest as a triviality and condemns the suspects before the evidence has been submitted, a defense minister who denies his participation for two weeks and lets his undersecretary take the blame without accepting the political consequences of the discovery of his own complicity:

this is the nucleus of a crisis of confidence that could well become a crisis of German democracy.

"The damage to all efforts at political education at school and at university level is immeasurable," Bracher declared. "This is practical instruction that inspires cynicism or resignation, not understanding of the nature and problems of a democracy. . . . The affair has nonetheless had a positive aspect: it has illuminated these dangers and tendencies and inspired a comprehensive discussion that one can only hope will continue."

Congratulations followed, from, among others, two deputies of the FDP and one of the SPD, several secondary school teachers, a student of the University of Bonn, and Major General Count Baudissin of the Bundeswehr. *Le Monde* requested permission to reprint Bracher's letter as an interesting specimen for "our French readers who seldom have occasion to learn what civil courage animates the younger German academic generation."

A housewife in a small town in Lower Saxony, who at least signed her name, charged Bracher with overlooking the main point. "This is a *very serious matter of treason*," she wrote. "Can't you distinguish what is more important from what is less important? And you are a professor, responsible for the academic youth of our nation?"

A correspondent in Darmstadt who signed his name in an illegible scrawl and enjoyed the anonymous exhilaration of addressing a real German professor with "*Du*," the intimate pronoun, was still more explicit. "That professors feel they have to take part in this long-term, *Spiegel*- and Communist-inspired witch-hunt against the government, and particularly against Strauss, only demonstrates what an all-time low the profession has reached," he declared.

The same day, November 13, the *Frankfurter Allgemeine* and the *Deutsche Zeitung* warned the CDU/CSU, with winks at the Hessian election returns, that if they persisted on the path they appeared to have taken, more election losses were likely. In a letter to the London *Times*, Lord Robert Boothby warned his countrymen against getting further involved in the negotiations with the European Economic Community in progress under Edward Heath's direction in Brussels. The Adenauer government's performance in the *Spiegel* affair, Boothby declared, proved conclusively that the Federal Republic was no longer a democracy "in the sense that we understand that term."

"In these circumstances," he continued, "I venture to submit that we should now break off the negotiations for entry into the Common Market and await the day when we can become the linch-pin of an Atlantic Union which will be genuinely democratic, and strong enough to negotiate an agreement with Eastern Europe, including the Soviet Union, that might ultimately prevent the extermination of mankind."

It was reported a few days later that Boothby had telephoned Sir William Haley, the editor of the *Times*, on Sunday to propose his letter, then brought it around in person at four that afternoon. Haley had the letters column reset to make room for it. Boothby conceded as much in a second letter that appeared the day after the first. He was merely trying to strengthen Heath's hand by pointing out that Britain could yet pull out of the Brussels talks, he admitted with a merry wink.

On November 14 Cologne journalists charged Höcherl, Strauss, and Adenauer with treason in the form of damage to the Federal Republic's reputation as a state where law prevailed. The West German branch of the PEN Club wired Adenauer demanding clarification of Ahlers' arrest and its political consequences.

A day later Rudolf Krämer-Badoni, a co-signer of the PEN Club telegram, unburdened his heart, which had hitherto belonged to Adenauer, in a column in the *Welt*. "The government doesn't look like a conspiracy against the *Spiegel*," he noted gloomily. "Would that this were the case. Then, at least, there would be demons sitting in Bonn. No, it was all as banal and miserable as anyone could imagine. It was a group of fiddling dilettantes, without a plan or a trace of awareness of the seriousness of the situation, who even failed to realize that they were thrashing around in a china shop."

While a session of Amnesty International in London indicated concern, the *Welt's* Hans Zehrer groped for a historical analogy. In effect, he argued, the Federal Republic was at the end of its Wilhelminian period. Adenauer was Bismarck, Globke the *éminence grise* Holstein, and Augstein the political publicist Maximilian Harden, who, at the beginning of the century, had caught the imperial regime with its pants down. The first time it was a tragedy, Zehrer observed, but this time it was a farce. The next phase, he predicted, would be a recapitulation of Weimar, beginning with a coalition of CDU/CSU and SPD. He hoped that it would succeed better this time than last.

On November 19, as the FDP convened in Nuremberg, fifty-three of one hundred and eighty professors at the University of Tübingen demanded cabinet changes to restore public confidence in the government. Colleagues at the Technical Institute in Stuttgart endorsed their statement later in the week. At the University of Kiel, Christian Democratic students demanded that Strauss be dropped. In Bonn six hundred Liberal and Social Democratic students staged a demonstration whose parade route included the Defense Ministry.

On the initiative of Bracher's colleagues Flume and Ballerstedt of the law faculty, sixty-three professors of the University of Bonn addressed the Bundestag. "The treatment of the *Spiegel* affair by the government is worse than a series of technical errors," they declared. "It was unworthy . . .

"Many people in Germany think first of the damage done to the reputation of the Federal Republic abroad. More serious, we feel, is the political devastation at home. Bad political style is like a chronic disease. It paralyzes the powers of good, surely not missing from our parliaments, parties, and civil service. It prevents the formation of a secure public consciousness (*Staatsbewusstsein*).

"Among our duties as university teachers is the task of educating the academic youth of our nation to its public responsibility (*an den Staat heranführen*). Incidents like those of the past weeks stand in direct opposition to such efforts. Under the circumstances, we cannot stand silent.

"We hope that the Bundestag, in a common effort of all parties, will have the strength to restore the credibility and legitimacy of our political processes."

Signatories ranged from the liberal Bracher to the historian Walther Hubatsch, who, according to academic legend, was given to flying a red, white, and black imperial flag from his house on the Kaiser's birthday.

Non-signatories regretted that the statement neglected to condemn the abuses of journalistic freedom that had led to the affair, or even objected to professorial expressions of political opinion per se—"questionable, if not to say dangerous," one wrote the authors of the statement. In a letter to the *Deutsche Zeitung*, Professor F. W. Bosch pointed out indignantly that, if sixty-three professors had signed, over one hundred and forty had not, including the entire faculty of Catholic theology. Opponents of the statement were particularly indignant that one of its authors had used the university's nonpartisan addressograph to distribute copies to the faculty.

The Bonn statement was followed by an address to the Federal President by West Germany's political scientists. "The damage done to the spirit of the constitution is severe and bound to shake the confidence of the citizen in parliament and government," they wrote. "Its restoration seems to us possible only if responsible ministers accept the consequences of their, however explicable, failures."

At a matinée the Sunday before the Bavarian election, members of Munich's municipal theater, the *Kammerspiele*, quoted passages from their federal constitution, the Virginia Bill of Rights, and the French revolutionary Declaration of the Rights of Man, from Aristotle, former Chancellor Heinrich Brüning, Macchiavelli, Hitler, Goebbels, the sociologist Max Weber, the Viennese journalist Karl Kraus, Erich Kästner, and St. Augustine. One read the Swiss Red Cross representative Carl J. Burckhardt's description of his visit to Ossietzky, the Nobel Peace Prize winner, at the Oranienburg concentration camp.

From Shakespeare, Angelo's speech in Act II, Scene 2, of *Measure for Measure* was cited:

The law hath not been dead, though it hath slept;
Those many had not dared to do that evil
If the first man that did the edict infringe
Had answer'd for his deed; now 'tis awake;
Takes note of what is done; and like a prophet,
Looks in a glass[6] that shows what future evils,—
Either now, or by remissness new-conceiv'd,
And so in progress to be hatch'd and born,—
Are now to have no successive degrees,
But where they live, to end

In America, Ekkehart Krippendorf, one of Berlin's angry young political scientists, published an anguished letter in the New York *Times*. "The affair should serve as an overdue eye-opener to all those who nourish the comforting illusion that, with certain exceptions, the Bonn republic is basically politically sound," he wrote.

"In recent years *Der Spiegel* has become the most outstanding rallying point of the intellectual and moral opposition to the Adenauer establishment," he declared, "the only widely read magazine with an outspoken critical attitude toward certain fatal trends in West Germany." It was time for the United States to come to the aid of an embattled democratic minority, Krippendorf proposed.

His letter was duly answered by an American reader, Charles R. Foster of De Pauw University. "What is most encouraging to those of us who deplore the police state aspects of the *Spiegel* affair," Foster pointed out, "is that the German press has almost unanimously condemned the actions of the justice and defense ministries. Moreover both the Social Democratic and the Free Democratic parties, which together represent almost a majority of all Germans, have protested vigorously in and out of parliament."

In Bonn, a few days before the Bavarian election and "after the resignation of F. J. Strauss in the form of the resignation

[6] "Spiegel" is the German translation.

of the whole cabinet," as he wrote, Hans Meyer, a young lawyer, addressed an American friend directly.

"Strauss will no doubt be Minister of Justice in the next government," he observed. "He can then do officially all the things he has hitherto had to do as Minister of Official Assistance. Beyond this, he is exceptionally well qualified by his total lack of prejudice in questions of jurisprudence, not to mention legality. It can be assumed that he has acquired the necessary expertise— which, as everyone knows, should at least be equal to that of the average voter—in the course of his own litigations.

"To the affair itself: the government turned out to be both brazen and stupid and for once—that's something!—didn't get away with it. So much for the surface. The resultant racket was scarcely appropriate to what had happened to the *Spiegel,* Ahlers included, but appropriate, if anything, to what happened in the Bundestag where the Chancellor once again played a shrill first fiddle. (Offense is the best defense—which, of course, is no operating principle for a concert-master.) It was certainly appropriate to the way in which the press—lovingly preoccupied with its own affair, which coincided uniquely with that of German democracy—had set the politically active part of the population in motion. And three-quarters of them had known for years anyway that it was time for an end to the old governor's government. Unfortunately it now looks as if the old gentleman's position is stronger than it was in 1961 since he has more undivided support from the CDU/CSU, and Mende need have no scruples either, considering that the FDP has also noticed that its big moment is still to come . . .

"Should one vote SPD again? A party that gets nervous at the slightest gleefully malicious hint that it might also be susceptible to treason? How is a party supposed to govern when it has so little confidence that it can't even fend off an attack from the aging Adenauer as it ought to?

"I refuse to weep any tears for the *Spiegel.* Its circulation gains are not inconsiderable, and it will no doubt soon announce its bankruptcy—I mean when Adenauer stops and Brandt starts trying to govern. I am more and more convinced that Adenauer can get along without the *Spiegel*, but not the *Spiegel* without Adenauer. To which I should add that Adenauer means a twelve-year program that has heretofore created the impression that it, and the whole political apparatus, is—as the Nazis used to say—hard as Krupp steel, tough as leather, etc."

In France the political imagination was fired by Döring's cryptic reference to the cold war of the intelligence services. "There are those who go so far as to suspect that the United States, via the Gehlen agency, wanted to strike a blow at the Minister of Defense," reported Henri de Kergolay of *Le Figaro*. While very few similar speculations turned up in the British papers and the intelligence-service aspects of the affair went largely untouched in the U.S. press, the story turned up with minor variations in *L'Express* and even the satirical *Canard Enchaîné*. To the extent to which it was not already clear, it became increasingly evident as time went by whom it was the French talked to in Bonn, or, more accurately, who talked to them.

The Federal Information Office overlooked the affair altogether in the English-language edition of its *Bulletin*, intended for distribution in the United States. It turned up, however, in *The German View*, published by the German embassy in London. German judicial procedure was different but not necessarily worse than other peoples', the embassy declared in the Federal Republic's defense. If there had been any irregularities, they would have their consequences, it asserted, and pointed ostentatiously to criticism of the government at home as well as abroad. Like Adenauer, the embassy referred to the *Spiegel*'s circulation gains and Augstein's uninterrupted attacks on Strauss from his cell.

In a petition to Gerstenmaier on December 4, 285 staff members of the University of Heidelberg demanded extensive legal reforms in treason proceedings. There were, in total, protest demonstrations at eighteen universities and institutions of higher learning. The faculties of nine universities and twelve other institutions of higher learning submitted staff petitions.

In mid-December a quiet demonstrator painted out "Von

Ossietzky-Strasse" on a Stuttgart street sign and painted in "Aug-stein-Strasse."

Surveys reflected the state of public opinion at the end of 1962. Of the three great events of late 1962, 55% of the population was most excited by the Cuban crisis, 44% by the *Spiegel* affair, only 1% by the Chinese campaign in India. Interest in Cuba was less and interest in the *Spiegel* affair greater in relation to the size of the community in which respondents lived. In towns of under 10,000, 60% were most excited by Cuba, 38% by the affair. In towns of over 100,000, only 48% put Cuba first, 51%, the affair. In the Federal Republic minus Bavaria 54% named Cuba first, 45% the affair. In Bavaria it was 62% for Cuba, 36% for the *Spiegel* affair.

To the question "In your opinion, how did the government deal with the *Spiegel* Affair?" an average of 22% answered "correctly," 48% "not altogether correctly," 29% "largely incorrectly." By a significant margin—34% compared to 25%—men were more inclined than women to criticize the government. Support for the government increased with the age of the respondent. Of respondents between fifteen and thirty, 17% found the government's performance "correct," of those between thirty and fifty, 20%, of those over fifty, 27%. Not surprisingly, support for the government was greatest in towns of under 10,-000, lowest in towns of over 100,000. In the north of the Federal Republic, 32% gave the government the lowest score, in Bavaria 26%.

Questioned on what they found most offensive about the affair, 10% named the night action, 15% the arrest of Ahlers, 25% the government's evasiveness, 12% the intervention of Strauss, 6% the fuss in the press. Of those who identified themselves with the CDU/CSU, 45% considered the arrests of Augstein et al. justified, of those who identified themselves with the SPD, 26%, of those who identified with FDP, 37%.

Polled on their feelings about the West German judiciary, 67% of the declared CDU/CSU supporters, 42% of the SPD supporters, and 54% of the FDP supporters indicated their confidence in the objectivity of the Solicitor General's office. In early December 1962, 14% of the CDU/CSU supporters, 37% of the SPD supporters, and 24% of the FDP supporters felt that the rule of law was in jeopardy.

Polled on general social attitudes, 57% of the total sample declared themselves in favor of journalistic treatment of defense matters and against a government monopoly on defense information. Of the *Spiegel* readers, 70% declared themselves in favor of reports on defense, a view shared with 70% of the SPD supporters but only 51% of the CDU/CSU supporters.

Questioned on what they considered the most serious of all crimes, 79% named murder, 15% treason, 5% blasphemy.

As definition of their feelings about treason, 5% identified it with criticism of existing laws, 23% with resistance during the Third Reich, 43% with publication of military secrets, 83% with divulgence of military secrets for money.

While 50% of the total sample did not consider resistance to the Third Reich treasonable, the figure rose to 61% among the declared *Spiegel* readers and 55% of the SPD supporters. Among CDU/CSU supporters, the figure was 49%.

Questioned on the relative culpability of source and journalists in the event of publication of military secrets, 62% declared the source more guilty and 6% the journalist, while 25% considered the responsibility equal. For *Spiegel* readers, the proportions were respectively 73%, 4%, and 19%; for SPD supporters, 71%, 6%, and 18%; for CDU/CSU supporters, 58%, 7%, and 18%.

Although the squabble over the publication of the report inspired some interest in early 1963, and the pre-Lent Carnival season produced a bit of satirical reminiscence, the resolution of the government crisis, the dismissal of Strauss, and, above all, the Christmas holiday, took most of the remaining steam out of the affair.

Munich's Julius Cardinal Doepfner recalled the affair distantly in his New Year's sermon, warning against the confusion of liberty with license, and against subversion (*Zersetzung*) of public opinion. *Der Mittag* in Düsseldorf recalled it by naming Döring the previous year's Most Courageous Deputy. Shortly afterward, the paper was bought out by Springer and the award was not repeated. It was also learned in early 1963 that a Bundeswehr private who hung a photo of Augstein in his locker had been ordered to remove it by his lieutenant. The private protested to the Bundestag's Commissioner for the Armed Forces, who reversed the lieutenant's order.

In January it was reported that one Karl Friedrich Basedow had registered the film title, *The* Spiegel *Affair: For now we see through a glass, darkly* (I Corinthians 13:12). The film was supposed to be a study of public reaction to the affair, and a psychological investigation of the participants. But nothing was ever heard of it again.

VII.

THE INSTITUTIONAL AFFAIR

Democratic states guarantee their citizens a free press. But they also guarantee themselves the right of self-defense against both attack from without and subversion from within. In 1962 the West German press was not only guaranteed by Article 5 of the federal constitution with its affirmation of the citizen's right to information on the basis of "generally available sources," its freedom was largely realized in statutory law, spelled out in greater detail than it is in Britain or in many states of the United States.

Statutory law explicitly defended editorial offices against search and confiscation.[1] It also granted the journalist immunity from testimony, and thus legal protection of his sources. To be sure, federal law qualified the privilege. Paragraph 53 of the procedural code grants "journalists, editors, publishers, printers, and others concerned with the production or publication of a newspaper or periodical" the right to refuse testimony concerning "the person of the author, source or contact of a publication liable to prosecution," with the proviso that "an editor of the journal concerned has been convicted or is liable to be convicted on account of said publication." But in at least one of the Federal

[1] Cf. p. 81.

Republic's constituent states, Bavaria, journalistic immunity from testimony was virtually absolute.

In Britain, Desmond Clough of the *Daily Sketch* and Reginald Foster and Brendan Mulholland of the *Daily Mail* were convicted of contempt in early 1963 for refusing to name their sources before a royal tribunal. The case originated in the Vassall affair.[2] The tribunal, convened to investigate security procedures, requested that the reporters name the civil service sources they claimed had been aware of Vassall's homosexuality before his apprehension for espionage. All three refused to do so, were convicted and jailed.

In 1957 Marie Torre, author of a regular TV column in the New York *Herald Tribune,* was sentenced to ten days for refusal to name a source. Her appeals were denied in 1958 by a federal court of appeals and the U. S. Supreme Court. In 1966 Annette Buchanan, managing editor of a student newspaper, was convicted of contempt for refusal to name a source at the University of Oregon.

Similar convictions were improbable in Germany, even where prosecuting authorities were prepared to face the risks of requesting them. In 1962 Leo Bermel, local editor of the *Solinger Tageblatt,* reported that the drop-forge industry was to be removed from the industrial town of Solingen. In the subsequent investigation of alleged violation of official secrets, Bermel was asked to name his—presumably local—sources. He was warned specifically that Paragraph 53, the statutory provision for protection of sources, did not protect him since he himself did not face the charge. Bermel's refusal to disclose his source, potentially the basis of a test case, was followed by the decision of Solingen local officials to drop their charges.

The test case followed, however, in 1964. Arnold Geib, the chief bookkeeper of Bucerius' *Stern,* refused to name the sources of a story suspected of having been acquired by bribery of prison officials. He was convicted and sentenced to a fine of

2 Cf. p. 117.

DM 500 or twenty days. The Federal Constitutional Court, referring explicitly to Article 5, overruled the conviction.

Legal speculations after the *Spiegel* affair pointed to a potential conflict. On the one hand, it was argued, Paragraph 55 of the procedural code with its guarantee against self-incrimination, in combination with Article 5 of the constitution, sufficed to cover anything. The journalist was constitutionally entitled to publish on the basis of "generally accessible sources." But what, after all, were "generally accessible sources"? Without further specification, it was contended, the journalist had not only the right but, in his own defense, the obligation to plead Paragraph 55. Not only did this close the holes in Paragraph 53, it rendered it practically superfluous. On the other hand, it could also be argued that there was no defense at all against Paragraph 108 of the procedural code: "If, on the occasion of a search, objects are found that have no connection with the object of the investigation, but point to the perpetration of another punishable offense, they may be confiscated."

But this was theoretical. In practice, German press law was short of comprehensive precedents for lack of test cases. What precedents there were tended to support and extend the rights of the press. In principle, the German press was as free as it chose to be. In their respective ways, the successes both of the *Spiegel* and the *Bild Zeitung* were positive evidence of the freedom of the West German press.

The twilight zone of defense journalism was negative evidence. What was commonplace in the United States and Britain was largely unknown in the Federal Republic. Albeit for different reasons, neither prewar nor postwar Germany had ever experienced the publication of a Gaither report[3] or anything comparable to

---

[3] The Gaither report, commissioned by President Eisenhower, was submitted in November 1957. Under the chairmanship of H. Rowan Gaither of the Ford Foundation, a committee including Robert Lovett, William C. Foster, Paul Nitze, Isidor Rabi, Jerome Wiesner, and James T. Kilian submitted American defense policy to a radical and comprehensive critique. Their conclusions were classified as top

Anthony Verrier's comprehensive and devastating critique of the British Army of the Rhine published in May 1962 in the *Journal of the Royal United Service Institution.*

Questioned in December 1962 on their hypothetical willingness to publish an article like Verrier's, a panel of reputable and not easily intimidated German editors equivocated. Only one, Jens Fedderson of the SPD-owned *Neue Rhein Zeitung,* answered with an unqualified yes. Three, Adelbert Weinstein, Emil Frotscher of the *Frankfurter Abendpost,* and Hermann Proebst of the *Süddeutsche Zeitung,* answered with a qualified yes. Frotscher indicated that he would omit numerical and technical details, Proebst that his decision would depend on both legal access to the sources and his own estimate of the public need for information. It was not his job, he emphasized, to make things easier for spies. Countess Marion Dönhoff of the *Zeit* hesitated to answer at all. British editors, she observed, had official security notices ("D-notices") to guide their decisions. Robert Haerdter of the *Stuttgarter Zeitung* answered with a qualified no. Verrier's article, he argued, belonged in a technical journal. There was more in it than the normal reader could be expected to want to know.

In part, this reticence was a by-product of the *Spiegel* affair, but only in part. The affair itself was uniquely German. But the problem, or at least the potential problem it represented, was universal. Even in peacetime all the news is not fit to print, as American editors well realized, at the latest during the Cuban crises of 1961 and 1962. Carl Rowan, himself a distinguished reporter during his career at the Minneapolis *Tribune* and later deputy assistant secretary of state for public affairs, noted the potential difficulties at a panel discussion at New York University in 1961.

---

secret. Although even the names of committee members, let alone their conclusions, were classified, both had become public before the end of November 1957. Stewart Alsop's New York *Herald Tribune* column was followed by comparable pieces in the Washington *Post,* the New York *Times,* and *Time.*

"I know that were I to meet a Communist agent and give him information bearing even the lowest security classification, most of the newspapers in the nation would literally howl for my scalp," Rowan observed. "Yet, not a day goes by but what some newspaperman is not invoking the 'public's right to know' in an effort to get information of the very highest security classification."

Ironically, while German politicians debated freedom of the press in late 1962, American newspaperman debated security. But "I want the press to go on criticizing government, branding needless secrecy wherever it exists," Rowan also told the 1961 panel. "I don't think it is going to hurt us an awful lot, and if you criticize responsibly—and reserve some of the criticism for the press itself—it can do not only the communications industry but our entire nation an awful lot of good."

It was hard to imagine a similar statement from Rowan's German colleagues—Schmueckle, a career officer, and Hase, a career diplomat. It was equally difficult to imagine a journalist like himself in their jobs. Felix von Eckhardt, the Bonn government's first official spokesman, was an exception. Eckhardt, now a CDU deputy, had not only been a newspaperman himself—he was the son and grandson of newspapermen. But in general, government reservations about journalists were matched by journalistic reservations about the government. For the seventeen years of CDU administration that began in 1949 and ended in 1966, Strauss's invitation[4] to Ahlers was exceptional, Ahlers' rejection typical. Ahlers' subsequent acceptance of an offer to become spokesman not for the Defense Ministry but for the whole government was a case for itself in a way that the Kennedy administration's appointments of Pierre Salinger as White House spokesman, Arthur Sylvester as Defense Department spokesman, or Rowan himself were not. A onetime city editor like James V. Forrestal, or a *Times* correspondent like Lord Chalfont (Alan Gwynne-Jones), in ministerial office, have no real German counterpart.

[4] Cf. p. 55.

In Germany, as in most European countries, soldiers, diplomats, civil servants, and journalists remain soldiers, diplomats, civil servants, and journalists.

A traditional German respect for the *Fachmann*, the trained specialist, in general, and the military in particular, was paradoxically reinforced by the consequences of World War II. America's ascent to world power and responsibility in 1945 engaged even American intellectuals. Historically skeptical of the military, American public opinion rose to the new situation, superimposing an untraditional interest in military affairs on its traditional misgivings: war was indeed too serious a business to be left to the generals. Germans went the opposite way. With Germany's decline from great-power status and the debacle of Europe's most uncontested military tradition, most Germans tended to follow their intellectuals in the direction of anti-militaristic apathy. A small minority became all but literally generals without an army. These were the officers of World War II whose experience and perspectives to all intents and purposes ended with 1945. In the half-generation between 1945 and 1962, the nation of Clausewitz had become a nation of spiritual civilians.

Only one major newspaper, the *Frankfurter Allgemeine*, maintained a full-time defense correspondent in 1962. It was not until 1964 that the *Spiegel* first engaged a defense correspondent of its own. Ahlers and Schmelz were, strictly speaking, political reporters who wrote about defense. For the specialized reader in Germany there was neither a *Bulletin of the Atomic Scientists* nor a *Survival*, the journal of the London Institute for Strategic Studies. At best there was a *Wehrwissenschaftliche Rundschau* and a *Wehrkunde*. The former was largely written and edited by retired generals. The latter, although the product of interested civilians, was slanted mainly at a readership of active and reserve Bundeswehr officers in the middle ranks. Between 1961 and 1964, historical articles comprised half the *Wehrwissenschaftliche Rundschau*, a quarter of *Wehrkunde*. Such few strategic analyses as appeared—10 of 135 articles in the *Wehrwissenschaftliche*

Rundschau, 24 of 372 in *Wehrkunde*—were almost without exception by foreign authors or reprints from foreign publications.

Although Germany was ineluctably the theater of any future European war; although the rearmament debate of the early 50s had raised the political temperature like few debates in German history; although by weight of numbers and military potential Germany, with the exception of the United States, carried more weight than any other single member of the alliance, its only significant contribution to the political-strategic debate of the late 50s and early 60s was Helmut Schmidt's *Defense or Retaliation.*[5] Schmidt himself conceded to an interviewer that he knew of only one German journalist, Theo Sommer of the *Zeit*, who could hold his own in a room with men like Harvard's Henry A. Kissinger or Alastair Buchan of London's Institute of Strategic Studies.

If the press, public, opposition party, and government parties had no very great interest in raising the threshold of official sensitivity, both the Minister of Defense and the ministerial bureaucracy had reasons to maintain it where it was. In principle, the minister was anything but hostile to the press as such, and used it with gusto and a certain skill. In 1962 Adelbert Weinstein was worth reading less for what he said than for the authority with which he said it.[6] But Strauss was as sensitive as the next man to criticism, and the natural habits of the German bureaucracy tended to shield him from it.

"Our bureaucracy seals its doors hermetically," Max Güde, the former Solicitor General, observed in a TV interview in 1962, "and the reporters peep through the keyholes." Control of sources is, however, the first line of bureaucratic self-defense in more countries than just Germany. In 1962 U. S. Assistant Secretary of State Robert Manning and Assistant Secretary of Defense Arthur Sylvester, himself a former newsman, had gone further than Bonn's Defense Ministry had ever gone when they required staff members to grant interviews only in the presence of an

[5] Cf. p. 58.
[6] Cf. p. 61.

official auditor, or to submit formal reports on such interviews as they granted. At the end of 1965 Manning's order had been withdrawn but Sylvester's was still in effect. But in the Federal Republic, bureaucratic self-defense was reinforced by the penal code, which extended control of sources to potential control of journalists.

There was still nothing inevitable about the *Spiegel* affair. In the course of it, more or less obvious national-character arguments—"The Germans never learn," etc.—were joyfully seized for a variety of purposes, both by foreign teutonophobes and domestic masochists. But they were no more valid than they had ever been. Their invocation was naïve, disingenuous, or outright deceptive. The spectacle of East German official eyes filled with tears of solidarity with the free press would have brought a snicker to the lips of Goebbels' ghost.

By the same token, the affair was not an accident, a conspiracy, or a tyrannical escapade. The exclusion of Stammberger, the responsible minister, from the proceedings, and Strauss's intervention in Spain were obviously "somewhat beyond the limits of legality"[7] and led, however laboriously, to consequences. But they were also outside the formal action.

What would have happened to Augstein, Ahlers, and the *Spiegel* if the Minister of Justice had been a Christian Democrat and Ahlers, like Schmelz, had been able to return home voluntarily, is hard to imagine. "If Strauss hadn't got mixed up in it, we would have had them," Hans Globke, Adenauer's undersecretary, mused in an interview with the author.[8] Legality, not illegality, was the heart of the problem. The affair might have raised doubts about whether the Federal Republic was a free country. But it left no doubts at all that it was a country of law.

It was the law in its concrete form, the institutions, and the men who administered it, that made this traditional goal of German liberalism so problematic. The rule of law per se, with its procedural rules, specification of infractions and prohibi-

[7] Cf. p. 116.
[8] At Globke's home in Bonn, February 1, 1966.

tion against prosecution of offenses not already fixed in law, is the first premise of civil freedom. Bad laws can be better than no laws. Thus Globke himself, who in 1935 published a commentary on the Nazi race laws, could argue in court testimony in 1966 that, for all their injustice, the laws had saved the victims from unrelieved arbitrariness. But laws, like fashions, lose their justification as seasons and circumstances change. In 1962 large numbers of Germans learned with a shock that the legislative *haute couture* of the nineteenth century was no longer adequate cover.

The general problem was the relationship of the citizen to a state that claimed with more success than any of its predecessors to be a liberal democracy. The particular problem was the Federal Republic's official secrets (*Landesverrat*) provisions. In principle, they went back to 1871. The specific provision that supported charges against Augstein and Ahlers was virtually unchanged. As Paragraph 92 of the penal code of 1871 it specified that "Whosoever deliberately communicates to a foreign government or publishes official secrets, fortification plans or documents, official papers or dispatches, such that he knows them to be secret with respect to this foreign government or essential to the security of the German Reich, is to be punished with a prison sentence of not less than two years."

As Paragraphs 99 and 100, effective since 1951, they specified that "Official secrets as defined in this section are facts, objects or information, particularly documents, drawings, models or formulae, or intelligence concerning them, whose secrecy with respect to a foreign government is essential to the security of the Federal Republic of Germany or one of its constituent states.

"Whosoever shall deliberately permit an official secret to reach an unauthorized person or who publishes one, and thereby endangers the security of the Federal Republic of Germany or one of its constituent states, commits treason as defined in this section.

"Whosoever betrays an official secret shall be sentenced to prison for treason."

Conviction in 1962 entailed a sentence of up to ten years.

While the effective equation of publication of official secrets with sale of them, and the basic disregard for motivation, not to mention the ambiguity of "security," were latent dangers in the text from the beginning, the history of treason prosecution in Germany revealed with remarkable clarity to what extent the most high-principled "government of laws" was also a "government of men."

In 1900 there had been six treason convictions in the German Reich; between 1896 and 1914 there was a total of 19. All of them had involved spies in the classical sense. None of them had involved journalists. While the Second Empire had had its press martyrs, proceedings against them were generally based on such relatively harmless charges as *lèse majesté*.

All this changed with the coming of the Weimar Republic. Constitutionally the first liberal democracy in German history, the Weimar Republic was characterized judicially by an oppressive authoritarianism that turned the paragraphs into weapons. In 1921 there were 111 treason convictions; in 1923, 1200 proceedings and 137 convictions; in 1924, 1081 proceedings and 516 convictions. In the first two months of 1925 alone, there were 755 proceedings including 20 against journalists. In the course of the year there were 561 convictions. Even where ultimate conviction was unlikely, proceedings were introduced for their cautionary effect, and invariably against the pacifist left. In 1923, 30 investigations were introduced against journalists. In 1925 they averaged 10 a month.

The most famous case of "journalistic treason" in the Weimar Republic was the conviction of Carl von Ossietzky in 1931. Ossietzky, publisher of the radical-pacifist *Weltbühne*, had commissioned a critique of illegal German air rearmament in 1929 with specific references to cooperative development with Spain and the Soviet Union, and budgetary manipulations involving the Lufthansa, Germany's civil air line.

He was charged with treason by the Minister of War, Groener. What made the conviction particularly dubious was not that Ossietzky had published official secrets, something he himself did not deny, but the question of whether the published secrets should have been classed as secret at all, since without exception they violated treaties to which Germany was a party. In declaring Ossietzky guilty of jeopardizing the security of the German Reich, the court accepted a definition of security that contradicted explicit treaty obligations and Article 4 of the Weimar constitution, which gave international law priority over German law.

Weimar precedents, particularly Ossietzky, played an understandable emotional role in the *Spiegel* affair. From beginning to end, the affair resounded with historical associations, appropriate and inappropriate. In November 1962 the *Spiegel* published a history of treason prosecution in Germany, which, although signed by Hermann Renner, a member of the staff, was actually written by Fritz Bauer, Hesse's chief public prosecutor, a man with a particularly vivid memory of the Weimar Republic, who had emigrated during the Third Reich.

Predictably, the treason paragraphs also played an important role during the Third Reich. The 1934 reform of the penal code added treason by negligence (*fahrlässiger Landesverrat*) to the list of judicable offenses, thus sparing judges the difficulty they had hitherto faced in proving deliberate intent. While U.S. and French law contain similar provisions, prosecution is explicitly confined to civil servants and officers—for example, to an officer who loses his briefcase. German law, however, contained no such limit and the provisions of the Nazi era were carried on into the Federal Republic, although the penalty was reduced from life imprisonment to two years with the additional possibility of a fine.

The traditional treason provisions were finally suspended by the Allied Control Council in 1946, only to awake to new life under the most unfavorable circumstances conceivable. In 1945 Germans faced a *tabula rasa*. With the traditional forces of conservatism discredited and the forces of nontraditional, i.e., Nazi, conservatism thoroughly routed, a minority of politically interested Germans enjoyed a unique consensus. Now, if ever, was the time for change. But the moment passed. The treason paragraphs came up for debate not in the summer of 1945, but in the summer of 1951, in the midst of a European cold war, a cold civil war, and, above all, of the war in Korea, which made West Germans aware of their vulnerability as nothing else had done. On July 11, 1951, the traditional treason paragraphs were restored to German law in all their comprehensiveness, including the provisions of the Nazi era. A single significant reform was added under pressure from the SPD. Mindful of the precedent of the Ossietzky conviction, the Bundestag provided that a Bundestag deputy could, where his conscience so demanded, reveal official secrets providing he felt them to be in violation of the constitution. By implication, citizens in possession of official secrets whose constitutionality they doubted could report them to their deputies for public discussion. To date, however, there has been no test case, and the *Spiegel* affair failed to provide one.

A second potential test case arose in 1963 when Werner Paetsch, an employe of the Office for the Protection of the Constitution, publicly reported that the Office had been tapping West German telephones in violation of constitutional guarantees, and that it employed former officials of the Gestapo. Paetsch, however, went not to a Bundestag deputy but to Josef Augstein. He was tried in November 1965, but for violation of official secrets like any employe of the Office, not for treason.

The Federal High Court ruled that it was his obligation to report his misgivings to his superior or a Bundestag deputy, but in no case directly to the public. It was his duty, the court declared, to "take the minimum risk." Paetsch was given a four months' suspended sentence.

The problems remained what they had been before. But specific implications and practical consequences were largely a matter of academic speculation. In this respect, like many others, Bonn was not Weimar. Postwar Germany was again in a state of cold civil war, but the war was largely carried out between West German state and East German "state," and not, as it had been during the 20s, when nominally republican judges pronounced antirepublican law, between social groups and parties. It was claimed that West German journalists, including *Spiegel* reporters, had periodically expressed devil-may-care skepticism about their professional situation. "Whatever we do, we have one foot in jail," Schmelz is supposed to have said to Gerstenmaier's secretary after the appearance of the Fallex article. But until the affair, this was romantic hyperbole. Risks there may have been. But where the press was concerned, there were again no test cases to demonstrate and elucidate them.

In non-press cases, however, the course of postwar precedents had already produced some new cautionary results. "Security of the Federal Republic of Germany" turned out to be as nebulous as "security of the German Reich" had been. The definition of secret was at least as difficult. With considerable psychological insight, postwar legislators had retained the traditional "material" definition of secrecy in preference to the "formal" definition current, for instance, in American law. Secrecy was determined not by the rubber stamp of a ministerial security officer but by the well-considered and theoretically objective judgment of a court. Paradoxically—or seemingly so—a document explicitly stamped secret might turn out in law not to be. An unclassified document, on the other hand, could be found essential to the security of the Federal Republic, at least theoretically.

The inadequacies of such a definition, in a system otherwise distinguished by the fastidiousness of its definitions, was deliberate. It was also not without justification in a country whose civil servants, even more than most, inclined to the view Russell Baker attributed to Philip J. Farley, a onetime special State Department adviser on disarmament: "I realize, of course, that a free press is the bulwark of a democracy, but it is very difficult conducting the affairs of government when things appear in the newspapers."

The disadvantages were, however, obvious, at least for the hypothetical journalistic defendant. The question of secrecy, nominally a question of the respective citizen's judgment, could be answered ultimately only by the judge, since only he was authorized to establish the necessary relevance to the security of the Federal Republic on which secrecy was based, and on which conviction or acquittal depended. Postwar precedents were reason enough for skepticism. West German judges showed little inhibition in determining secrecy. Yet another hazard of treason prosecution in the Federal Republic was that exclusive jurisdiction was reserved to the third senate of the Federal High Court in Karlsruhe, and from its decision there was no appeal.

In 1954 the court established that the willingness of persons with security clearance to talk was itself a violation of secrecy, irrespective of whether they had done so, or what they might have said. In 1956 it decreed that the names and activities of the civilian sources of the various intelligence agencies—the Office for the Protection of the Constitution, etc.—as well as the names of employes were a secret. The Paetsch decision in 1965 seemed to indicate that the previous Gestapo membership of Office employes was also a secret. A 1957 decision suggested that, under certain circumstances, the foreign policy of a political party could be considered secret information. In 1958 it was established that secrecy about the light armament of the *Bundesgrenzschutz*, a kind of inland Coast Guard subordinate to the Ministry of the Interior, and the personnel of its units, was essential to the security of the Federal Republic.

Two famous decisions in 1955 extended the definition even further. One, the basis of a so-called confirmation theory, established that information demonstrably known to a potential enemy was nonetheless still in the realm of official secrecy, since its report or publication presumably confirmed and thus verified what might hitherto have been known but not necessarily believed. The other, which led to a so-called mosaic theory, involved an agent of East Germany who had catalogued publicly accessible technical data. The Federal High Court ruled that the individual contents of the catalogue, themselves not secret, had become secret *in toto* in the process of cataloguing. Both precedents were of potential relevance to the *Spiegel*.

The practical problems of the decisions were reflected by

Hermann Teske, former editor of the military journal *Wehrkunde*. "In 1958 I was offered a largish article on the U. S. Strategic Air Command by a young journalist," he wrote the *Spiegel* in August 1966. "The article was full of precise data on numbers and locations. Examination of this unusually interesting piece by General Kammhuber, at the time commanding general of the *Luftwaffe*, produced the conclusion that, in his words, publication was a violation of official secrecy of the gravest sort. The author, questioned on his sources, replied that he had collected all available data on the Strategic Air Command from the foreign and domestic press for a number of years, and compiled his study from the results. I decided against publication. A few months later the article appeared in another military journal. No one said a word about it."

The theoretical problems of the decisions troubled law professors like Werner Maihofer of the University of Saarbrücken and Ulrich Klug of the University of Cologne. Both pointed to the apparent incompatibility of the treason provisions with the constitutional guarantee of a free press. The constitutional guarantee, Klug contended, necessarily limited the applicability of the treason provisions as such, and qualified the relevance of evidence even within the realm of their applicability. In any case, he maintained, it qualified the gravity of the charge: even if formally guilty, a journalist could not be as guilty as a spy.

Maihofer's critique was still more radical. Not only did the treason provisions conflict with the constitutional guarantee, he argued in a letter to the *Frankfurter Allgemeine*, it was conceivable that they conflicted with the guarantee of equality before the law as well, by granting the government a *de facto* monopoly on defense information with no comparable access for press and public. Finally, he contended, they conflicted with the provision *nulla poena sine lege*. Since the "material" definition of secrecy left it to the Federal High Court to decide whether official secrecy had been violated, it was altogether possible, even probable, that the journalistic defendant was unaware of publishing official secrets until long after he had actually done so.

Involuntarily, the Solicitor General's office did its bit to justify public doubts. It was self-evident to the most innocent *Spiegel* reader that the Fallex article justified suspicion, a spokeman declared testily in the first days of the affair. But if this were so, why a delay of nearly three weeks in initiating proceedings? Because the complexity of the treason provisions required the most painstaking investigation before proceedings could be initiated, was the answer.

The problems posed by the treason paragraphs were further complicated by the procedure applied to them. In 1871 it was relatively easy to recognize a secret. In 1962 it was difficult, if not impossible. The difficulty was not only a matter of technical complexity, although this was problem enough from the beginning: in 1871 as in 1962, judges were judges, not engineers or generals or politicians. The basic problem was the technical acceleration of modern defense planning itself. Since modern defense depends on technical progress, and technical progress depends on publication, the paradoxical premise of modern defense tends to be not secrecy but its opposite. For technological reasons alone, there tend to be fewer and fewer secrets. Political considerations reinforce the tendency. The strategy of deterrence on which NATO and thus the Federal Republic depend presupposes not minimum but maximum publicity; this led to publication of the results of NATO exercises—of "Holdfast," for instance, two years before "Fallex 62"—of ICBM sites, and of rocket and other weapon performances.

Well aware of both the formal and the practical problems it faced, the Solicitor General's office sought expert opinion. But it sought it from the source that was in some ways least qualified to provide it. West German judiciary procedure explicitly bars judges from proceedings in which either party even suspects prejudice. No comparable provision limits the prosecuting authorities. A Defense Ministry *Gutachten* in its own minister's cause—and, as it appeared, explicitly marked "provisional" and based on an inadequate survey of relevant comparative sources—sufficed to support charges, and thus the most radical action against a journalistic enterprise in recent West European history.

Even had there been no occasion to doubt the objectivity of the Defense Ministry, it was questionable whether the ministry's opinion sufficed. What might have been justified in the days of national armies was not necessarily appropriate to integrated forces in a fourteen-nation alliance; and NATO *in toto*, rather than the Bundeswehr alone, was the subject of Ahlers' article. The Bundeswehr, of all NATO forces, was the one army entirely integrated in the alliance. In the absence of a NATO protest, it could well be asked whether there were grounds for prosecution at all. In any case, there was reason to question the wisdom of neglecting the foreign press. The *Süddeutsche Zeitung* later observed that the Solicitor General's office behaved as though it believed the presumptive enemy should not learn from the German press what it already knew from, for instance, the American.

The federal attorneys accepted—or were made to accept—the legitimacy of the questions. But this was only after the event, after the formal arrest of five journalists and the temporary detention of two more, not to mention the fall of a government.

Their reply was both formal and practical. Formally, they argued, NATO secrets were only part, albeit the major part, of West Germany's restricted material. West German jurisdiction also extended to the security of the Bundeswehr per se, and to the security of allied forces in Germany.

Nevertheless only the Defense Ministry was approached for a *Gutachten*, not NATO headquarters or the headquarters of the U.S., British, French, or Belgian troops stationed on German territory. Could one assume that Wunder's *Gutachten* spoke for all of them? There was also no effort to consult the BND on the relevant question of exactly what a presumptive enemy could be assumed to know, or the Federal Information Office, whose library, at the very least, had more to offer than the eight foreign papers filed and catalogued by the Ministry of Defense. Under direct questioning, the Solicitor General's office

argued that official secrets are by their nature "active," not
"passive," i.e., a matter of intrinsic content rather than of
who might be privy to them. As to the question of prior publication, this was a problem for Wunder and the Defense Ministry,
Kuhn contended.

NATO, however, was later directly invoked by the prosecution.
But despite speculations about a Norstad complaint to Adenauer
before the Fallex article had even appeared—though after the
appearance of the Fallex critiques in the *Frankfurter Allgemeine*
and the *Deutsche Zeitung*—the only tangible evidence of NATO
concern seemed to be a letter to Strauss from General J. E.
Moore, chief of staff at SHAPE. In early December 1962 *Newsweek*'s "Periscope" claimed that a NATO complaint had started
the affair. But the complaint, if it existed, never turned up in
the Solicitor General's evidence. In November 1964 the *Sunday
Telegraph* reported that General Lyman Lemnitzer, Norstad's
successor as commander-in-chief of NATO forces, denied that
the Fallex article had contained any secrets at all.

Moore's letter indicated that his attention had been called to
the fact that secret NATO documents had been discussed in the
West German press. "Appropriate action" was requested. But
the date of the letter, October 26, the day of the action in
Bonn and Hamburg, left some room for speculation about who
had brought the matter to Moore's attention and why. It also
made obvious that official NATO complaints had played no role
in the initiation of proceedings.

A subsequent letter from the U. S. Judge Advocate's office in
Heidelberg denied outright that the Fallex article had in any
way jeopardized the security of U.S. troops in Germany. The
delayed arrival of Moore's letter and the content of the Judge
Advocate's cast a curious light on both German law and German
procedure which claimed responsibility for NATO and for foreign
troops on German soil and at the same time failed to accept
the logical consequences. If Article 99, as was claimed, embraced
—and by extension distinguished—Bundeswehr secrets from
NATO secrets and, *inter alia*, U.S. secrets, consistency alone

seemed to demand at least three *Gutachten* or at least appropriate qualifications in the one submitted. But there was nothing of the sort.

What there was instead was a second omnibus *Gutachten* to supplement the first. It was provided only under pressure and a year after the action had begun. As before, the choice of the author lay with the Defense Ministry. The second *Gutachten* differed only marginally from the first. This time the author, Kurt Gerber, was a brigadier general, unlike Hopffgarten, whose promotion from colonel followed completion of the first *Gutachten*. Gerber—also unlike Hopffgarten—could offer relatively recent staff experience at SHAPE, although the experience was now several years behind him, and at the time of his appointment, he was commander of an infantry school in Bavaria, not within the ministry like his predecessor.

He also did not have a reputation for uncritical admiration of Strauss. On the other hand, he admitted to uncertainty about the dimensions of the publicly available military literature. His working capacity was further impaired by recent eye surgery. The material on which his *Gutachten* was based had to be read to him.

The second *Gutachten* was submitted in March 1964. It concluded that Ahlers' article had contained not forty-one but ten secrets. Of these, five had previously been cited in the first *Gutachten*. Gerber, again without checking prior publication elsewhere, added five of his own. The Solicitor General's office claimed that the discrepancy was largely arithmetical. Gerber had grouped alleged secrets that Wunder and Hopffgarten had enumerated individually. They did not contest the revealing fact, however, that Gerber's "secrets" did not coincide with Wunder's and Hopffgarten's.

Gerber's *Gutachten* was supplemented by two others. One from the Federal Information Office, authorized by the Federal High Court in March 1963 and submitted in July, was relatively noncontroversial. The government librarians covered basically the same territory already covered by the *Spiegel*, and reached roughly the same conclusions. The sources of the Fallex article in both the domestic and foreign newspaper and periodical literature were demonstrable to the point of plagiarism, they reported. They conceded that Ahlers' article at certain points had gone beyond other published sources, in both detail and changes of context. Whether this was in itself significant, they said, would have to be checked by military authorities; but the qualification was a matter of professional reserve. Hase himself, the civil servant ultimately responsible for the *Gutachten*, left no doubt of its intent. "Were its conclusions pro-prosecution or pro-*Spiegel?*" he was asked by a visitor. "Pro-*Spiegel*," he answered emphatically.

The second of the supplementary documents was a military *Gutachten* demanded by the *Spiegel*. The Solicitor General's office understandably denied the need for it. The Defense Ministry under von Hassel then refused to qualify the *Spiegel*'s first German candidate, Colonel Hellmuth Roth, whose NATO staff service through the summer of 1962, along with his command of English and French, seemed to qualify him for the task at least as well as his predecessors. A second proposed candidate, Alan Gwynne-Jones, defense correspondent of the London *Times* and since 1964, as Lord Chalfont, Britain's Minister of Disarmament, was rejected by the Solicitor General's office with the argument that he was not liable to West German security control. A third candidate, the Bundeswehr's Lieutenant General Burkhart Mueller-Hillebrand, was found acceptable by the Solicitor General's office in December 1964, and by the Federal High Court in March 1965. Between March 1961 and March 1965 he had been deputy chief of staff at SHAPE, and thus Moore's direct subordinate. Mueller-Hillebrand submitted his *Gutachten* in December 1965. He concluded that Ahlers' article had contained no secrets.

The ambiguities of the law and inadequacies of procedure in dealing with it were finally complicated—perhaps beyond complete solution—by the institutional apparatus charged with dealing with them. In part, the institutional difficulties were formal.

In part, they were a fundamental problem of postwar German society.

The formal problems were rooted in the nature of the Solicitor General's office. Indirectly an organ of the executive, theoretically an independent and autonomous organ of the state,[9] the Solicitor General's office faces and presents a permanent dilemma. It has no political responsibility and limited recourse either to political support or control, but it is called upon to execute political justice. The result, since the reinclusion of the state security paragraphs in the penal code in 1952, has been potential, and in many cases actual, embarrassment for the government and frustration for the Solicitor General's office.

The presumable key to the dilemma lay in Paragraph 152 of the procedural code: "The public prosecution is obliged to introduce proceedings in the case of judicable violations when adequate evidence is available."

This, the so-called "principle of legality," was conceived as a guarantee of equality before the law. In Germany, of all countries, it was easy enough to appreciate its intention. It was also easy to appreciate the aversion to its alternative, the "principle of opportunity." It was not for public prosecutors to make political decisions, most Germans had concluded with the horrific examples of the Weimar Republic, let alone the Third Reich, before their eyes. The result, however, was that they made them nonetheless.

In practice, the "principle of legality" was an automatic mechanism as inexorable and uncontrollable as the broom of the sorcerer's apprentice. Infraction of the law demanded charges. They could originate with a private citizen, the police, or in the Solicitor General's office. Charges required formal internal inquiries, internal inquiries justified warrants, warrants justified investigatory arrest and, in the case of the *Spiegel* action, a month-long search of editorial files. It was a source of minimal comfort that the final decision lay with a court. The Dreyfus

[9] Cf. p. 97.

affair had at least begun with a conviction. The *Spiegel* affair began with the decision—or, as the Solicitor General's office might argue, with the obligation—to prosecute. A government and much of postwar Germany's laboriously acquired moral capital virtually disappeared in the wreckage that followed. "Every time I look in the mirror in the morning, I think, 'There's the man who brought down a government,'" Buback mused to a visitor in early 1966.

The Solicitor General's office had no doubt that its decision would have consequences, although it was scarcely aware of what they might be. It could at least be argued that the institutional capacity of the Solicitor General's office to make such a decision demonstrated, however involuntarily, the extent to which the Federal Republic had realized equality of its citizens before the law. The argument would have had more force, to be sure, had there been precedents for similar prosecutions in more or less equivalent situations. The arguments later used to justify the *Spiegel* action—inaccessible leaks in the West German executive, concern in Washington, Germany's reputation in the Western alliance—would have been at least as appropriate applied to Julius Epstein's revelations on the current state of Western Berlin policy in the *Rheinische Merkur*. The federal attorneys might reply that there had been no charge from outside—like, for instance, von der Heydte's—to draw their attention to the Epstein article. But it was a tip from within their office, not from von der Heydte outside, that had drawn their attention to Ahlers' piece in the *Spiegel*. In any case, it could be questioned whether an institution with the peculiar combination of strength and weaknesses that characterizes the Solicitor General's office was the right place for such decisions to be made at all.

Even if, as the Federal Constitutional Court later argued, the crucial decision lay not with the federal prosecutors but with the investigating judge of the Federal High Court who approved their application for search and arrest warrants, the basic problem remained. It had only been removed another step. If the necessary combination of political judgment and concrete expertise involved in such a decision could not be presupposed about the federal attorneys, with their access to appropriate consultants elsewhere, it could be expected still less of a single judge without it. Absolute in theory, judicial independence is relative in practice. Not even the Solicitor General's office argued seriously that the application for warrants could have been rejected.

But this was only part of the problem. West German intellectuals are fond of denouncing a postwar "restoration" of traditional conservative forms and values. The affair proved beyond any serious doubt how fragile and limited the "restoration" had been. Prussia-Germany, like France and Britain, had enjoyed a civil service tradition. Perhaps only in Prussia-Germany had the civil service not only claimed but virtually monopolized talent. The disaster of the Prussian-German state was also a disaster of the civil service tradition. Talent in the Federal Republic gravitated not to but away from the state.

One needed only to compare the elegant teak-furnished, thick-carpeted offices of the *Spiegel* with the shabby austerity of the Karlsruhe agencies to appreciate the distance between state and society. The *Spiegel* hearings before the Federal Constitutional Court in January 1966 were an unintentional demonstration in applied sociology. The courtroom itself, with its wooden benches and plaintively modernistic brass light fixtures, might have been the lecture hall of a provincial normal school. It was the home of Germany's highest court. The plaintiff was represented by three professors of law and a baron, high-priced talent in high-priced suits, all effectively mobilized against the state. Germany had never seen anything like it. In a country that for at least two centuries had known too much state rather than too little, where absolutism, to the misfortune of German posterity, had worked only too well, this had its advantages. The unattractiveness of public service, the mediocrity of the bureaucracy, are, paradoxically, among the glories of postwar Germany.

But the inherent problems were conspicuous in October 1962. For judges and federal prosecutors alike, Karlsruhe was less the summit of a career, even a public career, than a fortuitous assignment, a job like other jobs. The unoccupied office of the Solicitor General, the chief federal prosecuting officer, was itself a symptom. Far more than any society constitutionally committed to the rule of law can afford, it was a job no one wanted. Meanwhile the lower ranks were peopled by honorable mediocrities between forty and sixty-five, who took their lunch tickets to the canteen, had not been at the top of their class, who learned their constitutional law from men who had despised the Weimar constitution and, during the Third Reich, learned to live without one. Dedicated to the service of a state that had suffered its crucial defeat as long ago as 1914, admittedly unaware that Ahlers' article in 1962 was largely intended as part of a debate of which they were just as unaware, they were—like most Germans, to be sure—uncertain of the state they served and uncertain of themselves. When Hopf, widely regarded as the personification of the traditional Prussian virtues, appeared on October 20, they listened with much respect and few reservations.[10]

Problems of law combined at this point with problems of procedure, problems of institutional authority and, finally, problems of human insight. The result was a critical mass. Under the circumstances the explosion was not inevitable, but it was also not surprising.

[10] Cf. pp. 71–72.

VIII.

THE END OF THE AFFAIR

The affair made its first appearance in court while the Bundestag was still debating it. On November 7 *Spiegel* attorneys appeared in Karlsruhe to request an injunction from the Federal Constitutional Court. The *Spiegel* claimed that it had been subject to censorship the night the action began, protested the methods of the police, and demanded the return of confiscated material and the use of its offices. The court needed two days to reach a decision. Files and offices were being released for use anyway, it declared. While confiscation of the proofs[1] could conceivably be interpreted as censorship, there seemed to be no danger of repetition. In any case, the court argued, the *Spiegel* demands were imprecise to a point that precluded a discriminate response by the court. What files, after all? What offices? How, on the basis of the suit, were files and offices *in toto* to be distinguished from relevant evidence? More important, the court declared, the dimensions of the issue involved questions of principle that could scarcely be answered *ad hoc*. It was reluctant to prejudice its own future decision with an injunction that in any case struck it as superfluous.

A new effort before the Federal High Court (*Bundesgerichts-*

[1] Cf. p. 80.

hof), the adjudicating instance in political suits, met a similar fate a few weeks later. The decision identified the police action with the *Spiegel's* treatment of "Fallex 62." It declared itself satisfied with the relevance of the evidence seized, and pointed, in effect, to "a clear and present danger." There was legitimate suspicion that official secrets had been violated, the court contended. The general political situation—presumably meaning the Cuban crisis—made suspicion all the more justified. It denied that freedom of the press was in jeopardy, confirming, on the contrary, the executive's right to search, confiscate files, and occupy *Spiegel* offices on the basis of existing statutes. In early December the *Spiegel* again requested an injunction and was again turned away.

"We never had a chance," recalled a *Spiegel* attorney of his client's efforts before the Constitutional Court. "But we wanted to show them we were there." The subsequent appearance before the Federal High Court could at least be justified as a matter of legal form. The Federal Republic's judicial pyramid rises to a double peak, the High Court and the Constitutional Court, whose jurisdiction is confined to constitutional cases. Rejection by the former, which implied exhaustion of the only instance authorized to adjudicate the official secrets statutes, was the necessary condition for the *Spiegel's* return, with a constitutional case, to the latter.

It was May 1965 before the High Court issued its next major decision on the affair. It was August 1966 before it had again passed the Constitutional Court.

In the meanwhile, the High Court began its preliminary investigation of testimony and confiscated evidence in December 1962. It also lost its presiding judge, Heinrich Jagusch. The episode was peculiar even by the bizarre standards of the whole affair. On December 7, the day the High Court rejected the *Spiegel's* second request for an injunction, it was announced that Jagusch was to transfer from its third senate, responsible for political offenses, to its fourth, responsible for traffic offenses, at the end of the year. The transfer announcement seemingly coincided with an inquiry from the *Spiegel's* Munich bureau about Jagusch's political past. The inquiry, in turn, appeared to have been inspired by East German charges.

Rather remarkably, Jagusch was considered a "left liberal" by those who knew him well. Of illegitimate birth, he had been active in trade-unionism and the SPD as a young man. But in 1933 he had joined the NSDAP and studied law on official scholarships. He had written his dissertation on the Third Reich's mass labor organization, the German Labor Front, then served in the army during the war, losing an eye. A postwar denazification court in the British zone classified him as "exonerated." But, considering his subsequent position, he had sufficient Nazi past to inspire curiosity about why the East Germans had discovered it only in late 1962.

As it happened, Jagusch was the guiding spirit of political prosecution in the Federal Republic. It was generally believed that the "mosaic" and "confirmation" theories were his work. He had presided over the convictions of the former deputy Frenzel and of Otto John, former chief of the Office for the Protection of the Constitution, who had mysteriously appeared in East Berlin in 1954 and as mysteriously reappeared in the Federal Republic two years later. There was reason to doubt his sympathy for the *Spiegel.*

In the spring of 1964 the *Spiegel* published two articles strongly critical of West German security legislation. The second of them recalled the Ossietzky case. With pointed reference to the still-pending *Spiegel* prosecution, the author expressed the fervent wish that the High Court's judges would not repeat the disastrous errors of their Weimar predecessors. Both articles were signed "Judex." But "Judex," as Ernst Müller-Meiningen reported in the *Süddeutsche Zeitung,* was in fact Jagusch. Jagusch at first denied it, then confessed. The next day he requested his retirement. In November, Minister of Justice Bucher reported that disciplinary proceedings had been introduced against him for failing to report his Nazi past in his personnel papers.

In January 1963 the district attorney's office in Bonn had

introduced proceedings intended to illuminate the arrest of Ahlers. The Bundestag deferred a decision on Strauss's immunity pending the results. In April, a bit anticlimactically, the government found a Solicitor General, Ludwig Martin, to fill the vacancy Güde had left nine unexpectedly turbulent months before. In May, over the protests of the Solicitor General's office, an investigating judge of the High Court introduced a new precedent, requiring that transcripts of all testimony, irrespective of security classification, be made available to the defense attorneys; the Solicitor General's office had hitherto agreed to show but not release them.

All the while the respective investigations continued. In November 1963 Franz Drügh, the Bonn district attorney, announced his intention of asking the Bundestag to withdraw Strauss's immunity to permit investigation of the charge that he had assumed unjustified official prerogatives the night he intervened with the Spanish authorities. It was reported that Hopf too was being investigated. In an interview in late November, over a year after the affair had begun, Bucher indicated discreet surprise that the High Court's preliminary investigation was still going on. But it was going well, he added. In mid-December the Bundestag withdrew Strauss's immunity. It also withdrew the immunity of Jahn[2] and of Merten, the chairman of its defense committee.

Gerber's *Gutachten* was a source of further delay. In June 1964, Solicitor General Martin indicated that there was a possibility that the main defendants, Augstein, Ahlers, and Colonel Martin, might yet be tried before the end of the year. In October, just short of the affair's second anniversary, Federal Attorney Loesdau announced that it would soon be decided whether there would be a formal indictment. The indictment of Augstein, Ahlers, and Colonel Martin was finally submitted on October 16, 1964.

The Strauss investigation in Bonn went less smoothly. Strauss's reluctance to testify did not make matters easier. He failed to

[2] Cf. p. 148.

understand the specific charges raised against him, he said. A voluminous memorandum, prepared in his name by CSU staff lawyers, implicitly suggested that the district attorney in Bonn should learn his business. Rather than presume on the time of innocent people, he might do better to investigate the source of the charges, it recommended. It noted that German penal law also made provision for false charges. All the familiar stops were pulled out again: official assistance, the extradition inquiry via the Foreign Ministry on Saturday morning, the immanence of treason, Hopf's contact with the federal attorneys. "Nothing could be more unpleasant for me than that I be forced to take legal steps to achieve my rehabilitation," Strauss threatened on page 60. "Only one thing is illegal—the introduction and conduct of proceedings against Secretary Hopf, Colonel Oster, and *de facto* against me," he announced on page 67. "Your subtle argumentation is difficult for a layman to understand," he observed by way of conclusion. The sixty-nine-page memo of March 1964 was followed by a forty-seven-page one in mid-September.

In mid-October 1964 Arthur Straeter, North Rhine-Westphalia's CDU Minister of Justice and the Bonn district attorney's superior, publicly criticized what was reported to be Strauss's fourth failure to appear to testify. He would get one more chance, Straeter announced testily. Otherwise the investigation would be closed without him. On October 22 Strauss finally appeared. "Strauss," Bucher reported on TV a week later, "has invented a brand-new legal concept, 'objectively illegal proceedings.' I must admit I never heard of such a thing as a law student. Maybe it means something like the department of municipal sanitation pronouncing a death sentence . . . And then he says he presented two memos of something like one hundred and twenty pages, but he failed to understand the charges raised against him. I ask myself what exactly he said in those one hundred and twenty pages."

In January 1965 the Solicitor General's office announced that it was dropping charges against Becker and Engel; in February the charges against Conrad and Josef Augstein were dropped, and in March those against Jacobi and Wicht. On May 14 the Federal High Court dismissed the indictment against Rudolf Augstein and Ahlers. Güde had predicted in March 1964 that Ahlers and Augstein would be brought to formal trial. In November he had gone a step further, recommending that the trial be deferred rather than held, as would otherwise happen, on the eve of the 1965 federal election. The proposal made a very bad impression on the Federal High Court. Interior Minister Höcherl, however, had also done a bit of predicting as host to the foreign press corps on a Rhine excursion in the summer of 1964. "There is not going to be an Augstein-Ahlers affair," he told them. "The only affair is the affair of Colonel Martin."

In its decision to drop charges against Ahlers and Augstein, the court argued that it was indeed possible that the incriminated Fallex article contained a couple of official secrets—although it indicated reservations about Gerber's *Gutachten*. It refused to accept, however, that either Ahlers or Augstein had acted deliberately. "It is to be noted," the court added, "that in cases of so-called journalistic treason, the proof of motivation demands a more thorough investigation than in the case of spies and agents."

Ahlers, the court reported, had declared from the beginning that his article had corresponded to the current level of public information. In principle the court agreed. This had certainly been the case with the majority of ostensible secrets designated by the Defense Ministry in the original *Gutachten*. It also included ostensible secrets subsequently mentioned by Gerber. Other points had been demonstrably weakened in the composition of the article. Ahlers had no occasion to anticipate that his article *in toto* constituted an official secret. Awareness of precisely what points of his Fallex critique might be of use to an opponent, the court declared, presupposed a familiarity with military intelligence that could scarcely be expected even of a specialist like Ahlers.

Where Augstein was concerned, the court saw no alternative to accepting his claim that he had no reason to believe the Fallex article contained official secrets. Military affairs were not his business, Augstein had testified. The court was unable to prove the contrary. Under the circumstances, Augstein and Jacobi had left the matter of security to Ahlers. Considering Ahlers' reputation among his colleagues for excessive caution, and the fact that Augstein had no conceivable motive for jeopardizing himself, Martin, and the *Spiegel*, it could be assumed that his confidence in Ahlers was legitimate.

With respect to the article itself, the court was skeptical that the "mosaic" theory had any application. Journalistic effect was the object of the article, not military intelligence. The sources were conspicuous enough to sophisticated readers. It could be assumed that any intelligence service would be able to compose the Fallex article itself without help from the *Spiegel*. The polemic content of the article further reduced its value as a source of secret information, the court contended. Ahlers' use of technical expressions proved nothing to anyone familiar with his past. His oblique reference to "NATO strategists," to "staff officers in Paris," etc., was a matter of journalistic convention. Even at points where a high military source could be recognized, there was no reason to conclude that this source had checked Ahlers' text for accuracy, the court argued.

It was further held to the defendants' advantage that the manuscript had been passed openly around the editorial offices and the library. The article had twice been announced with accurate indications of what it would contain. Such information as the defendants had acquired and not included in the article had also been passed around the office, and beyond this to a Bundestag deputy. But there was neither indication nor likelihood that it had gone any further. There was no indication that Ahlers' secretary or the Xerox operators were aware of the contents of the original "*exposé*."

In conclusion, the court observed that neither Ahlers nor Augstein claimed that the material they published was in contradiction to current NATO policy, let alone unconstitutional. Nor did they claim that their intention of provoking a reassessment of NATO strategy would have justified the publication of official secrets. Court and investigation costs were to be borne by the state. But there was no question of compensation for Augstein and Ahlers. They were acquitted "for lack of evidence" and not because of "proven innocence." It was the first time the Federal High Court had ever dismissed an indictment without trial. The CSU's *Bayern-Kurier* claimed victory nonetheless. If the court was prepared to dismiss charges with the indicated reservations, it declared, there was clearly no justification for sustaining charges against Strauss.

Three weeks later, in the second major legal decision of the affair, the charges were, in fact, dismissed. But only the least critical of Strauss's admirers could take much comfort from the decision. The *Spiegel* might have published official secrets, the High Court had decided. Strauss had fulfilled the objective conditions of the charges pending against him, Drügh reported without qualification. Only Colonel Oster emerged from the decision with a clean bill of health.

Strauss, District Attorney Drügh concluded, had unambiguously arrogated to himself the functions not only of the prosecuting authorities but of the Foreign Ministry. Only the police would have been justified in approaching Pozo Gonzáles, only the Foreign Ministry—or theoretically the federal government—in approaching Spanish counterparts about Ahlers' deportation. "The responsibilities of the Defense Minister and the Solicitor General's office are so different that there can be no question of official aid." Hopf's arrangement with the Solicitor General's office had confined itself to *Spiegel* sources within the Defense Ministry.

Strauss's responsibility for Ahlers' detention, the decision continued, was also illegal. The warrant for Ahlers' arrest was for the police, and only the police, to execute. Its execution in Spain was out of the question in any case. Ahlers had been held on the basis of Spanish, not German, law, and then only because the Spanish authorities had been misinformed. "Anyone who orders the detention of a suspect by deceiving a foreign official about the facts relevant to his decision is behaving illegally even where an arrest warrant, issued by a German judge, exists,"

Drügh remarked. "This illegality is in no way qualified even if the foreign official, on the basis of the erroneous information given him, is authorized to act." Nor was Drügh prepared to accept Strauss's claim of emergency. Detention, in the name of emergency, was hardly justified on security grounds, he stated. Security had no priority over civil rights in a case where, as Strauss claimed, the only object was getting Ahlers to testify about alleged sources in the Defense Ministry. "In any case," he added, "it can be questioned whether Ahlers' detention, considering his right to protect himself against self-incrimination, was the appropriate way to deal with leaks in the Defense Ministry."

Strauss had claimed, Drügh reported, that he had intervened only to propose to the Spanish police that they investigate the possibility of holding Ahlers, on the basis of Spanish law, as a means of persuading him to return home voluntarily, or at least as a preliminary to deportation. Testimony by Oster, by Feit of the German Embassy in Madrid, and by Pozo González had contradicted this.

Strauss had also claimed that Hopf told him he had already asked the police in Bad Godesberg to notify Spanish police of Ahlers' arrest warrant, and had subsequently confirmed that this had been done. Hopf, Strauss testified, had not mentioned official doubts about the legality of this. If this were true, Drügh said, it could be questioned whether Strauss had deliberately misled the Spanish police or encroached on the official preserves of other agencies. But it was hard to believe, considering Strauss's Bundestag performance of November 7–9, 1962, he contended. He also found it curious that Oster had been ordered on November 7 not to answer questions put to him by the embassy's chargé d'affaires. It was still more curious that Councillor Schnell, the Defense Ministry's corruption investigator, who happened to be in Madrid between November 6 and 9, had been in touch with Oster and had advised him on what he should tell the chargé in case of interrogation.

Strauss's contention could nonetheless not be disproved. There had been no witnesses to his phone conversation with Hopf. Hopf, in turn, refused to testify. There was also the theoretical possibility that Strauss had misled the Bundestag for fear of reinforcing the (in fact unjustified) suspicion that he had himself initiated the *Spiegel* action for reasons of revenge, thus weakening his own political position. Another theoretical possibility was that Hopf really had misled him, and that he wanted to protect Hopf. Under the circumstances, Hopf's refusal to testify could mean that Hopf had wanted to cover Strauss. But it could also mean that he had been concerned about covering himself.

There were reasons to justify suspicion of Hopf alone, the report continued. Beyond Strauss's testimony and his own refusal to testify, there was his conspicuous initiative in dealing with the federal attorneys from the beginning of the investigation, and his activity the night of October 26-27. It was also Hopf who had been in contact with the police in Bad Godesberg and with the Ministry of Justice, and Hopf alone who had been specifically warned of the obstacles in the way of pursuing Ahlers abroad. It was significant that he had neglected to call either Kuhn or the Foreign Ministry after being warned. But while this constituted evidence for the possibility that he had failed to notify Strauss, possibly to spare him future embarrassment, Strauss's own peculiar behavior made it impossible to prove that he had really been misled. Strauss's testimony alone was no adequate proof to the contrary.

On the other hand, it was impossible to prove complicity if only because there was no conclusive evidence that, subjectively, both had *not* been the victims of errors of judgment—reinforced, as they claimed, by the needs of the moment. Both Hopf and Strauss maintained that had they not acted they might well have been prosecuted for dereliction of duty. Drügh confessed to skepticism about this. "Nonetheless," he concluded, "it cannot be disproved that the defendants believed, on the basis of erroneous assumptions, that the detention of Ahlers was justified by the state of emergency. They thus acted in legitimate error. Considering further that the defendants were exposed to particular strain due to the Cuban crisis, which threatened to lead to war and made the apparent source of official leaks within the Defense Ministry seem especially dangerous, with inadequate time for further reflection on their action, the question of whether their error was avoidable would possibly have to be answered negatively." Ahlers had the legal option of requesting reconsideration of his case. But he chose not to take it. Life went on, he said. He disliked the idea of appearing vengeful.

Applause for the decision was sparing. "Did the district attorney, who must surely have worked on his decision in close contact with the Ministry of Justice in Düsseldorf, dismiss charges with an altogether clear conscience?" asked Robert Strobel in *Die Zeit*.

"Would he have done the same had it involved not the chairman of one of the government parties, but just a simple citizen? One can imagine what influences might have been at work in Bonn and, still more, in Düsseldorf."

There was even indignation from the *Bayern-Kurier*, though not for the same reason. It claimed that the Bonn district attorney's assertion that Strauss had objectively infringed on other people's offices and personal freedom was not only wrong-headed, but unconstitutional. The Bundestag had not withdrawn Strauss's immunity to enable the district attorney's office to investigate the possibility of Strauss's role in an illegal arrest, it declared.

In any case, thanks largely to Hopf, Strauss was clear in time for the election. In mid-July what remained of the charges against Jahn were also dismissed.

It was again over a year before the Federal Constitutional Court produced the affair's third major decision. It rejected the *Spiegel*'s charge of unconstitutionality. The eight judges divided evenly on the issue put to them. The decision included the first published dissenting opinion in German legal history.

The court concurred on the significance of a free press as a fundamental aspect of the free opinion guaranteed by Article 5 of the constitution. Within limits, it also concurred that journalistic sources were entitled to some protection. But there was no question about the constitutionality of the official secrets paragraphs of the penal code. And, the court maintained, there was no fundamental incompatibility between them and freedom of the press. Both had a common purpose, the preservation of the Federal Republic as a democratic state, governed by the rule of law. There was no validity to the argument that security interests had priority because the existence of the state was the necessary condition of a free press, a key sentence declared. Security of the Federal Republic referred not only to a certain administrative apparatus but to a political order based on the criticism and approval of its citizens. Public information and public safety were complementary, the court declared. Where practical conflicts arose, neither had priority. Both must be weighed against each other.

At this point, the opinions went separate ways. Four judges argued that there had been a breach of constitutionality. They began with the distinction between journalism and espionage. It was not only the right of the press to discuss defense but its legitimate task, the dissenting judges declared. While not all military information was suitable for publication, the limits of the official secrets paragraphs could be applied to the press only with care. The "mosaic" theory was altogether inapplicable to the press, they contended. Synthesis and interpretation of facts were what the press was for. Nor, they argued, could the concrete question of military security be left to the military alone. "The legitimate interest in public discussion of military problems ordinarily does not presuppose familiarity with details," they observed. "On the other hand, such a discussion can hardly be conducted without a minimum understanding of the facts involved in the problem."

Where the Fallex article was concerned, the judges found it was necessary to establish whether the information contained in it was already under public discussion, whether its objective jeopardized the security of the Federal Republic, and to what extent the facts reported were consistent with the objective of the article. None of these had been considered in the preparation of the search warrant, they argued. Their critique began with Wunder's *Gutachten*. It extended to the judge who had issued his warrant on the basis of it, and to the Federal High Court which had accepted the *Gutachten* in rejecting the *Spiegel's* request for an injunction. In none of these cases had there been any serious consideration of Article 5.

The supporting judges argued, on the contrary, that the search would have been constitutionally questionable only if it had been based on the "mosaic" theory, and, beyond this, if the applicability of the theory in press offenses had already been explicitly declared unconstitutional.

Like Wunder himself, the issuing judge had, however, assumed that, precisely because of the limited evidence of prior publication, he was dealing not with "mosaic stones" but with "original," i.e., unpublished, secrets. Under the circumstances, they maintained, the question of the constitutionality of the "mosaic" theory was irrelevant. There was no question at this point that the official secrets paragraphs of the penal code were themselves unconstitutional.

The court again concurred, with a scarcely mistakable wink at the Bundestag, that existing laws made conflicts between prosecuting authorities and journalistic enterprises all but inevitable. It was, they agreed, the judge's function to consider the conflicts bequeathed him by the legislature before issuing his warrant. But they also denied that the search warrant was purely arbitrary, as the *Spiegel* had originally claimed it was. The Defense Ministry had unquestionably been interested in the case. But the initiative and subsequent conduct of the action had remained where it belonged, in the hands of the Solicitor General's office.

Where the formal acceptability of the search warrant was concerned, the opinion again divided. Search was justified, the dissenting judges argued, where suspicion centered on the editors of the *Spiegel*, not where it was directed at third persons—the Defense Ministry suspects referred to not only by the federal attorneys but by Strauss himself. They balked at the comprehensiveness of the warrant: all offices in Bonn and Hamburg, seven floors, 117 rooms including 77 editorial offices and 18 rooms of library, with no concrete indications at all of what was being sought in them. The dimensions of the search as such jeopardized the further existence of the *Spiegel*, they contended. "Nor can it be argued that the *Spiegel* nonetheless managed to appear without interruption during the entire month of the search," they observed. "This happened only because other papers came to its help." The search threatened all *Spiegel* sources without discrimination. It involved not only the *Spiegel* but, by extension, all German papers, which would have occasion to think twice before looking into defense matters in the future.

The search was nonetheless theoretically permissible, they agreed. Whether it was justifiable in practice remained to be established. Journalists were not spies, they again observed. The Cuban crisis, which followed, not preceded, the start of the investigation, was no excuse. There was also little justification for the assumption of Augstein's complicity. Augstein's feud with Strauss proved nothing in particular, they argued. It was also doubtful whether any journalist as intelligent, experienced and concerned with his reputation as Augstein was prepared to take the risk of deliberate publication of official secrets.

The assumption of Ahlers' guilt was at least as questionable. Precisely because Ahlers had experience enough to sense a secret when he saw one, there was little reason to think he would so baldly publish one. It could also be assumed that he had experience enough to distinguish between formal rubber-stamp security classification, and official secrets in the sense of the penal code. It could not be maintained that examination of just these premises was the point of the action. And even if it were, the dissenters argued, an omnibus search was not the way to go about it. They found no justification at all for the bribery charge.

Where the treason charges were concerned, no search was necessary, they contended. If the charges had any objective validity, this could be established only by a court on the basis of the offending publication. The search was justified only as a means of finding evidence about the suspects' motives. But this too was dubious, they argued. If the suspects were really in possession of official secrets, common sense suggested that their offices were the last place they would keep them. Interrogation and investigation within the Defense Ministry were at least as good a method of establishing the suspects' motives. "It can be expected that the state first cleans its own house," the dissenters observed. The search had begun before this was even tried.

Under the circumstances, they could only reproach the High Court again for its abstract treatment of the constitutional issues in November and December 1962. "The gravity of a treason charge and the potential danger to public security as the result of an official secrets leak cannot suffice to permit fundamental neglect of the guarantees necessary to a free press and to justify every kind of police measure," they declared. While freedom of the press could not be allowed to be a cover-all for security offenses, such offenses must at least be proven. In the *Spiegel* case, there had been no such proof. On the contrary, the purpose of the investigation was to establish it. If the charge of treason sufficed to suspend the normal assumption that suspects are innocent until proven guilty, there was no place left for a free public discussion of defense at all.

"The significance of a free press requires that investigating procedures be subject to rigorous controls, and at the same time demands a thorough examination of the practical conduct of such proceedings by the Federal Constitutional Court," they wrote. "To the extent that constitutional rights demand it, even important considerations of practicality must be sacrificed and the resulting technical inconvenience accepted."

The supporting judges accepted without qualification the constitutionality of the search warrant. The Solicitor General's office had more than met its formal obligations in requesting *Gutachten* at all, they argued. It was hard to imagine a more qualified source for the *Gutachten* than the Defense Ministry. Wunder had been independent in his judgment, was not specially selected for this particular case, had consulted others of his own choice more familiar with the subject than himself, and had referred to the library. His *Gutachten* did all that could be expected of it. It was not intended as the basis of a verdict or even an indictment, but only as a guide to the action of the Solicitor General's office.

The Solicitor General's office had not followed Wunder's judgment blindly, they continued, nor had the judge who issued the warrants. The only issue was whether an investigation was justified, not whether Wunder was right in every particular. Under the circumstances, they declared, it was impossible to demand the same degree of certainty of the investigators that would be demanded of a court pronouncing a verdict. The press, they maintained, was entitled to no special privileges.

An investigation led almost inevitably to a search, they continued. The evidence produced by a search was relevant in determining the official secrecy of the published material, the collaboration of the *Spiegel* with sources in the Defense Ministry, and the motives behind the Fallex article. In ordering the search, the federal attorneys had considered the operation of the *Spiegel*. They also considered that the case involved serious suspicion of an offense against the public security, something "in any case not inferior to the freedom of the press." Where the press encroaches on military security, the supporting judges argued, "the equilibrium shifts: the public need for information recedes if only because the reader, for lack of adequate technical training, is incapable of forming an independent opinion anyway, in part because this kind of familiarity is unnecessary in forming a political opinion."

Treason demanded quick and thorough action as a matter of principle, they observed. They also accepted the Cuban crisis as a relevant factor. The documentary evidence likely to be found in the search was far superior to testimony by the suspects, they argued. The investigation, moreover, was directed at Ahlers and Augstein not as receivers of information from elsewhere, but as themselves the violators of official secrecy. The Defense

Ministry's interest in its own security leaks must not be confused with the federal attorneys' interest in the *Spiegel*, the supporting judges wrote. Their suspicion was legitimate. The question of security involved was no less a matter of the constitutional order than the guarantee of a free press. To assume that the press represented a special case in security matters was not to interpret but to transcend the law. It was not the Constitutional Court's function to legislate.

The right to a free press, they continued, could not be exploited to prevent prosecution of security offenses that jeopardized the existence of the state itself. "So permissive a view of journalistic freedom necessarily has negative consequences for the credibility of the Federal Republic within an integrated alliance like NATO," they claimed, "whose members, for all that their legal systems derive from similar historical premises, permit a far more intensive protection of military secrecy than does the Federal Republic."

This brought the court to the *Spiegel*'s charge that the formal imprecision of the search warrant had violated constitutional premises. The dissenting judges again took exception to the warrant's extraordinary comprehensiveness. Neither time nor place of the alleged offense was indicated, they observed. The bribery charge was confined to a repetition of the legal text that supported it. In principle, the search warrant justified the confiscation of anything.

The supporting judges replied that the grounds for the charge of official secrets violation were satisfactorily indicated in the arrest warrant issued at the same time as the search warrant. Greater precision in the terms of the search warrant was anyway impossible. The federal attorneys—as the investigation had proved —were in no position in October 1962 to anticipate what would be found where. The supporting judges agreed with their dissenting colleagues that the bribery charge was inadequate. But the treason charge, they observed, justified the search in any case. There was no reason to believe that the bribery charge had had any significant effect on the dimensions of the search.

They agreed that the search warrant was in fact vulnerable to formal criticism. But they argued that this in no way compromised its constitutionality.

The mixed decision again found a mixed response. The government press, not surprisingly, felt vindicated. This included *Bild*. "*Spiegel* Turned Back," it announced—although on its back page. *Spiegel* supporters were divided. Ehmke, the *Spiegel's* counsel in Karlsruhe, was not at all displeased. "As an attorney, I would naturally have preferred a 5–3 'victory,'" he wrote an acquaintance. "But legally and politically this decision is much nicer. With 5–3 we would have had a typical compromise decision." Jens Feddersen, editor-in-chief of the SPD's *Neue Rhein Zeitung*, applauded the decision. Formally, the state had won, he wrote. But the *Spiegel* was the moral winner.

Die Zeit saw hope: "After four of eight judges have so clearly criticized the federal attorneys, the investigating agencies will surely be considerably more skeptical in the future about yielding to whispers from the executive and *Gutachten* from the 'official authorities.'" Bishop Lilje's *Sonntagsblatt*, once Ahlers' employer, saw confusion—but confusion over existing legislation. "The boundary between the citizen's right to information and the state's to security is as unclear as ever," it observed. "The risk of overstepping it remains with the journalist."

The *Süddeutsche Zeitung's* Ernst Müller-Meiningen saw black. "Certainly, not everything that conflicts with a law is necessarily unconstitutional. But the accumulation of measures of the crudest nature, all of them directed against a magazine, its publisher, its editors, its editorial and business offices, its entire library, is and remains . . . brutal violation of a journalistic enterprise. If this, apart from all the individual offenses, is not a flagrant attack on the constitutional guarantee of a free press, our name is Hopf, or Strauss, or Adenauer."

In the *Kölner Stadt Anzeiger*, Hans Gerlach saw an even blacker outlook. "For the future, this decision will have incalculable consequences," he wrote. "Even more than before, the discussion of those questions that determine war and peace will be complicated in Germany. . . . Compared with this, it scarcely matters that the *Spiegel* lost and Strauss finally won. More disturbing, if anything, is the fact that four judges of our country's most important court, after all the failures, all the errors and crimes that German authorities have committed in this century (all of which they themselves have experienced), can still believe so unshakably in the justice and wisdom of those who govern us."

On October 27, 1966, in the last major decision of the affair, the Federal High Court decided to drop proceedings against Colonel Martin. "Extensive investigation leads to the conclusion that further proceedings would, beyond the jeopardy caused by the defendant's action, compromise the security of the Federal Republic," the court declared in an official statement.

In December 1966 it finally dismissed charges against Schmelz, the last of the *Spiegel* defendants. Only in the case of the Tunisian consul, Conrad, did the court rule "proven innocence," and thus establish a claim to compensation for arrest and detention.

While the political affair had largely burned out by December 1962, smoke and occasional sparks appeared from the ashes for years afterward.

The Jahn-Merten investigation smoldered on outside after flickering out in the committee rooms. The old FDP-SPD solidarity was still intact in October 1963 when FDP members of the Immunity Committee refused to cooperate in lifting Jahn's immunity before the investigating public prosecutor made available to them a transcript of Schmelz's testimony. The CDU members announced that they were scandalized.

Shortly afterward, it was reported that the mysterious second document had gone astray via the SPD's Willy Berkhan. Merten produced a hitherto misplaced receipt. But the receipt was dated October 1962 and was evidently older than the photocopy found in Schmelz's possession. The receipt was then misplaced again. Berkhan and Merten left the defense committee, protesting their innocence in the whole affair. Its representatives having meanwhile come to terms with the public prosecutor, the Bundestag now proceeded to lift Jahn's immunity at the same time it lifted Strauss's. The CSU protested the injustice of it all. The SPD, clean as a hound's tooth at least in its aspirations, warmed itself in its feelings of moral austerity. Only Mrs. Jahn confessed in an interview to some bitterness.

Nearly a year later the matter flared up once again with Bucher's decision to authorize further prosecution, although it was clear that whatever Jahn had done, it had scarcely jeopardized the existence of the Federal Republic. Under pressure from both sides—from the CSU for his hesitation in acting, from liberal opinion for acting at all—Bucher defended his position before his FDP colleagues. His hand had, in fact, been forced by one of the special cases in German law. Felonies, e.g., publication of official secrets, are governed by the "principle of legality." Misdemeanors, however, like publication of nonvital, classified material, are governed by the "principle of opportunity." The option lies with the Minister of Justice. Bucher could have dismissed charges against Jahn. He chose not to. He had concluded that the case—still nominally an official secrets charge—had no leg to stand on, he said. But the Solicitor General's office and the Ministry of the Interior were of a different opinion. To take a stand against them would look like protection of Jahn. It was also likely to lead to a nasty election campaign in 1965 with Strauss's *Bayern-Kurier* declaiming that Jahn was a traitor, Bucher a friend of traitors, etc. There was also no justification for risking yet another cabinet crisis practically on the eve of the next election. Jahn could at least take comfort in the opportunity afforded him for full rehabilitation. This rehabilitation duly followed.[3]

By this time, the FDP had sustained two conspicuous losses. In January 1963 Döring was stricken with a heart attack while driving from Bonn to Düsseldorf. He died shortly after his ar-

[3] Cf. p. 209.

rival at the hospital. His party commemorated him with the foundation of an annual prize for demonstrations of courage in public life. (The FDP's Theodor Heuss, the Federal Republic's first President, was the first recipient of the Döring prize; Hildegard Hamm-Brücher, known, as Rosa Luxemburg once was, as "the only man in her party," and, as an expert on school policy, one of the few interesting women in German public life, was subsequently honored. In 1967 the prize was to go to Augstein. The hall was rented, the orchestra engaged, Frau Hamm-Brücher scheduled as speaker, when the committee reconsidered. Augstein—like Hamm-Brücher—had been active at the party's 1967 convention in Hanover in a campaign against Mende's leadership. The Döring prize was not awarded. Augstein learned of the change of plan from the newspapers.) The East German television too commemorated Döring with a play that suggested broadly that the hero, a courageous young deputy, had been murdered by unspecified others, afraid that he knew too much. In June 1964 Stammberger, bitter about the alacrity with which the FDP had sacrificed him in December 1962, joined the SPD.

While Stammberger moved laterally, Hopf moved up. In June 1965 he was confirmed as the Federal Republic's chief auditor. Hitherto an undersecretary, he was now formally subordinate to no one.

The most dramatic piece in the affair's shambling epilogue was the story of Franz Josef Strauss. In early January 1963 Father Lorenz Freiberger, editor of the Munich diocesan paper, addressed an open letter to his old friend Strauss. Strauss was in a personal crisis, Freiberger suggested. It might be worth considering a long vacation. Perhaps Strauss might like to try writing a bit of history. It was something he had occasionally mentioned with a certain rueful nostalgia about his unfinished dissertation. The *Frankfurter Rundschau* reported that Freiberger's letter enjoyed the full sympathy of Munich's archbishop, Julius Cardinal Döpfner.

The counterattack began almost immediately. At the CSU's annual Ash Wednesday rally in the little village of Vilshofen, it was obvious that Höcherl had come to praise Strauss, not to bury him. "There can be no doubt that he will come to the top again where his natural ability is bound to lead him," Höcherl announced to cheers from his audience. He was seconded by Franz Xaver Unertl, a hardy perennial of Bavarian politics, who declared with feeling that the entire affair would never have taken place at all had Strauss been born in "Prussian" Düsseldorf. He recommended that diocesan papers stay out of politics.

Shaken into action, the party machine produced a censure resolution condemning Guttenberg for his role in the coalition negotiations the previous fall. Catholic lay organizations were meanwhile campaigning discreetly for Guttenberg to succeed Strauss as party chairman. But Guttenberg himself was against the idea, and no other candidate appeared in his place. Party headquarters withdrew their subsidy from the student magazine that had earlier urged Strauss's resignation.

In June, in an interview with the Israeli journalist Amos Elon in Jerusalem, Strauss produced yet another version of his role in the affair. The Spiegel was the Gestapo of our times, dpa quoted him as saying. Its library housed thousands of personal files. "When you consider Germany's past," he said, "everybody has something to hide. The result is blackmail. I was compelled to act to do something about it." Approached for further elaboration on his arrival in Madrid a few days later, Strauss announced that he had been misquoted. He had only been quoting a colleague, he said, who believed that the Spiegel ran "a sort of private Gestapo."

In July, in a tumultuous session at the German Museum in Munich, Strauss was overwhelmingly re-elected chairman of his party. Guttenberg, who announced his intention of voting against him, was booed by the delegates. In a speech on his own behalf, Strauss emphasized his humble origins. He was, he observed with an obvious allusion to Guttenberg, not a millionaire either by birth or by pursuit of wealth. To the delight of his audience, he added that the church should mind its own business and stay out of politics. The combination of poor-boy-made-good with anticlericalism was apparently irresistible. The vote was 550 for Strauss, 85 against, with 42 abstentions. Bavaria's Minister-President Alfons Goppel declared that, when a man of Strauss's age said that he had not lied in November 1962, he had to be believed. "We have to believe him that he did not lie," he said. "There are differences between lies. There are subjective lies and objective lies."

Strauss returned to the fray in Bonn. His relentless opposition to Schroeder in general and to West German ratification of the nuclear test ban agreement in particular—nominally because the Western powers were willing to accept East Germany as a cosignatory—was the overture to his new role in German parliamentary life. By the time the Erhard government was installed in the fall of 1963, taking over virtually intact both the policies and the personnel of the Adenauer administration, Strauss was, in effect, leader of the opposition. The opposition continued unabated until Erhard's removal from office in October 1966. If, as the affair had seemed to prove, it was impossible to govern with Strauss, it was also apparently impossible to govern without him—at least as long as the CSU was prepared to elect him chairman.

A series of victories over favorite enemies was a kind of bonus. A Munich court awarded Strauss DM 25,000 damages in July 1965 and charged Augstein ¾ of the court costs. It ruled that Augstein had failed to prove corruption, but also that Strauss, as plaintiff, had failed to prove the opposite. Augstein was required to retract claims that Strauss had become rich in office and that "Uncle Aloys"—whose doctor reported he was unavailable to testify—had brought Strauss a suitcase full of cash.[4] He was not required to retract the charge that Strauss was corrupt, had peddled influence in armaments contracts, and split Fibag profits with Kapfinger. He was, however, required not to repeat them. Augstein appealed the decision. The appellate court upheld the verdict and increased Augstein's share of the costs from ¾ to 9⁄10.

[4] Cf. p. 47.

Strauss's victory over Augstein was supplemented with one over the FDP. The FDP, which conducted its 1965 campaign on a pro-Erhard, anti-Strauss platform, produced eight million copies of an election brochure, advertising itself as the party of law and order. The FDP, the brochure suggested pointedly, was the citizen's best defense against illegal midnight arrest in Spain. Strauss, his qualified acquittal by the Bonn district attorney's office in his pocket, demanded an injunction against circulation of the brochure. The injunction was granted.

Above all, there were no apologies, either from Strauss, or from the government. "I might have done things otherwise," was as far as Strauss was prepared to go. The suspension of charges against Ahlers and Augstein in May 1965 prompted the SPD to query the government's view of the matter. The government refused to give way. The new CDU Minister of Justice, Karl Weber, interpreted the Karlsruhe decision to his party's advantage. The court had indicated that suspicion was justified, Weber declared. It was justified still. The indestructible Höcherl insisted that he had spoken only of suspicion in the famous debate of November 1962. The claim that he had spoken of "traitors" was wrenched out of context, he claimed. He had meant only "the defendants." Under pressure from journalists, Hase indicated that he felt the press should have easier access to the military establishment and that it was time for a reform of the official secrets paragraphs.

A year later there was another flurry when the presidency of the Federal High Court became open. Judge Kurt Weber publicly claimed he had been passed over because the Ministry of Justice, formally responsible for the appointment, took exception to his role in the 1965 decision. It was not impossible, most commentators agreed—but it was also not very probable.

Adenauer himself was privately conciliatory. "Were you really locked up?" he asked Ahlers in an interview after the 1965 election. At their next meeting, Ahlers brought along a copy of the first volume of Adenauer's recently published memoirs for dedication. "To Herr Ahlers," Adenauer wrote in the book. "Consider this the end of your trip to Spain," he said to Ahlers as he handed back the book.

In the meantime, it appeared that Ahlers had come to terms with Strauss. "Strauss has changed," Ahlers wrote in early 1966— not in the *Spiegel* but in the CDU-subsidized *Civis*. It was not so much Strauss's politics that had changed, Ahlers contended, as Strauss's personality. "Temperament and vitality remain," Ahlers said, "but will and determination are more fragile than they appear. There is also a perceptible uncertainty, a willingness to question himself, a quest for confidence where he once sought only collaborators. All this results in a complicated picture but creates the impression, in one way or the other, of an unfinished story whose conclusion is as unpredictable as the route it is likely to take on its way."

The prognosis was confirmed by events. On October 27, 1966, four years almost to the day after the start of the affair, and the day the Federal High Court suspended its case against Colonel Martin, the FDP resolved to leave the Erhard cabinet. The government collapsed.

When the fog had cleared three weeks later, it was seen that CDU/CSU and SPD had finally formed their "grand coalition." Strauss, now Finance Minister, was back in the government. As he had been since the fall of 1965, Höcherl was Minister of Agriculture. In power for the first time since 1930, the SPD named Jahn Parliamentary Undersecretary for Foreign Affairs, and Ehmke, the *Spiegel*'s attorney, as Undersecretary in the Ministry of Justice. Ahlers was invited to return to the Federal Information Office as press spokesman for the new government. After a short hesitation, he accepted. Unlike Augstein, he had been a proponent of the "grand coalition" "for nearly twenty years," he said. He also felt that any journalist who turned down an offer to join a government lost his moral right to criticize.

"Is that really so?" Augstein replied. "Is it disloyal not to take a position in the new government? Have we reached such an economic emergency after seventeen years of CDU government that it is disloyal to conceive of a government without a CDU Chancellor?"

He nevertheless wished Ahlers luck. "The *Spiegel* owes him a lot, just as he, ironically, owes it the *Spiegel* affair," he wrote in a rueful editorial farewell. "We would have preferred that he not become government press secretary but remain a *Spiegel* editor, loyal to the state, and, as far as I'm concerned, a proponent of the 'grand coalition' for another twenty years."

On January 2, 1967, the *Spiegel* published a *"Spiegel-Gespräch"* with the new Finance Minister. Brawand and Augstein himself were the interviewers. The discussion, civil but cool (the accompanying photo seemed in fact to show Augstein in his overcoat), included Germany's relations to the United States and its European neighbors, the future of the German economy, the complexities of the West German budget, the problem of increasing nationalist frustration and the possibilities for an integrated West European defense system.

"Bonn is now in the Kiesinger era," Walter Henkels observed in the *Frankfurter Allgemeine* a few days before the interview appeared, "and we have the assurance that we will continue to live in it into the new year. The likelihood of seeing Ahlers and Franz-Josef Strauss on the same government bench seems a bit fantastic. But Bonn was practically plunged into inner turmoil as it heard that Rudolf Augstein of the *Spiegel* had been to see Strauss during the Christmas week. The reporter no longer dares to utter reservations about Strauss. Strauss asked him to see him sometime. Isn't he the most significant Bonn politician whom the fourth estate has ever misjudged?"

IX.

THE AFFAIR IN RETROSPECT

It had, as Aristotle might have said, its moments of pity and fear. It had its moments of heroism. It even had its heroes: Krämer-Badoni, the writer who swallowed his pride; Bausch, the deputy; Dräxlmaier, the rural mayor; and the student Christian Socialists of Munich, who swallowed their loyalty. The FDP's Döring, the Social Democrats in the question periods, the students who marched and the professors who protested, *Die Zeit*, the *Frankfurter Rundschau*, the *Süddeutsche*, the *Stuttgarter*, and the broadcasters distinguised themselves for public courage in a country where that is anything but a traditional virtue.

They had their effect, but the effect was increasingly hard to assess as the shock receded. As time went on, explaining what good came of it at last became increasingly like explaining the Battle of Blenheim to little Peterkin.

The ending was happy. The defendants were acquitted one by one. Although only one of them was compensated for his inconvenience, the rest had at least the moral satisfaction that not a single one of them was brought to formal trial. The *Spiegel* itself emerged without a visible scratch. Five years after the affair its circulation had nearly doubled. Advertising volume, by and large, kept pace. The *Spiegel* brought suit for damages. It was asked without irony whether it could succeed in proving that it had sustained any. If there was no real catharsis, no public apology, Adenauer's successor Erhard voluntarily assumed the symbolic responsibility of granting the *Spiegel* a formal interview. So, finally, did Strauss, and then Adenauer. A handwritten note from the former Chancellor, acknowledging Augstein's critical but fundamentally sympathetic review of the second volume of Adenauer's memoirs, led to a long conversation in early December 1966. An interview with the *Spiegel* appeared the following March.

There were those who claimed that the *Spiegel* lost its old bite, that the consequences of the affair could be seen in its news columns if not in its annual balance. Marginal staff defections, including Jaene, one of the original defendants, and Hermann Renner,[1] may have been evidence for the claim. But a long and distinguished line of victims, including Erhard, his Defense Minister von Hassel, and his undersecretary, Karl Gumbel, the FDP *in toto*, and the SPD more often than not, could have testified to the contrary. A whole-hearted *Spiegel* exposé of official ineptitude in the care and management of Starfighters in 1966 reflected continued interest in defense. A 1966 story with evidence of massive corruption and collusion in tank procurement in the early 50s, implicating a former high official of the CDU and close associate of Adenauer's, was reassuringly in the *Spiegel* tradition for those who wanted reassurance. Its opposition to Strauss, purged of its obsessiveness, which no one could really regret, went on as before.

The happy outcome for the defendants, both individually and collectively, was matched by the evident health and well-being of their opponents. Whatever else it may have been, the affair was evidently the good wind that blows nobody ill. In January 1966 the Karlsruhe audience tittered as witness after witness diffidently corrected the court as he presented himself, in order to register the change of status that had followed since the affair.

Federal Attorney Buback, seconded to the Solicitor General's staff in 1962, had been accepted as a regular member. He was now, as *Oberstaatsanwalt*, a rank higher. Councillor Wunder was

[1] Cf. p. 185.

now Director Wunder, Police Commissar Schuetz now Councillor Schuetz. Hopf, the Federal Republic's chief auditor,[2] was not only no man's subordinate but *ex officio* a guardian of public rectitude in the highest salary bracket.

Of those not in the courtroom, Hopffgarten, Oster, and Schmueckle had quietly advanced to brigadier general. Schnell, true to his name, was now *Ministerialrat*, two notches above his original position. And then there was Strauss. Ironically, the casualties, such as there were of them, came not only from the more distant ranks of the protagonists but from the bench between them, for example Judge Heinrich Jagusch and, at least by his own testimony, Judge Kurt Weber.[3] As a result of the affair not Höcherl but the ministers Balke, Lemmer, and Starke, who had nothing to do with it at all, lost their seats in the cabinet. They were joined by Stammberger, whose most conspicuous guilt was his innocence.

There were no voluntary resignations. The buck passed on and on, from the executive to the prosecuting officials, from the civil service to the legislature to the courts. The legislature tolerated lies, the government insubordination, its spokesmen the humiliation of being made to assume public responsibility where they were not responsible. Undersecretary Carstens of the Foreign Ministry was not asked to resign,[4] Hase did not resign. Like Hopf, Walter Strauss, Undersecretary in the Ministry of Justice, was promoted. It appeared not only that Strauss was guilty, but that he was uniquely guilty. With his departure, the affair turned, if only by default, into what the government had always claimed it was: a matter for the judiciary. The parties and the voters alike successively waved it out of the political arena and on its way to the courts. It was not the first time that Germans had passed their political problems to the judiciary. Nor was it the

[2] Cf. p. 253.
[3] Cf. pp. 200–201, p. 219.
[4] Cf. p. 87. On being named Minister of Defense at the end of 1966, Schroeder in fact took Carstens to the Defense Ministry with him.

first time that the courts, with the shrug of a Solomon, had passed them back.

In the end, each of the basic decisions trailed ambiguity behind it. Ahlers and Augstein were acquitted but not rehabilitated. The question of official secrecy was raised but not answered. In effect, Hopf and Strauss were convicted without being arraigned. An unprecedented split decision confirmed the constitutionality of the police action. But its legality, by implication, was left in doubt. Colonel Martin, formally absolved of charges, was given no opportunity to demonstrate either his innocence or his conscience in open court.

There was not even any very conclusive guarantee that there might not be another affair. On December 16, 1964, Adelbert Weinstein of the *Frankfurter Allgemeine* reported that the Federal Republic had considered the use of atomic mines along its eastern boundary. Augstein, who had again alluded to the 1961 "war study"[5] in the *Spiegel* of November 18, 1964, seized upon the mine story in an editorial that appeared on January 6, 1965.

On January 21 Federal Attorney Loesdau reported that both Augstein and Weinstein were under investigation for treason. This time, at least, dpa confirmed that Minister of Justice Bucher had been notified first. This time suspicion also extended to Weinstein who was, incidentally, a reserve lieutenant colonel. This time Augstein was invited to appear in Karlsruhe to testify at his convenience, not that of the police.

On December 22 the charges against Weinstein were dismissed. A year later, dismissal of the charges against Augstein followed. The case against Weinstein had been suspended, Federal Attorney Kuhn announced, for lack of concrete evidence. But the case against Augstein was dismissed on the same grounds that had supported dismissal of charges against Colonel Martin: the risk of jeopardizing national security in continuing the prosecution.

At the government press conference on January 23, 1965, Hase again found himself facing the lions. Existing legislation, com-

5 Cf. pp. 52–54.

bined with the "principle of legality,"[6] was not enough, he conceded. Perhaps the law itself was at fault? Hase's implication, like
the decisions of the Karlsruhe courts, passed the buck back to
the Bundestag, where it was to remain. In the course of 1964
and 1965, Berlin, Lower Saxony, Bremen, Hamburg, Baden-Württemberg, and Schleswig-Holstein joined Bavaria in passing legislation intended to strengthen the press's position vis-à-vis the
executive. But despite a barrage of warnings and proposals from
the Federal Republic's constitutional lawyers, judicious head-shak-
ing and finger-waving by a series of Ministers of Justice, beginning with Bucher, and steady fire from the press itself, there was
no comparable federal initiative. An SPD draft disappeared in
committee, legislative initiative apparently exhausted itself in a
series of hearings in the spring of 1966. Five years after the affair,
West German security legislation was unchanged. "Treason" by
journalists was still indistinguishable from "treason" by spies.

This was not without its advantages. "Would you favor a reform of existing statutes that would distinguish journalists from
spies?" Ahlers was asked by an interviewer in late 1965. "No," he
replied. "If there had been such a law, we would probably have
been convicted." Given the basic tendency of government reform
proposals, the press had little reason to regret the Bundestag's
inertia. Draft proposals for a "constitution of national emergency"
submitted by Höcherl in May 1963 included provisions for an
"advisory council" of journalists and civil servants, also authorized
to meet in peacetime, and for a "press commissioner" with extensive powers.

In 1966, apparently with the support of the Ministry of Justice,
at the time under the CSU's Richard Jaeger, an alumnus of the
"Abendländische Akademie,"[7] Solicitor General Ludwig Martin
recommended his own reform: to give the Solicitor General the
authority to summon the joint senates of the Federal High Court
in cases where one of the existing senates had rejected his brief—

[6] Cf. p. 195.
[7] Cf. p. 64.

as, for instance, the third senate had done in rejecting the case against Augstein and Ahlers. No comparable appeal was foreseen for the defendants.

Höcherl's proposals were shattered by the combined—if not exactly identically motivated—resistance of the Ministries of Justice and Defense, and the skepticism of the press. Martin's disappeared with Jaeger's departure from the Ministry of Justice in late 1966 and the advent of the Social Democrats Heinemann and Ehmke.

Other questions raised by the affair remained unanswered. Döring suggested in the Bundestag[8] that it would be well worth the trouble to inquire which intelligence agencies had worked with the *Spiegel* and which had worked against it. However, with the most conspicuous problems solved, Wicht acquitted, and Gehlen still in office, the suggestion was not followed up. The three federal intelligence agencies continued to exist as before, with a minimum of supervision and coordination. This was not to say, as the American experience continually reminded German legislators, that a coordinated agency on the CIA model was necessarily the answer to their problems. But after a substantial affair of its own had done much to discredit the Office for the Protection of the Constitution in 1963,[9] and former Gestapo agents, turned East German spies, were discovered in the BND, there was reason to wonder whether the risks and hazards of a new organization might not be preferable to the chronic embarrassments and self-perpetuating vested interests of the old ones.

Unsolved as well, or negatively solved at best, were the internal and external problems of the Bundeswehr, and their corollary, the indestructible dilemma of West German defense. In the last analysis, "flexible response" was little comfort if it were in Germany that NATO forces were to respond flexibly. But if deterrence failed, massive retaliation was also no solution. What then was the purpose of the Bundeswehr? The debate over the Bundeswehr, like the debate over West Germany's internal security leg-

8 Cf. p. 114.
9 Cf. pp. 118, 186.

islation, was virtually as old as the object itself. Whether facing the problem of West German security or its subsidiary, the problem of West German forces, Hassel took office with his administrative, logistical, and above all strategic work cut out for him. In August 1963 he publicly conceded that "Fallex 62" had proved the inadequacy of the Bundeswehr.

If Hassel's tenure in office failed to produce a great debate,[10] there was at least a small one, beneath the confining wraps of domestic politics. In the course of it, the strategy of massive retaliation was reappraised, and West German policy effected a quiet withdrawal from the more exposed positions of the Strauss era. Multilateral control of nuclear weapons served for a time as an alternative to the original Starfighter program. Schroeder and Hassel followed the multilateral fleet to its grave in December 1964, and indeed beyond it, in the face of opposition from the original nuclear party—now the "European" or "Gaullist" party, depending on the context—led by Strauss and Adenauer. In the summer of 1963 Strauss led the resistance to the nuclear test ban treaty. Two years later, Adenauer shook his party in mid-campaign with a spectacular warning against the dangers of a nonproliferation agreement between the United States and the Soviet Union, presumably at German expense. Adenauer's certain trumpet was effectively amplified by Springer's *Bild* and *Die Welt*. Resistance to a nonproliferation agreement continued into early 1967. But it was hard to find a rational relationship between the limited if real justification for German concern and the arguments marshalled to support it. Foes of the agreement conjured up memories of the Versailles "Diktat" of 1919. In his first post-affair interview with the *Spiegel*, Adenauer himself recalled Secretary of the Treasury Henry Morgenthau Jr.'s wartime plan for the destruction of German industry. A nonproliferation agreement, Adenauer declared, would be "Morgenthau squared."

Beyond the at least partially understandable West German

[10] Cf. p. 62.

obsession with security—the keynote sounded by both major parties in the 1965 election campaign—all was as unclear as before. In September 1963 the alliance formally accepted the obligation of forward defense.[11] At the same time, the alliance's original premises were becoming more and more obsolescent. Both NATO and the Franco-German alliance of January 1963 had to be repeatedly patched up with string and tape. France meanwhile discontinued universal military service as Britain had already done, and limited itself to a professional army. At the same time, Britain's unending financial crisis threatened removal of the Army of the Rhine and even Belgium considered withdrawing its troops from Germany. In the spring of 1967 a combination of congressional pressures, balance of payments problems, anticipated détente in Europe, and the exigencies of Vietnam finally led to the *de facto* withdrawal of two brigades of U.S. troops and four squadrons of fighter-bombers.

While increasing numbers of thoughtful West Germans began to wonder whether there might not be something to be said for following France and Britain in dropping conscription in favor of a professional army, various outside pressures suggested that the Federal Republic, with 450,000 men under arms, might well have to continue to maintain if not to increase them. Washington's concern with Bonn's proposal in July 1967 to drop 60,000 of its troops in the interest of a balanced budget was symptomatic.

All this time Hassel struggled on like a political Laocoön with the problems bequeathed to him by his predecessor. The radical divisions of his party as well as the obvious hazards of the office of Defense Minister effectively obstructed any early replacement. Problem mounted on problem. The West German navy sprang leaks, though it was by no means the only navy in NATO to do so; some fifty Starfighters fell from the skies like hailstones. Considerable numbers of West Germans had the impression that Secretary of Defense McNamara regarded the purchase of massive quantities of new equipment—naturally made

[11] Cf. p. 57.

in U.S.A.—as the only salvation for its ground forces. Meanwhile Hassel, with some American encouragement, doggedly pursued projects like the multilateral nuclear fleet and nuclear mines for the German zonal boundary. His theory, at least in part, was, as he expressed it, "Co-determination does not imply co-ownership, but co-ownership implies co-determination."

Increasing resistance, both at home and abroad, testified to the difficulties and unresolved intricacies of German politics. West Germany, as Theo Sommer has observed, regained its sovereignty in 1954 with a partial renunciation of its sovereignty. Its security, more than that of any other NATO partner, not only depended on the North Atlantic alliance and the American deterrent, but was virtually identical with them.

As the deterioration of the alliance continued, Germans became increasingly aware of what this involved. Self-help, the theoretical alternative, whether based on regional, that is, West European, cooperation or on German territorial forces, was not a real alternative. Increased cooperation, for instance with France, depended on the qualified goodwill of France's President. Strauss himself had learned as early as 1957 how qualified this goodwill could be. In any case, it meant replacing one dependence with another, incomparably less reliable one. Autonomous self-help was also out of the question, whether in the form of more conventionally armed troops in an economy known to search for workers as far afield as Turkey and North Africa, or of a nuclear program likely to exceed the tolerance both of the federal budget and the Federal Republic's neighbors.

"With the possible exceptions of the United States and the Soviet Union, everybody's army is 'conditionally prepared for defense,'" Helmut Schmidt remarked to an American visitor in reference to Ahlers' Fallex article. As in 1962, the question was to what extent Germans were both prepared and willing to accept the implications of this.

In the 1950s the Bundestag, faced with the psychological problem of German rearmament, had risen to the occasion. The rearmament debate of 1956 was one of the finest hours of postwar

German democracy.[12] For the first time, the principles of civilian control of a citizen army were written into German law. But their execution was left to the professionals, whether military or civil service. This, a crucial root of the *Spiegel* affair, by and large continued to be the case after the affair. Helmut Schmidt himself lectured on defense problems at the University of Hamburg during the summer semester of 1966. But his appointment as SPD floor leader in the Bundestag set an end to this and he had no successor. In May 1967, *Die Zeit* reported that fifty student political scientists at the Free University of Berlin had been initiated in the mysteries of Inter Nation Simulation, computer-supported nuclear decision-making in sandbox dimensions[13]; the retired Admiral Ruge accepted a chair in naval strategy at the University of Freiburg at the foot of the Alps. In Hamburg the physicist and philosopher Carl Friedrich von Weizäcker organized a small group of scientists to study the possible consequences of war for the Federal Republic, while semi-private institutes in Bonn and Munich presented occasional reports and organized periodic seminars on questions of defense and disarmament. But if the German public responded to oppressive drill sergeants and the boom of flying, not to mention falling, Starfighters, it still lagged behind the French or British, not to mention American, public in its sensitivity to the more basic problems of defense.

Among the major parties, the CDU ostensibly backed real civilian control in the person of its Defense Minister while conceding to an increasingly frustrated army the decorative symbols of "tradition" denied it in the 1950s. The SPD, put off by the endless improvisations of Hassel's civilian staff and neurotically sensitive to the anti-military tag repeatedly hung on it since 1919, appeared to take the side of the generals. In either case it was doubtful whether this was the way to run NATO's second largest defense establishment, let alone a satisfactory basis for the

[12] Cf. Fritz René Allemann, *Bonn ist nicht Weimar*, Cologne and Berlin, 1956. Allemann's book, perhaps the best ever written on postwar Germany, has never been translated into English.
[13] Cf. *Die Zeit*, May 9, 1967.

civilian control envisaged by German legislators a decade before. By the spring of 1966 it appeared that there was opposition to Hassel's policy even in his own government. Strauss himself was against any West German co-ownership and advised cooperation in form only, co-determination of nuclear policy within the alliance without access to the weapons themselves. The FDP talked about "political solutions," Helmut Schmidt about a German seat on a crisis management board and "negative co-determination" —meaning a veto over use of nuclear weapons from German soil or on German targets. Before the end of the year, beleaguered by demonstrating generals, deserted by his colleagues, and defenseless against daily barrages from the press, Hassel followed Erhard out of office. The defense impasse was an impasse of both foreign policy and domestic politics. Erhard's successor, Kurt Georg Kiesinger, found Hassel a quiet post at the Ministry for Refugee Affairs.

Kiesinger's accession to power at the head of the grand coalition so noisily debated and laboriously rejected four years before was the last of the significant by-products of the affair. Its very existence illuminated again how few of the problems thrown up by the affair had been solved in the intervening years.

Bonn was not Weimar. Fritz René Allemann's truism was proved again in the course of the affair. A treason charge was no longer the *ultima ratio* of German politics. Unlike their fathers, students had unequivocally demonstrated for the republic. Unlike their predecessors, judges, with all their reservations, had ruled against the government. But the basic political problem of finding a majority, if not a consensus, was there as before. If Germany had become more of a democracy than ever before, Germans still had some way to go in learning the rules of the game.

The marvellous schizophrenia of the Free Democrats, the Liberals in a liberal democracy, was a key to the issue. If the FDP was a major factor in resolving the affair, it was also a factor in provoking it. The party had been thoroughly terrified by its anti-Adenauer courage in 1956–7. It might be argued that its subsequent role as the bourgeois anticlerical appendix of a bourgeois antisocialist government was imposed on it by its voters. It had nonetheless accepted the role and its responsibilities. Its "collapse" after the 1961 election was unavoidable. It fought Adenauer, then accepted him, resolving to oppose him from within. Given the imperatives of survival, the position had a certain logic. But it was no ticket to popularity, as the affair proved. The affair presented the FDP with an opportunity to reconsider, but the reconsideration was too little and too late. At the end of 1962, commentators credited the FDP with a victory. But it was, in the long run, a victory without dividends. Ultimately, the affair was the failure not of a Defense Minister, or of a Chancellor, but of a government. Above all, it was the failure of *the* governing party, the CDU/CSU. The appropriate response was a new government. It was a response the FDP refused to accept. Once again, as it had done repeatedly since 1848, organized German liberalism saved its skin at the loss of its face. If the great coalition was brought together in 1966 by the CDU/CSU's desire to share the risks and the SPD's desire to share the power, a common aversion to the FDP united all partners.

The grating dualism of the Federal Republic's first party, the CDU, and its fourth, the CSU, was another key to the problem. It was also the key to Strauss. Sensitive Germans continued to be aware that Strauss's recovery and rehabilitation was anything but a testimony to their political self-respect. The fate of John Profumo, whose lies in the House of Commons in 1963 had ushered him out of British public life altogether, continued to attract as much attention in Germany as it did in Britain. The Denning Report on the Profumo scandal, the British government's ritual exercise in public expiation, may have afforded Britons embarrassment. Germans, their eyes turned to their own government's *Spiegel* report,[14] could find only admiration for British style and candor.

[14] Cf. p. 148. A cartoon in the *Stuttgarter Zeitung* showed two civil servants in a ministerial corridor. "What do you think of the *Spiegel* report?" asks the first. "The same as you do," replies his colleague. "Please desist from further seditious remarks," answers the first.

But the question was not only one of style but of structure. Germans had their reservations about Strauss. Bavarians did not, or could not. As they had since the war, CDU-inclined Bavarians found only the CSU on their ballots. Bavarians who wanted to elect Erhard in 1965 had no alternative but to support Strauss, who opposed him. But while they divided on issues, CDU and CSU were wed in power. So long as the CSU elected Strauss, so long as Bavarians elected the CSU and the CDU depended on Strauss's party in forming the governments that kept both of them in power, the realities of German political life left little room for British fastidiousness.

The dilemmas of multiparty parliamentary democracy and an electorate that resolutely refused to comprehend them impelled the SPD, the Federal Republic's formal opposition, to its own reconsiderations. The alternatives were more of the high principled opposition that had carried the party to four consecutive defeats between 1949 and 1961, or the path Wehner had been the first to blaze in 1962—coalition, at virtually any price, with the parties the SPD had four times failed to beat. They opted for the latter. The result, an apparent violation of the rules of parliamentary democracy, was in fact their consistent expression. CDU and CSU, parties and government, ridden with dissension, exhausted, and discredited by the affair, seemingly faced less opposition than before. But the less things changed, the less they remained the same.

The Federal Republic had been created in 1949 with a double mandate, Western integration and national reunification, theoretically in the boundaries of 1937. The Adenauer government had taken office with a double program, free enterprise and welfare. The compatibility of these goals, whether foreign or domestic, was seldom questioned—least of all in the CDU/CSU. The latent inconsistencies contained in themselves all the characteristic ambiguities of the Federal Republic, the remarkable combination of laissez-faire and subsidies that bemused economists, the historic disparity between national self-effacement and intransigence that bemused the diplomats. The assorted anomalies of West German life reposed between them: "restoration" and a cold social revolution, "bourgeois" government and a consumer society, national pathos and supranational zeal, utopian intellectuals and "the end of ideology," liquidation of the past and denial of it. The system was as viable as its premises: the cold war; the western alliance; an economy like the Volkswagen, the "small wonder" that so appropriately symbolized it, that "ran and ran and ran."

The system went on. Its premises did not. The discrepancies became increasingly evident. The Adenauer era really ended in 1961. It ended again in the last months of 1962, again in 1963 with the old man's resignation from office, again in its nostalgic reincarnation under Erhard, again with the demise of the Erhard-Adenauer government in December 1966.

The creation of the grand coalition four years after the affair, the marriage of parties that had governed the Federal Republic almost as long as both had existed with an opposition that had seemingly ceased to oppose, was apparent capitulation. In fact, it was the most radical break the Federal Republic had seen. It was not, as Johannes Gross observed, the changing of one constitutional government in favor of another, but a change of regime.

Whether it would succeed was an open question. But the efforts of its first hundred days—whether in the application of a judicious neo-Keynesianism, of confident if tacit repudiation of the country's twenty-year attempt to ignore Eastern Europe, even of careful self-assertion against the demands of the traditional American Big Brother—were evidence of a new departure.

So was renewed discussion of an electoral reform that only the SPD and the CDU/CSU were likely to survive. Should they succeed, it was clear to all concerned that, for better or worse, neither they nor the Federal Republic would ever be the same again. "At the end of the grand coalition," Johannes Gross prophesied, "the two major parties will face each other without polemical power, neither of them nearer to the state than the other, neither suspect of conspiracy against the national interest, both of them embedded in consensus born of a common administration, without utopian hopes, leveled off in normality like the parties of England and America."[15]

In retrospect, the affair was epilogue and overture at the same time. Once under way it refused to end. "The affair," Anatole France wrote of the Dreyfus affair, "rendered our country the inestimable service of gradually confronting and revealing the forces of the past and the forces of the future." This, in principle, the *Spiegel* affair did for the Federal Republic. If the appropriateness of "forces of the future" remained to be verified, "forces of the present" at least were beyond serious doubt.

The affair confronted Germans with virtually every question of their postwar existence. Could bourgeois government still be justified in a country of middle-class consumers? Could a modern industrial society continue to govern its affairs according to the statutes of 1867 and the *Weltanschauung* of 1914? Was the stability that, until 1962, had seemed to distinguish the second German republic so favorably from its luckless predecessor, really stability? Or was it sclerosis?

George Bailey of the *Reporter* was moved to quote Professor Teufelsdrokh from Carlyle's *Sartor Resartus:* "What would Majesty do, could such an accident befall in reality; should the buttons all simultaneously start and the solid wool evaporate, in every Deed, as here in Dream? *Ach, Gott.* How each skulks into the nearest hiding place; their High State Tragedy (*Haupt- und Staatsaktion*) becomes a Pickle-herring Farce to weep at, which is the worst kind of Farce, *the tables* (according to Horace) and with them the whole fabric of Government, Legislation, Property, Police and Civilized Society *are dissolved* in wails and howls."[16]

If, five years after the affair, the questions had not yet disappeared, neither, reassuringly, had the wails and howls. The issue, at least, was joined.

[15] Johannes Gross, "Hundert Tage Kabinett Kiesinger" in *Die Zeit*, March 7, 1967.
[16] Cf. *The Reporter*, December 6, 1962.

DATE DUE

9/13			